The
Facility Manager's
Guide to
Finance and Budgeting

David G. Cotts
Edmond P. Rondeau

AMACOM

American Management Association

New York • Atlanta • Brussels • Buenos Aires • Chicago • London • Mexico City
San Francisco • Shanghai • Tokyo • Toronto • Washington, D.C.

To the memory of Art Hahn, a friend and mentor to us both!

Special discounts on bulk quantities of AMACOM books are available to corporations, professional associations, and other organizations. For details, contact Special Sales Department, AMACOM, a division of American Management Association, 1601 Broadway, New York, NY 10019.
Tel.: 212-903-8316. Fax: 212-903-8083.
Web site: www. amacombooks.org

This publication is designed to provide accurate and authoritative information in regard to the subject matter covered. It is sold with the understanding that the publisher is not engaged in rendering legal, accounting, or other professional service. If legal advice or other expert assistance is required, the services of a competent professional person should be sought.

Library of Congress Cataloging-in-Publication Data

Cotts, David G.
The facility manager's guide to finance and budgeting / David G. Cotts, Ed Rondeau.
p. cm.
ISBN 0-8144-0562-2
1. Facility management. I. Rondeau, Edmond P. II. Title.

TS155.C647 2003
658.2'00681—dc21

2003010067

Printing number

10 9 8 7 6 5 4 3 2 1

Contents

Preface

Every book, especially a technical book, needs a purpose. This book is the collaboration of two extremely experienced facility managers, but more than that, two colleagues of long standing (more than twenty years). Perhaps even more, this is the work of two friends who feel strongly about facility management and about its being practiced well. This book was written because we often see facility management not being practiced well. In addition, we often see facilities being managed well, but facility managers not being given the credit for being good managers. This bothers us and has caused us to reflect on the root causes of these real problems.

In this book, we examine at some length the current business environment and how facilities and facility managers fit into that business milieu. Simultaneously, we look at the reasons why facility managers fail, are perceived as being less than astute managers, and, perhaps most troubling, do not follow good business practices. Following this exposition of what we see as troubling problems *that continue to go unaddressed*, we offer, we hope, good business practices in the variety of facility management business functions that will help you become an all-star.

Your authors bring varied backgrounds to this work. One's career is founded in planning and design, with strong practice in corporate real estate. The other's management experience is in heavy construction, operations, and maintenance. One has primarily private-sector experience; the other's career has been split between government and the private sector. Both have long experience in the education and training of facility managers, and both have written landmark books for the profession.

If you glance through the table of contents and the book itself, you will find that we go beyond financial management. This is a book about integrating facility management seamlessly into the business processes of the company. In addition, we try to raise the consciousness of facility managers so that they will manage their department in support of corporate goals and view themselves as business leaders within the company.

Occasionally the reader will say, "Why did these guys put this here? It obviously belongs in Chapter 5 (or 7 or 9)." Organizing a book requires you to put topics into discrete places, whereas facility management (and its supporting financial management) is completely intertwined. Perhaps the best example of this is the way we treat technology. At one time, you addressed FM hardware and software by putting CADD in the chapter on design. Now technology and automated processes (the Internet, e-commerce, CIRM, and so on) are involved in every aspect of the financial management of facilities. Our general rule is to introduce theory early in the book, but to discuss its application in depth under the FM function to which it applies. We hope this works for you.

Frequently you will see us refer to FMForum (*www.fmforum.com*). This is a site, founded by Peter Kimmel, devoted to communication among facility managers. We find this site invaluable while we are researching and writing. When we have a question, we go to FMForum, and we usually get an answer to our query within days—and from a facility manager who is currently practicing. Another invaluable resource for getting FM answers is Jim Elledge's column, "Tricks of the Trade," in *Today's Facility Manager*.

Both of us have published previously, and there are three conventions that we use in this book that knowledge of will make us more understandable to you, the reader. At times, we use *FM* as an abbreviation for both *facility management* and *facility manager* unless it is not self-evident which is intended. Second, this book is for both private- and public-sector facility managers, so when we say *company,* we mean both *company* and *government agency.* This is ever more relevant as the practice of facility management in the public and private sector becomes more and more similar. Also, we use either *he* or *she* when referring to facility managers to avoid the awkward *he/she* pronoun construction.

One final word of explanation about the title and text of this book: Throughout the book, we will concentrate on financial management and on giving you financial management skills as they relate to the various functions of facility management. However, we have taken the liberty of the generalist and applied a more liberal definition of financial management. Our goal is to move the reader to run his department as a business, to address management in business terms about the facility management department, and to think like a businessperson at all times and in all situations.

Acknowledgments

No book is the sole product of an author, or even several authors. For this reason, we wish to thank all of those whose wisdom and research contributed to the factual material in this book, particularly Shari Epstein of the International Facility Management Association, Michael Hoots of the University of Southern Colorado, and Stormy Friday, president, The Friday Group. Shari never failed to respond to requests for research help, and Michael and Stormy's ideas are undoubtedly reflected here intermixed with our own, since we have worked with them on many projects over the years.

In addition, we wish to acknowledge the editorial assistance of Linda Willard Cotts and of Neil Levine, our senior editor at the American Management Association, who coaxed, cajoled, and badgered this book into its final form.

1

The Facility Department Within the Corporate Business Structure

Pulse Points

- *Facility managers need to have the same level of business skills as their colleagues.*
- *Facility managers must know their business—both the FM business and the business that they support.*
- *Facility managers need to be major players in strategic business planning.*
- *Facility managers should use programmatic planning and budgeting.*
- *Facility managers should be able to manage a capital development program using capital budget evaluation tools.*
- *Facility managers should know their costs of doing business.*
- *Facility managers should use performance metrics, one of which is unit costs, to evaluate their departments and each function performed.*
- *Facility managers should be able to make sophisticated business arguments in terms that their business colleagues and upper management understand.*

Keywords

Cost center, CAFM, capital budget evaluation tools, facilities business planning, programmatic planning and budgeting, budget, annual expense, capital expense, annual budget, capital budget, chargebacks and allocation, life-cycle costing, depreciation, benchmark, ratio analysis, cost reductions, cost avoidances, lease-versus-buy, managing by metrics, cost of ownership, business case

Introduction

During our professional activities, we often observe a large number of facility managers and speak to facility managers' bosses and colleagues concerning their perceptions of facility managers. Three troubling conclusions based on these observations and contacts have prompted us to write this book:

1. Facility managers are less sophisticated in financial management than most of their colleagues at an equivalent management level.
2. Upper management does not view facility managers as contributors to the corporate bottom line or even as being particularly conscious of that bottom line. They certainly do not view facility managers as business innovators.
3. Facility managers are often unaware of how they are viewed.

While these observations may be both subjective and presumptive and are not scientific, we do believe that facility managers generally ignore business reality and that many of them have failed to develop adequate financial management skills. They have done this at their own peril, and we know of cases in which facility managers have lost their jobs largely because they viewed themselves only as technical managers. In contrast, after surveying the company's investment in bricks and mortar and the size of the annual FM department budget, upper management wanted a business-oriented manager. This is enough of a problem that one of the leading FM trade publications convened a group of facility managers representing the major professional organizations in June 2001 to discuss how facility mangers can better interface with or perhaps even join upper management.[1]

The purpose of this book is to enable facility managers, while continuing their superb work as technical managers, to gain financial management skills, to sensitize them to the business environment in which they must compete, and to show them how to promote their departments in terms that business-oriented upper management will understand.

Public Versus Private Sector

Having had extensive FM experience in both large government agencies and the private sector, we are struck by how the approach to facility management in those two types of organizations has merged, so that it is less dissimilar now than at any other time in our lifetimes. In fact, as consultants, our first recommendation to facility managers in either sector will be, "Run your department as if it were a business." We will discuss exactly what that means later, but we ask facility managers to consider the following scenario:

> There will be a day on your local golf course when your boss has just sunk a three-foot putt and the president of a local outsourcing firm has just said, "Great shot, Mr. Boss, and have I ever told you how much we can save your company by outsourcing your facility management department?" If you think that can never happen at your firm, then you are a fool, and you are probably toast. There are people out there

who know how to run facilities as a business, and they have great credibility with the business leaders in corporations and government agencies.

Facility managers ignore this possibility at their own professional risk, but even when they acknowledge that something like this might happen, there are great obstacles to our managing in a businesslike manner: our education, our personalities, others' perceptions of us, and an ever-changing business environment.

Traditional FM Education

It is not surprising that facility managers are unsophisticated in applying business practice to facility management. Most of them have a technical education in engineering, architecture, or administrative management. Their education and training did not stress business principles or theory. Many of them have had little training in financial management. Our students' eyes often glaze over at the first mention of internal rates of return or the net present value of money. The authors of this book are typical. We were educated as an architect and as an engineer, respectively. According to the International Facility Management Association (IFMA), only 34 percent of facility managers have business degrees.[2] While that probably most accurately reflects the situation in North America, a 1997 Centre for Facilities Management Review confirms that the situation is the same in Europe.[3] In our discussions with academic policy makers and curriculum shapers, we unfortunately do not see financial management becoming a major curriculum addition to undergraduate programs in the near future.

Personality Issues

Recently on FMForum we posed the question, "What personality type will be successful in facility management?" and asked for studies to back up any response. We got only two replies, and both of them said basically, "We are looking for the same information. Please share it with us if you get any substantive response." Unfortunately, the one study of personality types among facility managers is very old. In general, it found facility managers to be overwhelmingly judgmental and analytical while somewhat introverted.[4] Given the preponderance of technical educations, is that surprising? Our observation is that those personality types predominate in the profession today. That is not all bad. A facility manager *needs* to be analytical. A facility manager *needs* to be capable of making a large number of judgments quickly. However, we find that too many facility managers want to build their departments so that they run like well-oiled machines. After turning on the machine, these facility managers then want to retire to their office to "clean up the paperwork," insulated from customers and problems.

If these educational and personality profiles fit, it is extremely important that facility managers begin a concerted effort to present themselves in a different light, because today's successful business manager is diametrically opposite in his approach to management: flexible, intuitive, and forward-thinking.

Perceptions

These differences between facility managers and other company managers have not gone unnoticed by their colleagues or by upper management. Historically facility managers have been viewed as being:

- Caretakers
- Naysayers
- Advocates for employee welfare
- Controllers
- Employee efficiency multipliers
- Heavily reliant on the purchasing department
- Service providers
- Producers of voluminous policies and regulations
- Project handlers[5]

As facility managers look at this list, they certainly are in agreement that most of these attributes are desirable in good facility managers. Perhaps FMs do go overboard on written procedures and fall back too often on arguments like, "No you can't have a second side chair in your office because the standard says that for your grade you get only one."

While the attributes in this list have historically been important for good facility management, today what is more important for them and for their departments is the question, "How are we perceived?" Generally we have found that the answer is, "Not well!" When we interview facility managers' colleagues and bosses, we are often struck by the frequency with which the FM is viewed as the guy who "always says no," "is not bottom-line-oriented," "is not supportive of my department," "doesn't really understand where our company is going," and "is too limited in vision." We suspect that some of these remarks are unavoidable (they go with the territory), but we have been struck by how widespread these perceptions are. If they are not contradicted, perceptions soon become reality, and that means trouble for facility managers within companies where they are so perceived.

We can quantify the problem. In 1997, only about 40 percent of top executives surveyed by IFMA viewed facilities (and by inference the manager of those facilities) as a resource to be used as a competitive edge. In the same survey, 90 percent of upper management felt that financial skills were paramount for facility managers.[6] The implications are that top executives are not convinced that FMs are managing an important business resource (so why should they treat the FM department as more than a bother?) and that they wish their facility managers had better business skills. When management has this view of facilities, is it any wonder that the most common complaint of FMs is lack of resources?

Thus, we conclude that, just to hold their own, facility managers need to move aggressively to show their business skill and to demonstrate their knowledge of how they contribute to the company overall. And just holding their own is not good enough because the business world is changing rapidly.

The Changing World of Business

It is really quite remarkable how rapidly changes occur in the business world (and in the government). What is even more remarkable is seeing facility managers try to adapt to this changing environment. Here is an anecdote that speaks to this point. One of the students in a recent seminar we were teaching was a facility accountant from one of the major technology equipment providers, a well-established company. She said that her firm (1) absolutely wanted to expense everything possible in the facilities area and was extremely reluctant to tie up any capital funds in bricks and mortar and (2) had an operating budget cycle of between four and six months. That's a far different management and financial environment from what we are familiar with for a firm that large. To be successful, the facility manager must be able to function within those financial guidelines and to offer world-class service while intensely managing the operating budget.

These business changes have both advantages and disadvantages for the facility manager. The lesson to be learned is that facility managers must note these changes, understand their impact on FM (and the impact that FM has on this changed financial environment), and manage accordingly. The purpose of this book is to help them do so. Some of the most significant of these business changes in the past decade are the following:

- Internationalization
- Rise of information management
- The quality movement
- Flattening of organizations and outsourcing
- Emphasis on the speed of delivery
- Focus on *cost reduction* and shareholder value
- Rise of the chief financial officer
- The payoff in the investment in automation[7]

To those we would add the following:

- The growth of e-commerce
- The start of the integration of facility resource information into corporate business data
- Globalization

Other additions to the "business" of facility management that substantially change the financial and business environment for facility managers are:

- Introduction of the concept of infrastructure resource management (IRM)
- The development of truly effective, *computer-assisted facility management (CAFM)* systems that are integrated with company business systems

All of these changes have financial implications, but several of them are particularly dramatic and worthy of amplification.

Many FMs can remember when the chief financial officer (CFO) was treated as a necessary evil, the bean counter. Now, because the success of the company and the job security of the CEO are often dependent upon shareholder value and quarterly performance against earnings expectations, the CFO has become a major corporate player. Note how closely connected the CEO and the CFO have been in the recent corporate scandals. A substantial number of facility managers now report to the CFO, but whether the CFO is the FM's boss or not, the FM needs to be constantly aware of how the facility management department affects shareholder value, expense ratios, indebtedness, and earnings.

There just is no denying that the FM department is a *cost center*. That is not a statement of philosophy but a fact. The facility manager should run the department like a business. Having said that, we remain a major indirect expense, e.g., overhead. Whether facility services are provided in-house or outsourced, it costs to provide them. (Several facility departments have been spun off to become outsourcing companies, but that is another issue.) Providing facility services to any single company or government agency is costly—it is generally a company's second or third highest annual cost.

Facility financial management is not easy. Since facility services are costly, facility managers will always be under pressure to reduce expenses. That is the nature of the modern business model. Improvements that the technically competent facility manager knows are needed may not be possible at any given moment because company funds are needed for other business improvements. Facility managers must watch their expenses like a hawk, and should understand, in detail, how facility expenses fit into the expense structure of the company. In addition, facility managers must be able to make financial arguments—for example, why plant HVAC equipment replacement is needed more than product R&D—or they will be doomed to failure.

Suddenly the terms enterprise resource planning (ERP) and business-to-business (B2B) are as pervasive in newspaper business sections and business journals as ISO 9000, reengineering, and quality management were five years ago. We will discuss these concepts later in this book, but, with our seventy years of combined experience in the field, we will say unqualifiedly that some of these concepts will, in fact, be integrated into the business life of international commerce and government. Others will be no more than the term (and/or business concept) of the day and will pass from the business scene. Facility managers need to be in the fray, learning about and analyzing these business concepts and applying them to FM rather than just grabbing the tag end of one of them after it has become accepted business practice within the company. As an example, in large organizations, facility managers should be aggressively pursuing e-commerce. We see great value in online procurement from companies specializing in FM materials. Even if an initiative in this area would be only a partial success, pursuing it would establish the FM as a business leader rather than a follower.

Having unsuccessfully tried to develop a CAFM system in the early 1980s that would both allow our department to manage its internal business (design, space, finances, project management, work management) and fit in seamlessly with the business systems of the company, we are pleased that such systems are now possible. Having a system for managing department finances that fits into the corporate financial system is critical; this will be mentioned over and over again in this book. We continue to observe situations in which a company has bought a companywide resource management system that has an inadequate interface for FM and corporate real estate. These systems expect you to change your business to go along with the way the software works. FMs, who are not managing a core business, can be especially susceptible to having this type of corporate information system forced on them. We are seeing greater success when the facility manager buys a CAFM system and then makes minor modifications to it to "feed" corporate systems. The final solution is compatibility between the enterprisewide management systems and the CAFM.

Perhaps the most exciting thing that is happening at this time is that FM professionals are starting to talk about managing strategically. The process has various names; infrastructure management, strategic asset management, and managing for competitive advantage are some common terms. We find this development interesting because it signals a willingness on the part of FMs and the FM profession to view their assets strategically, to ensure that they make facility decisions using the same financial management techniques as the other professionals in their companies, and to frame their facility decisions within the business framework of their company. We will continue to discuss these concepts throughout this book. They incorporate many of the skills and tools that we emphasize and demonstrate.

Business Skills of the Facility Manager

People without a complete educational background or even the most suitable personality type can still be successful facility managers if they are adaptable. FMs need that adaptability to keep pace with the business environment, which we believe will only accelerate in its tendency to change over the coming years.

This is the crux, the very core of this book. Through this book, we want to give facility managers the necessary skills to compete successfully and to manage the facility department within the business environment of any company or government agency.

In order to be a success, facility managers need to master the skills in the following list:

Business Skills for the Facility Manager

- Know your business.
- Know, and be able to use, the language of business.
- Understand, in detail, how you affect the business. Be able to translate business needs into FM requirements and to show how FM achievements fit business needs.
- In your practice and your communications, stress the importance and benefits of good facility management. Unfortunately, the research community will not help you much here. Most studies, for example, concentrate on such things as the "effect of the office workplace," which is only one part of the whole FM contribution. BOSTI's (Buffalo Organization for Sociological and Technological Innovation) work is an example of the latter.[8]
- Be able to use *capital budget evaluation tools*.
- Implement strategic *facilities business planning*.
  - Have a facilities plan that is complementary to every company/agency plan.
  - Use programmatic planning and budgeting.
  - Use annual work planning as a bridge between strategic planning and the *budget*.
- Be able to develop, execute, and evaluate budgets.
  - Annual or expense
  - Capital
- Like your business colleagues, expect to invest in business technologies.
- Understand the importance of being able to project and work to a budget and a schedule.
- Make your annual budget your principal facility management information tool.
  - Get a statement of accounts within the corporate system that reflects the programs that you want to manage (and the way that you work).
  - Work to make your CAFM system compatible with the corporate business systems.
- Be able to administer *chargebacks and allocations*.
- For major decisions, use *life-cycle costing*.
- Understand *depreciation* and its effects on your budgets.
- Understand your costs of doing business.
  - Identify those unit costs that drive your operation and put in place ways to collect them consistently and to analyze them.
  - Benchmark your drivers with yourself (over time), with competitors, and with others who are best in class.
- Understand ratio analysis.
  - Identify those ratios that are important to your management.
  - Understand how you contribute to those ratios and manage your contribution carefully.
- Identify and use best practices in all functions of facility management.
- Focus, like a laser, on cost reduction and on management improvements that will lead to cost reduction and *cost avoidance*.

- Reduce churn.
- As a lessee, sign favorable leases and get control of your leases.
- Actively manage your real estate portfolio.
- Be capable of making lease-versus-buy decisions.
- Be a skilled contracting officer and procurer of goods and services.
- Think of ways to make well-run facilities a corporate advantage where appropriate.
- Understand how you should manage, track, and report the ongoing performance metrics, stated in financial terms, for the success of your department and service providers.
- Implement a regular program to communicate these metrics and your success to management and to your customers.
- Become a skilled business communicator.
  - Become a skilled speaker and writer.
  - Couch all presentations to management in business terms.
    - Use financial arguments.
    - Always stress cost savings and avoidances, if any.
- Submit an annual report for the department.

If we could recommend only one thing, it might be that each facility manager make a copy of this list, laminate it, and make it a part of his or her action plan for the next two to three years. Some of the items will take that long to implement. We think that awareness of these skills is important, and that if every facility manager would practice them, the profession would move dramatically from one that seems to have a lifelong inferiority complex to one in which (1) facility management departments would be considered true business partners within corporations and (2) FMs would attain the recognition that they seek and deserve. This is true in both industries that are "bricks and clicks" and those that are "bricks and mortar" based and in government agencies.

Some of the skills in this list are self-evident. For those that aren't, we will explain them briefly, rolling them up into logical categories. These skills form the backbone of the remainder of this book. If FMs acquire these skills, they will promote those practices that Dr. Martha O'Mara describes as "enablers," which help to get things out the door better, faster, and at a lower cost.[9] Through this book, we intend to assist each reader to acquire each of those skills that she or he still needs in order to become a business leader within her or his company or agency.

Know Your Business

Most facility managers who have significant responsibilities know the technical aspects of their jobs. However, we would give them a low or failing grade on their ability to understand, in detail, how they affect the businesses that they support. In this regard, we find that FMs who support manufacturing businesses often have the best handle on exactly how they affect business output. Many of them know and are constantly recalculating the exact facility expense component of each manufactured product.

In addition, we find FMs trying to communicate with colleagues and upper management in "FM-speak" (cfm, lf, type 6 cable, etc.) when they should be using the language of business (ROI, IRR, expense reduction, etc.).

Facility Business Planning

Throughout this book, we will stress the importance of facility business planning. This is not master planning; this is planning how the FM department will support the business plan in one, three, five, ten, or more years. It is more than space planning; all programs of the FM department need to be planned. FMs need to plan how they work—what we call *programmatic planning*. From programmatic planning flows *programmatic budgeting*. Until the facility manager becomes a member of the company business planning team, he will be a reactor, and there will always be major costly mistakes made in the management of facility resources. The FM profession has not done a good job of assisting individual facility managers to conceptualize and quantify the impact of facilities on companies' and government agencies' business processes and bottom lines. The most recent effort is by Tim Springer and Steve Lockwood in the article "Strategic Facility Planning."[10] In this article, the authors spell out the impact of current business strategies on facilities and vice versa.

Facility Budgeting

Most facility managers have too limited a view of budgeting, both *annual budgeting* (often called expense budgeting) and *capital budgeting*. In addition, they tend to feel that their responsibility is primarily to get as many resources as possible (this *is* important) and then to stay within that budget. While those budget functions are important, we feel it is also important that FMs take a major role in budget development, in managing the budget during execution, and in conducting a budget post mortem (an evaluation) at the end of each budget year. In that evaluation, one criterion should be used: "How well did I (and my subordinates) do what I said that I was going to do, given the resources that the department was allocated?" Those FMs who use client service agreements and chargebacks need to have another skill: managing a chargeback budget and ensuring that costs are properly allocated according to transparent rules.

Technology and Company Business Systems

One major weakness of many FM departments is that they use a statement of accounts that does not reflect the way they work. In our consulting to major companies throughout North America, we have seen FM expense and capital budget reports that were superficial at best. These reports did not begin to provide the depth of information needed to accurately manage expense and capital budget programs. Without this detail, FMs cannot manage what they do not know and cannot provide reliable or believable ongoing performance reports to upper management.

It is worth the effort for the FM to work with the corporate financial department to get a suitable statement of accounts (reflecting programmatic budgeting). Once that is done, the FM should use the budget as the principal facility management information tool. Once that is accomplished, the FM, like other business leaders, should invest in those business technologies that will help in the management of all aspects of information needed to manage the department. Concurrently, the FM must work with the other business managers within the company or agency to ensure that FM information needed by other business systems is seamlessly available. This needs to be a "push" system, in which the FM provides other managers with the information they need, rather than some kind of packaged "pull" system (with a minimal facility package). There are vendors now selling enterprise-wide data management systems (generically called enterprise resource planning, or ERP, systems) that include real estate and facility management systems. Within the profession, we are now hearing about infrastructure management. There is nothing wrong with such systems per se, but they are often developed by an outside vendor or consultant who has never managed facilities and does not know what FM information other company business leaders need. The FM needs to stay in control of what data are to be gathered and managed (and, in turn, to manage carefully those functions and data that are visible to upper management). This sequence and a willingness on the part of the facility manager to manage his or her own destiny is a recurring theme of this book.

The Costs of Business

Though these voices seem to be disappearing, for a while there were a number of consultants trumpeting the idea that facility managers should view their departments as a profit center. We often wondered what facility departments they had ever managed. Except for two cases we know of where FMs actually spun off their corporate FM departments to become private businesses, FM departments are cost centers. Anthony Pizzitola, a facility leader for Tricon Global Restaurants, says that the FM department needs to be a cost savings center, which appears to us to be very close to correct. We want to encourage FMs to run their departments as a business, but these departments don't generate revenue. The FM department consumes corporate resources; it is the second or third greatest expense on the corporate ledger. For that reason, the FM needs to have a laserlike focus on expenses and to understand which expenses must be most intensely scrutinized. As we like to tell our fellow facility managers, "If you aren't watching your expenses, someone is, and you will be judged accordingly because expenses affect revenue, and that has a direct effect on shareholder value." Large consumers of resources, such as the facility department, will continually be scrutinized. That goes with the job.

Once the key expenses, or "drivers," as we call them, have been identified, the FM needs to ensure that the FM information management system accurately provides information on those expenses in a consistent manner and allows the FM to analyze them over time. Most of the drivers will be unit costs. Once the FM is convinced that those unit costs are being accurately captured and has examined them over time, the FM will want to *benchmark* with competitors and best-in-class organizations to learn how they produce superior products and services at a cost with which they are comfortable. After the FM has ironed out the inevitable problems, these benchmarking efforts can be used as the basis for a request for more resources or as a substantial business argument that the FM is using resources effectively and efficiently.

Best Practices

An area where we remain very critical of the facility management profession is the failure of FMs to use best practices. Too often, they insist on reinventing the wheel over and over and over again. While we cannot absolutely measure this, we contend that, in general, over the long run best practices will produce the best combination of effectiveness and efficiency. For a while, the IFMA sponsored best practices seminars, and, although we are experienced facility managers, we never failed to marvel at the policies, procedures, and techniques that we learned at these seminars from our fellow FMs. We realize that best practices are site-specific. One of our favorite examples of this came from a young facility manager who said that, under a management directive to cut costs, he had instituted a policy whereby individuals emptied their own trash baskets and got their offices cleaned only twice a week. Our evaluation of that proposal was that we would be fired concurrently with the announcement of such a policy at our companies. So, for us it was not a best practice, but it apparently worked for the presenter.

Recently we talked to the managers of a very large public FM organization, who knew, at the top level, that many best practices, lessons learned, and even outstanding research, all developed at public expense, were not easily accessible to others in their organization or to their customers. They realized the inefficiencies that this created, and they were looking for ways to correct the situation. This enters the realm of knowledge management, a catchword at this time. Service organizations all need to seriously examine how knowledge is managed within the organization, particularly if they are geographically dispersed, so that all parts of the organization can have access to the written and oral corporate knowledge of the organization.

Real Estate Considerations

In a large organization, a facility manager must have the skills to make lease-versus-buy decisions. That is basic. In addition, FMs in moderate-size and large organizations will, in all likelihood, be both lessors and lessees. Unfortunately, in both cases, facility managers, because they tend to use a variety of real estate middlemen, do not have well-developed business skills. An FM who does a substantial amount of leasing should never sign a standard lease. Instead, the FM should develop an appropriate lease with the help of the company legal department. An FM should be able to manage a real estate portfolio actively and should have an information system that is capable of highlighting critical lease events at a date when they can be acted upon appropriately.

Selling the Department in Business Terms

We are tempted to say that, of all the skills that a facility manager needs, being able to speak and write to colleagues and upper management in terms that they understand and being able to make financial arguments may be the most important. Sheryl Hansen of State Farm Insurance summed up the problem succinctly in a recent entry to FMForum, "However, because we are not 'core business,' there are times when we, of necessity, become less than 'full partners.'"[11] Thus, there is a natural bias against FMs to start with, even if they have strong communication skills. And most FMs are not skilled writers and speakers! To be a successful business manager, a facility manager needs to become a skilled writer and speaker. Quite frankly, many facility managers need to return to school and retake English 101 and Speech 101. For example, one of the comments of attendees about facility management presenters at World Workplace 2001, the principal international FM event, was, "Knowledgeable presenters but horrible public speakers."[12]

With regard to speaking, the IFMA has an effective handout, "30 Seconds with the CEO," that stresses the keys to effective business speaking, POP: understanding the *purpose* of your presentation, defining what *outcome* you want to achieve, and strategizing an effective *process* (see Appendix A). When in doubt, stress the bottom line and keep it short! Our colleague Nancy Sanquist calls this "thinking like a CFO . . . not a FMer."[13]

Each company or government agency will have a slightly different format and methodology, but the process that you will use to sell your FM projects and initiatives involves making a **business case**. A business case is just what the name implies. It explains, normally in primarily financial terms, how the initiative or project will add value to the company or agency. You must sell your initiative to the business leaders of your company using business terms and arguments. An excellent discussion of the methodology and the importance of linking your FM initiative to corporate strategies is contained in an article by Lynetta Baldwin and Eric Teicholz, "Making a Business Case at BellSouth."[14]

In the general approach to selling your department, stress the importance of good FM, the benefits of good FM, and how well-managed facilities can be a corporate advantage.

Another important communication skill, especially when talking to and with colleagues, is **ratio analysis**. Most senior members of the management of your company will be rated (and their bonus will depend) upon some sort of ratio (earnings/share is a common one). An FM should be alert to how the FM department can affect these ratios positively. Since other departments and managers are often judged on some ratio, perhaps you should develop one or two ratios that can gives upper management the ability to judge your department as others are judged (total cost of occupancy/staff, capital investment/sales, total occupancy cost/total administrative cost, and so on).

Finally, the FM should submit an annual business report to upper management. This report should again stress the importance, benefits, and corporate advantages of well-managed facilities. Keep it short and show, in financial terms, how the facility department is contributing to the corporate bottom line.

Managing by Metrics

Shareholders measure the corporation using financial metrics. It is only fitting that the facility manager should expect to be judged similarly. It is essential that the facility manager have the ability to develop performance *metrics* (stated in financial terms) for the department and any contracted service providers. In addition, the FM must communicate progress against those metrics to both management and the FM's customer base.

Recurrent Themes

These, then, are the learning objectives of this book, the skills that we recommend to you for business success as a facility manager. They are the themes around which we will develop subsequent chapters of this book. It is important to remember that these are not new skills that you need to learn on top of those technical skills that you have been taught. *These are the skills that you should have possessed all of the time* in order to succeed as the facility manager of a medium to large facility management department. Frans van Waardhuizen spells this out well in his description of the five different levels of functional facility management. At its highest level, facility management is fully integrated into the strategy of the company.[15] For two other approaches to managing facilities toward the business mission, see Richard Ness and John Hinks's excellent articles in the *Proceedings, Facility Forum 2001.*[16]

We are not yet where we want to be, or where we should be, in managing facilities as a business function. This is a call to action for our universities and for individuals and the professional organizations to ensure that we place as much emphasis on how to manage a budget properly as on how to select a CAFM system, and that we focus on how to decide between competing capital projects as much as on how to manage a custodial contract properly.

Figure 1-1. The Facility Life Cycle and the Cost of Ownership.

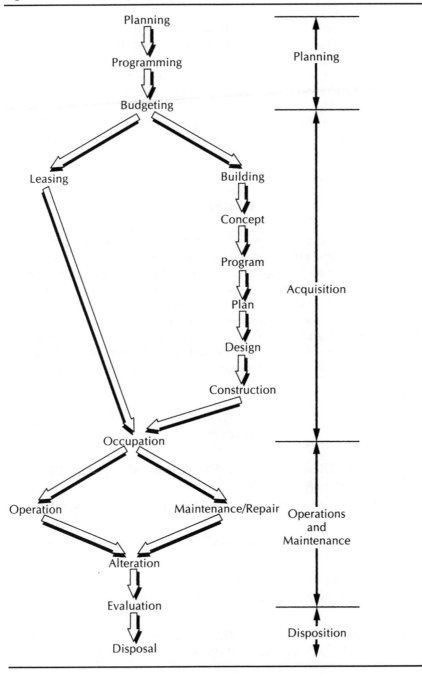

The Cost of Ownership

Figure 1-1 depicts the facility life cycle from the moment that a company decides to build, buy, or lease. That is known as the *cost of ownership*. Even disposal has a cost, as becomes obvious to the FM who has had to dispose of environmentally "dirty" sites. The greater a company's dependence on facilities and the greater the importance of the FM's job, the greater the expenses that must be managed through this life cycle. The business goal of the FM is to minimize expenses, to know the facilities the company owns and/or leases, to maximize the use of facilities, and to be able to justify the use of substantial company resources throughout that facility life cycle.

Conclusion

At Facility Forum '99, Nancy Johnson Sanquist, a long-time and perceptive observer of facility managers and our profession, said that she thinks it is necessary that we think like a CFO by "viewing the virtual and physical infrastructure . . . as a bundle of assets that—when selected and managed right—will generate substantial returns on your investment." As a result, she predicted that facility managers' duties will come to include an increase in financial strategy, an increase in investment management, an increase in performance management, a decrease in cost planning/budgeting, and a decrease in financial operations.[17] We think that is about right, although, as we will reinforce in Chapter 6, we need to stay focused on our costs.

Notes

1. Julie Liebowitz and Eileen McMorrow, "Show Me the Money," *Facility Design and Management,* June 2001, pp. 42–45.

2. *Profiles '98* (Houston: International Facility Management Association, 1998), p. 13.

3. *UK FM Employment Review '97* (Glasgow, Scotland: Centre for Facilities Management, 1997), summary.

4. Martha Whitaker, personal note, August 14, 1989.

5. David G. Cotts, *The Facility Management Handbook,* 2d ed. (New York: AMACOM, 1999), p. 8.

6. *Views from the Top: Executives Evaluate the Facility Management Function* (Houston: International Facility Management Association, 1997), pp. 1–4.

7. Cotts, pp. 8–9.

8. John Olson, "How Do We Measure the Facility's Contribution to Business Success?" *Facilities Design and Management,* August 2000, pp. 18–19.

9. Martha O'Mara, *Strategy and Place: Managing Corporate Real Estate and Facilities for Competitive Advantage* (New York: Simon & Schuster, 1999), p. 253.

10. Tim Springer and Steve Lockwood, "Strategic Facility Planning," *Today's Facility Manager*, August 2002.

11. Sheryl Hansen as quoted on the Internet site FMForum, December 27, 1999.

12. Comment from attendee comment report provided to presenters, World Workplace 2001, p. 4.

13. Nancy Johnson Sanquist, Presentation to Facilities Forum 98, Santa Clara, Calif., March 29, 1999.

14. Lynetta Baldwin and Eric Teicholz, "Making a Business Case at BellSouth," *Facilities Design and Management*, June 2002, pp. 14–16.

15. Frans van Waardhuizen, "Between Maintenance and Change: The Five Functioning Levels of Facility Management," *FMJ*, September/October 1998, p. 60.

16. Richard Ness, "Managing Toward the Mission—How Excellent Facilities Management Helps Organizations Achieve Success" and John Hinks, "Measuring FM Performance in Business Terms," *Proceedings, Facility Forum 2001* (Red Bank, N.J.: Group C Communications, 2001), pp. 145–158 and 159–174, respectively.

17. Nancy Johnson Sanquist, "Financial Forecasting for Infrastructure Management," *Proceedings, Facility Forum '99*, (Red Bank, N.J.: Group C Communications, 1999), pp. 141–142.

2

Basic Financial Concepts

Pulse Points

- *Facility managers must understand and be able to apply corporate finance to financial management.*
- *Facility managers must understand, and be able to explain to their management, the concept of the cost of ownership.*
- *The facilities department is a cost center.*
- *The facilities department budget is a significant portion of a company's overhead budget and will always be scrutinized carefully.*
- *Facility managers must understand the financial character of their company, since it affects attitudes toward asset allocation, debt management, and valuation.*
- *The facility manager should have a statement of accounts that reflects how he or she works, that can be fed by the CAFM system, and that is compatible with the corporate accounting system.*
- *The facility manager is one of the few managers who manages both an annual and a capital budget consistently and must understand the differences in developing, managing, and reporting each.*
- *Facility capital decisions should be made using capital budget decision tools that account for the time value of money.*
- *The facility manager should implement a two-tiered approval level for expenditure of funds.*

Keywords

Cost of ownership, expenses, cost center, financial ratios, asset allocation, valuation, balance sheet, assets, liabilities, revenue, expenses, cash flow, debt management, depreciation, capitalization, expensing, capital decision-making tools, approvals, overhead, direct expenses, indirect expenses, time value of money, payback, return on investment, net present value, internal rate of return

Introduction

The remainder of this book is devoted to presenting the business, and particularly financial, skills needed to become an effective business manager. In Chapter 1, we stressed the need for these skills. At the conclusion of this chapter, we hope that you will be motivated to implement them. We have tried to strike a balance in this chapter in determining what the facility manager really needs to know in order to be a good business manager. There are those who say that, because facility management is not a core business in most companies, facility managers are viewed as less than full business partners. Another group says that facilities should be viewed as an investment opportunity. We have tried to strike a middle ground, one that views facilities as assets but that also realizes that facility expenses tend to be the second or third largest corporate or agency expense.

To begin, we will introduce a number of financial concepts that are important for facility managers. Our aim is to make these concepts understandable, and we explain them in the context of facility management. Some of these concepts will be explored in more detail in later chapters; taken together, they supply the basis for the understanding of financial management for facility managers.

With these new concepts come new terms. Just as facility management has its terms of art, so does the financial world. Some of these terms are easily understood; some are complex. We have provided nontechnical definitions and used those definitions throughout the book. However, in doing so, we may lose some of the nuances of a term. Therefore, we suggest that, as always when learning a new subject, the best approach is to commit to memory a certain number of financial terms. Those terms will be **_bold italic_** in this and subsequent chapters. As a minimum, bookmark this chapter and the glossary for quick reference while proceeding through the book.

Financial Concepts

Alan Whitson, a favorite writer and speaker on financial management topics, summarizes finance in simple terms:

- Making money with money is easy.
- Finance is making more money with the same amount of money invested.
- The object is maximizing the return to the owners of the business.[1]

Simple, yes? However, in order to focus on the applications of corporate finance in facility management, FMs will find it helpful to understand some more detailed concepts. The financial concepts that we consider most important for the facility manager are these:

- The _cost of ownership_
- The pain of _expenses_
- Being a _cost center_

- The financial character of your company
- *Financial ratios*
- *Asset allocation*
- *Valuation*
- The *balance sheet*
  - Corporate *assets*
  - Corporate *liabilities*
  - Corporate *revenue*
  - Corporate *expenses*
- *Cash flow*
- *Debt management*
- Accounting practices
- The tax code and *depreciation*
- *Capitalization* versus *expensing*
- The *time value of money*
- *Decision-making tools*
- *Approvals* and approval levels

Many other important concepts could be included, but, in our opinion, these are the general financial concepts that have relevance in the practice of facility management.

In order to simplify, we will present the remainder of this book in terms of a corporation, not a sole proprietorship or partnership, differentiating the public sector where it is appropriate or needed.

The Cost of Ownership

At this point, FMs need to remind themselves that there is a cost of ownership (see Figure 1-1) and that the facility department is a cost center. That means that facility managers are in a continual competition for operating and capital funds to meet the business requirements of the company or government agency. Ultimately, funding decisions are made by upper management, the CFO and/or the CEO, who know little of facilities or facility management. An excellent overall summary of the financial context of that competition can be found in Tom McCune of AE Pragmatic's list of ten ways to secure necessary funding:

Learning to Get the Funding That Facility Managers Need

1. To a financial officer, everything is financial.
2. Learn the CFO's language.
3. Learn where you fit in the CFO's frame of reference.
4. Learn the time value of money.
5. If it is an expense, eliminate it. If you can't eliminate it, minimize it.
6. If it is an investment, maximize the return on it.
7. Cash is king.

8. Hedge all risks.
9. Don't ignore politics.
10. Emphasize the corporation's welfare, not your division's.[2]

McCune's excellent article "How to Speak to a CFO," which also provides other financial management concepts for facility managers, is printed in its entirety in Appendix A.

The Pain of Expenses

One way of looking at expenses is that they represent dollars that could be profit. Management understands well that there are *direct expenses* that are a component of the cost of the goods or services produced by the company, but it also realizes that there are also *indirect expenses* (*overhead*). While management understands the necessity for these expenses, it hates them with a passion. One of the characteristics of the modern corporate climate is a relentless attack on overhead expenses. The facility budget represents a significant part of overhead expenses and is always in the spotlight. For example, the CFO might well question moving from Class B to Class A office space unless the facility manager can prove with financial arguments that upgrading office space will result in increased productivity and/ or increased personnel retention. The FM, on the other hand, may just see the move as a sensible part of the mandate to promote employee well-being, a technical argument that may be neither appreciated nor accepted by the CFO.

Being a Cost Center

In this area, the public-sector facility manager actually has it much easier than the facility manager in the private sector. In the public sector, the facility manager's task during budget preparation is essentially getting an appropriate share of the organization's budget pie. In the private sector, it is not that simple.

Taking a macro view of corporate finances makes the financial quandary in which facility managers find themselves very evident. First, FM departments do not create revenue, nor do they turn a *profit*. Yet they are the lifeblood of any corporation, because without them the corporation cannot be viable in the long run. Second, FMs manage a large share of long-term capital assets, but upper management much prefers short-term assets, like cash. Third, FMs control at least a portion of corporate liabilities (examples might be mortgages and the financial and legal obligations of leases), which upper management views as bad. Fourth, and perhaps worst of all, FM departments are funded as overhead, an indirect expense that a CFO treats like cancer. On three of the four elements of this financial framework, facility managers are in the "bad" category, and in the fourth, revenue, FMs are a nonproducer. For a CFO, who is charged with the financial well-being of the company, there is a natural bias against the FM department and its activities. FMs need to realize that fact and understand how to work around it. So, when, on a bright Monday morning following the publication of quarterly earnings, the FM approaches upper management to request capital funding for a favorite project, she should not expect an automatically enthusiastic reception. She should expect tough questions and be prepared to argue for the funding of long-term assets that management knows are necessary for the long-term well-being of the company, no matter how reluctant management is to admit it.

Understanding when the deck is stacked against the FM and that there is a natural bias against giving the FM department either annual (expense) funding or capital funding underscores why FMs must be able to make their arguments in financial terms.

The Financial Character of the Company

Just as the financial approach of private- and public-sector FMs needs to be different, there will be differences in the financial nature of private companies, often historically determined by industrial sector. Private-sector facility managers need to understand that as well. From a financial perspective, being a facility manager for a closely held private company can be quite different from being a facility manager for a publicly traded corporation.

Another major factor in determining a company's approach to its finances is the company's method of financing. In arguing for more funding for FM, the arguments may be slightly different depending on whether the company is equity-financed or is primarily financed through the sale of bonds.

Because all companies have a financial nature, and because upper management tends to have a business background, it is essential that FMs learn to plan, measure, and communicate in financial terms. Some of this financial communication is done using financial ratios.

Financial Ratios

Ratios are used by outsiders to evaluate the corporation (earnings/share, P/E ratio) and are used within the corporation to measure such things as efficiency and effectiveness. Business managers understand that and realize that their success is measured using these ratios. Facility managers have not traditionally been measured by this type of yardstick, yet these ratios are important. For example, a company that is looking at a declining ratio of sales to total assets may not look kindly upon the FM's request for increased capital spending. FMs who wish to be successful should learn how they positively or negatively influence the important financial ratios for their corporation and should focus on and publicize how they can help to improve those ratios for their colleagues, upper management, and the corporation.

Asset Allocation

There are always competing demands upon corporate resources. Should the corporation build a new plant in Ohio, or should it commence a nationwide television marketing campaign? One way in which upper management will be judged is by how well it manages the financial resources of the corporation to make more money (see the quotation from Whitson earlier in the chapter). In a corporation, upper management has a legal mandate to increase shareholder value through the management of corporate assets. The process of deciding who will be allowed to incur expenses and short- and long-term debt is called asset allocation. Every manager, including the FM, is in the competition for resources, and it is often a contact sport. Asset allocation decisions may be made rationally or irrationally (there are always politics to consider[3]), but in a well-run company the person who can make the most rational argument for assets is likely to win more often than lose. Every day the FM is battling for capital, particularly at budget time, and he needs to convince management that the return on capital invested in the FM department is greater than the cost of that capital.

Valuation

Determining the value of any asset is both an art and a science. For instance, it could be the real property value of an asset, its workplace support value, or its return on corporate investment.[4] There are legal aspects to it (for example, your residence is assessed for tax purposes according to rules that judge each property equally), but value, like beauty, is often in the eye of the beholder. For instance, in the eyes of a buyer, the value of the physical assets of Acme Drilling will change radically the day that Acme files for bankruptcy. Some of the factors that influence the value of real property are age, location, market value, condition, adaptability, and historic value.

Tax laws can often be used to determine one valuation (how much has the asset depreciated?), whereas a buyer may be willing to pay quite a different amount. In general, valuation can be reached in one of three ways:

1. The cost approach (How much would it cost to replace this asset?)
2. The market approach (What is the selling price of a similar asset?)
3. The income approach (What rate will the asset return on the company's investment?)[5]

What approach the facility manager should use when calculating the valuation of a specific asset is case-specific and will be discussed at various places in the book. In most cases, however, the facility manager will not be determining what valuation approach to take. Once an approach has been determined, the FM's task will be to gather the data to properly value the asset in question. Danny Shiem-Shin Thien and Wes McGregor emphasize that proper valuation is critical for corporate survival and is the principal "push" factor for good facility management.[6]

The Balance Sheet

We have thus far avoided throwing out too many new terms and using too many technical terms in explaining the concepts. However, we have gone as far as we can without introducing some accounting terms, not for accounting purposes, but for the purpose of understanding corporate finances from the perspective of your management. The terms used here should be looked up in the glossary as they come up. For another explanation of this information, see Tom McCune's excellent presentation to World Workplace 1999, which is included as Appendix A.

Corporate assets are of two types and represent what the company has. Short-term assets, like cash, are highly valued. Long-term assets, like most of our facilities, are generally valued but always raise the CFO's question, "Why do we have our cash tied up in these?" FMs are most identified with long-term assets and because of that may spend some of their time answering the CFO's question.

Corporate liabilities represent what the company owes. Shareholders' equity, the value of company shares plus retained earnings, represents shareholders' confidence in the company. When the company went public, it did so because it realized that in order to really grow, it needed to use other people's money. However, most companies have other liabilities. Payables are one of these (and one that is managed diligently by the CFO). The liabilities that an FM is most often involved with are mortgages and long-term leases.

Corporate expenses represent what the company pays out. In the widget business, there is a cost of labor and materials directly tied to that widget (direct expenses). No one likes to pay these costs, but they are unavoidable. On the other hand, indirect expenses, particularly in the modern corporation, are the bane of a CFO. Guess who, it could be argued, manages the largest chunk of indirect expenses within the corporation? That's right, the FM. That is one of the reasons that facility managers really need to know their costs of doing business and to be able to attribute as much of those costs as possible to the direct production of goods and services rather than having them viewed as a big glob of *overhead*, another name for indirect expenses.

Corporate revenue represents what the company takes in. It would be great if FM's were major players in this revenue stream ("Hey, boss, I turned a profit this quarter."). Unfortunately, they are very seldom players in the production of revenue, at least in the way that accountants define their terms.

This may be one of the greatest problems in financial management: Others define FM. Management has a different financial frame of reference. And many FMs are ill-equipped to help change either the definition or that frame of reference.

Cash Flow

For the reasons mentioned earlier regarding the rise of the CFO, money is managed intensely in the modern corporation. (Did you ever wonder why those who owe you money don't pay for at least 30 days?) Cash flow is a major issue in both the public and private sectors. It may affect the FM when, despite the fact that a project has been approved, the CFO suspends or delays it because of a cash flow deficiency.

Public-sector facility managers, on the other hand, may, in fact, get an infusion of funding just before the end of the fiscal year if they are prepared to spend it well. In the public sector, funds tend to disappear on the last day of the fiscal year. In the weeks preceding that date, the organizational budget officer may well have excess funding authorization that she will be willing to release to a facility manager who is able to put it to use effectively before the end of the fiscal year.

Finally, FMs must understand that most financial analyses involve a display of the cash flows (savings and expenses) for a period of time. These cash flow analyses are the basis for the capital budget evaluation methods discussed in Chapter 5. It will be emphasized in that chapter that the results of these analyses will depend upon the time period analyzed (three, five, ten, or some other number of years). The decision on the number of years to be analyzed is set not by the FM, but by the CFO and/or the controller.

Debt Management

As important as cash flow management is, most businesses, even small ones, expand by using some amount of debt. Those of us who have ever tried to get a home loan realize that there are benchmarks and guidelines for how much debt an individual should be carrying. Similarly, CFOs are concerned about corporate debt. How management views debt tends to be situational and varies from industry to industry as well. However, be assured that the FM of ACME Financial Services who approaches his board with a proposal to design and build a new computer and call center costing $56 million will have the company's existing debt taken into account in analyzing that proposal. Like some individuals who are overleveraged with debt, companies can get into situations where their ability to increase their debt is limited. The facility manager in an organization like that may have the most worthwhile project with an outstanding technical and financial justification, but the company will not be able to implement the project because it has too much debt. That means that it is important for FMs to be aware of (1) what is, in general, salable within the company in normal times and (2) what is going on financially at the current time. For any project, there is a season.

Accounting Practices

"Finance is prospective; accounting is retrospective. Accounting is measuring, recording, classifying, summarizing and reporting transactions and financial events and the communications of this data to decision makers."[7] While an FM may look at that definition and say, "What has that got to do with me?" the devil is in the details. Failure to understand the effect of general and corporate accounting practices can have a profoundly negative effect on the functioning of the facility department. An FM should have (1) a general knowledge of double-entry accounting, (2) a statement of accounts that serves the department and reflects how it works, and (3) the necessary personnel and equipment to provide the retrospective financial information mentioned previously in such a way that he can properly manage the department.

In the next chapter, we will discuss in detail the need for a proper statement of accounts as the foundation for proper planning and budgeting, a statement based on facility programs. It is our observation that few facility departments have ever taken the time to get themselves a statement of accounts that (1) allows the department to budget as it works, (2) allows for uncomplicated assignment of internal responsibility for expenditures, (3) interfaces seamlessly with the corporate accounting system, and (4) makes the calculation of meaningful unit costs and benchmarks easy. Programmatic planning, budgeting, and accounting are best practices, yet they seldom occur. Most facility departments are saddled with a statement of accounts pressed upon the FM by corporate accountants that does not help the FM manage the department. In fact, most of the facility financial data by which the FM manages have to be twisted and modified in some way to fit into corporate statements of accounts. Remember, *it is better for the FM to have a statement of accounts that meets her operational and information needs 95 percent of the time and can be manipulated the other 5 percent of the time to meet corporate needs (special requests, ERP, or SAP, for example) than the other way around.*

Furthermore, how many FMs have to take the accounting information coming from their computer-assisted facility management system (CAFM) and translate it for corporate accounts? It is very difficult to fine-tune an information and work management system like a CAFM to produce precise accounting reports, but unless the FM department accounts the same way it works, doing this will be impossible. The reports from the CAFM should be able to be fed to corporate accounting without manipulation. That can be done only if corporate accounting is using a proper statement of accounts. It may take the personal intervention of the facility manager to achieve that.

Finally, the FM must understand the difference between departmental/corporate accounting and project accounting. We will discuss this in detail in Chapter 7. While facility management is not project management, any facility manager will, in the course of a year, probably manage a number of small projects and perhaps several large projects. There is no surer way to a disaster than to try to use corporate accountants and the corporate statement of accounts to manage a multimillion-dollar construction project. The appropriate way to account for a major project is to use Construction Specification Institute or other standard accounts and then, monthly or at the end of the job, transfer the project accounts into the appropriate corporate accounts.

Even with modern systems and good statements of accounts, we have found it best to have a facility accountant to serve as the bridge between the FM department and corporate accounting and among FM vendors, the purchasing department, and corporate accounting. This is not the typical clerk of the works found on a large project, but an accountant who is familiar with the FM vendors and the unique nature of FM accounts. In large departments, this individual is an almost indispensable assistant to the FM. If having a staff accountant is not possible in your organization, as an alternative have the corporate accountant who handles FM accounts colocated with the FM department. A knowledge of accounting and how it is conducted in the company can influence everything from how accurate the corporate numbers are (by which you are judged) to in how timely a manner the contractors are being paid (believe us, they work better when they are paid on time). FMs need not be accountants, but they ignore accounting at their own risk.

Depreciation

There are two reasons for depreciating an asset, an accounting one and a tax one. In accounting, expenses incurred in producing revenue during any given time period should match the revenue produced. This is called the matching principle. Theoretically, if we used up 15 percent of the useful life of a boiler in a year, then the boiler should be depreciated 15 percent for that year. Depreciating a capital asset represents an attempt to apportion the acquisition cost of the capital asset over the useful life (the period when the asset is producing revenue) of that asset. We have already discussed (under "Valuation") the fact that the value of an asset can be calculated in a number of different ways. In the simplest form of depreciation, a depreciable asset with an initial value of $30 million and a thirty-year useful life would have a depreciated value of $29 million [30 − (30/30)] after one year.

The other reason for depreciation is a tax reason. Several different depreciation methods can be used for tax purposes. Canadians, for example, have a flat rate of taxation on the depreciated value of an asset. In contrast, the U.S. government has created a whole variety of ways in which assets can be written off—i.e., depreciated—at a rate faster than their useful life, once that is determined. The method established by the IRS is MACRS, the Modified Accelerated Cost Recovery System. Categories of assets are written off over a predetermined number of years that does not necessarily have anything to do with the assets' useful life. For instance, in Virginia, one of your authors is allowed to depreciate the total cost of his computer and printer in one year, despite the fact that he expects it to have a useful life far beyond that. Politics aside (and they are never really aside), depreciation is a powerful consideration in a company's decision to invest in capital assets. This consideration is not present in public-sector decision making.

Depreciation may have another major impact on managers, such as the FM, who manage depreciating assets. In some companies, all depreciation charges (e.g., the $1 million in the depreciation of the $30 million asset mentioned previously) are paid back to the corporation each year through the centralized accounting of the CFO in a process that is invisible to the FM department. In other companies, there is an annual depreciation charge to each manager equal to the combined annual depreciated costs for all depreciable assets managed by that department that have not been already fully depreciated. The amount of this charge shows up in the FM department's budget the year following the completion of its first capital-funded project and continues through the depreciable life of the asset. This can become a significant expense item in the annual expense budget of an FM department that has an active capital program. Unless it is budgeted for, it reduces the amount of operating funds available to do additional work.

Capitalization Versus Expense

Every facility manager is familiar with an operating or expense budget. In addition, most facility managers either have an annual capital budget or manage an occasional capital-funded project. Which assets are to be capitalized is defined by tax law and by company policy. Capitalization of an asset directly affects the *balance sheet*. Capital expenditures are used to acquire goods or services that are expected to provide benefits over a period longer than one year. In the facility department, capital expenditures typically involve construction, acquisition, replacement, or modernization (including major maintenance). Most companies have some floor for capital requests. (We capitalize only goods and services in excess of $10,000 per purchase, for example.)

As mentioned in Chapter 1, some firms are averse to capital funding (some for philosophical reasons, but most for tax reasons). They will really stretch the envelope in order to be able to expense items that we have traditionally assumed were capital items. In construction and alterations, a methodology called tax engineering allows owners to depreciate some building components at a rate that is more accelerated than the rate used to depreciate the building itself. All companies will make a determination annually as to how much corporate resources, funds and or debt, they want to use to meet capital needs. That means that there is stiff competition, and the manager who makes the best financial argument (how you can make money by spending money) is likely to be the manager who consistently obtains capital funding authorization. We cover capital budget decision-making and prioritization tools extensively in Chapter 5.

FM expenses directly affect the corporation's income statement. A dot.com company that wants to put every possible dollar into development of its products is probably uninterested in investing in long-term assets. If it has to have bricks-and-mortar facilities, it prefers to lease them. If it is forced to build and own them, it may well prefer to pursue a design and construction strategy that allows the maximum amount of the design and construction cost to be expensed.

Facility managers need to understand that not all projects are equal in the sight of the tax code. Some projects are eligible for accelerated depreciation and may be more desirable to the CFO for that reason alone. Issues like depreciation and the replacement value of facilities will become increasingly more visible and important to upper management as companies implement ERP and asset management.

With regard to valuation, accounting, depreciation, and capitalization, it is important that the facility manager understand that the chief financial officer sets the rules and the FM implements them. If the FM feels that there is an inequity or sees a financial advantage to the corporation from using a different procedure, then the FM should argue the case to management. However, there is no easier way to get in serious trouble than to start inventing accounting rules or deciding what can or cannot be depreciated. Facility managers will certainly be asked to be the expert in implementing corporate financial procedures, but FMs do not make up their own financial rules.

The Time Value of Money

Would you prefer to take $100 from us today, or would you choose to take it from us in five years if you could be assured that we would still be there? Through most of our lives, if given the chance, we would take the $100 sooner rather than later. Since the Great Depression, we have been in a period of inflation, which deflates the value of funds over time. But there is yet another solid economic reason. Money in hand could be put to work in the business or invested. (This is what CFOs are doing when they do not grant FMs the funds they request.) If the money is used or invested wisely, within five years that $100 might be worth $125, $500, or even more. These situations exemplify the idea that money has value over time. This is an important concept that is the basis of the two important financial management tools presented in the next section.

Decision-Making Tools

This topic returns us to the familiar area of asset allocation. Because CFOs have to differentiate among competing requirements for funding (see the section on asset allocation), companies have developed a variety of tools to make go/no-go decisions on those competing requirements and/or to prioritize the requirements. Commonly, corporations have used one of the following decision-making tools, the last two of which are based on the time value of money:

- Average or annual *payback*
- *Return on investment* (ROI)
- *Net present value* (NPV)
- *Internal rate of return* (IRR)

When these tools are used, projects that are not worth the funds invested in them according to the company's criteria will not be funded at all. In addition, funding will go first to the proposal that is most likely to provide the best return to the corporation. We will show how to calculate and use these tools in Chapter 5.

An FM should be able to provide the necessary analysis to allow the calculation of an IRR, for example, for his projects. Use of these tools is a best practice, particularly when combined with life-cycle cost analysis.

Approvals and Approval Levels

Another best practice is the concept of a two-tiered approval level. The policy entails first approving a project or program and then separately approving the expenditure of funds on it. That situation is similar to what already happens in the annual FM budget. First the facility manager gets budget approved, then she approves individual expenditures as the year progresses, depending on cash flow requirements and cash availability.

For major projects, we recommend that the project first be approved in concept and that the project budget then be approved. Expenditures should be similarly managed. The facility manager should approve the *commitment* of funds for a specific purpose but should also approve the expenditure of funds (*expensing*) for that purpose. We will discuss this in detail when we discuss budget execution, but different approval levels for committing and expensing funds should be established within the corporation.

Automation and Use of the Internet

Before we close this chapter, we need to discuss two topics that cut across every successive chapter of our book: automation and the use of the Internet. We will mention automation and the Internet whenever their specific applications appear in ensuing chapters rather than devote a separate chapter to each. We do so because we see automation and the use of the Internet as needing to be integrated into the practice of good financial management within the FM department. It is absolutely necessary that each of the specific applications of automation and the Internet be integrated into a total management system. For example, in CAFM, the work management system should seamlessly feed into the budget management system. Similarly, data provided to upper management under ERP should be collected within whatever FM management system is used and be provided to corporate accounting without the need for hand manipulation at the FM department level. Integration and seamlessness are necessary in order to make automated systems and the Internet helpful to the facility manager and the FM department.

Automation

It is incomprehensible that any separately organized FM department will not be using either an Internet-based facility management system or a CAFM. We have been involved in developing comprehensive FM information systems since the early 1980s. Frankly, the technology just wasn't there at that time, so the FM functions have tended to be automated in a stovepipe fashion, one at a time. These systems are used both to improve processes and to produce information. Historically we automated by starting with CADD and space management systems, then adding project management, then work management, and so on. Mostly, however, systems were more often touted as being truly integrated than truly effective, and that was not totally the fault of system producers and integrators. As one of the top facility managers, Rod Stevens, said during a presentation at World Workplace 1999, "Technology problems are easy; the tough ones are business process problems (which are the majority)."[8] Now, whether you use computer-assisted systems or the Internet, it is necessary to integrate these systems for more effective and efficient management of our facilities and department. Interestingly, with the introduction of asset management and ERP, it appears that some upper managers have been exposed to more FM data. They now appreciate the management data that are stored in the FM department more than ever before. As Eric Teicholz states, "It appears that corporate management finally is convinced that technology is essential in order to better manage facilities. The questions now being asked relate to how best to implement technology and to integrate and align computer-aided facility management systems (CAFM) with existing corporate databases and systems."[9]

Use of the Internet

While it is obvious to us that the Internet could have a profound impact on the management of finances within FM departments, it is much less clear what those impacts will be. There are a number of FM departments that have developed, with their outsource partners, an Internet application that permits them to view and run financial reports at any time through a proxy server. This allows them to access data from their outsource provider's servers and has improved their access to financial information while reducing the mailing and copying of reports and improving communication between the FM department and its outsource partner.

Use of the World Wide Web is responsible for a large amount of current corporate productivity increases. There is no reason that this should not be true in FM also. For that reason, we will certainly address items like ASPs and business-to-business (B2B) commerce, but we will promote Internet solutions only when we know that someone has successfully implemented those solutions.

Conclusion

After reading these first two chapters, FMs should be thinking like CFOs and should be ready to look at FM assets that can generate a good return on corporate investments with good management. Each of the concepts mentioned here will have FM applications later in the book.

We have probably understated the importance of risk and risk assessment. The facility manager will be asked to provide financial information that will, for example, allow management to decide between owning a property, taking a long-term lease, or taking a short-term lease. Within the department, the facility manager will have to assess the risks of repairing a boiler yet one more time versus buying a new one given the existing funding situation. In both cases, hopefully the facility manager will have the data to present the best business case, but the ultimate decision depends upon weighing finances within a larger management context and then making a decision that either is risky but offers high rewards or is risk-averse.

Before we proceed, here is a final reality check. Despite the best arguments for any individual project, the timing may be bad. The CFO is constantly managing corporate financial indicators such as cash flow and debt load. An FM may have the best economically justified project ever developed within the company, but if cash is short and there is no desire to increase the debt load, the project will be dead on arrival or delayed. That means that it is important for facility managers to be aware of (1) what is salable within the company in normal times and (2) what is going on financially at the current time. For every project, there is a season . . . but it might not be this one.

In this chapter we have presented the financial principles needed by facility managers in lay terms. We hope that with this information and the glossary, FMs will feel comfortable in applying these concepts to facility financial management, the first element of which is facility business planning.

Notes

1. Alan Whitson, "Basic Finance for Facility Managers," Presentation to World Workplace 1999, p. 3.
2. Thomas McCune, *Proceedings of World Workplace 1999* (Houston: International Facility Management Association, 1999), p. 355.
3. Every public-sector facility manager should read George C. Leef's classic, "A Lesson in Political Management," *The Freeman*, December 1999, pp. 28–30, for a better understanding of how money is appropriated each year for facility needs and yet the backlog of maintenance, repair, and replacement continually rises.
4. Class notes for the IFMA course "Facility Financial Forecasting and Budgeting," 1999, p. 59.
5. Ibid., p. 60.
6. Wes McGregor and Danny Shiem-Shin Thien, *Facilities Management and the Business of Space* (New York: John Wiley & Sons, 1999), p. 16.
7. Whitson, p.3.
8. Rod Stevens, Presentation to World Workplace 1999, p. 13.
9. Eric Teicholz, "The Business Side of CAFM," *FM Journal*, March/April 1994, p. 27.

3

Financial Aspects of Planning

Pulse Points

- *For every company business plan, there should be a corresponding facility plan or annex.*
- *There can be no good long-term facility management without good facility business planning.*
- *The greatest opportunity for expense savings and avoidance lies in better facility business planning.*
- *Facility business planning is not master planning, nor is it merely space or capital planning.*
- *Budget the way you work; plan the way you budget (programmatic planning and budgeting).*
- *Facility managers need to be represented on the corporate strategic business planning team.*
- *All levels of the facility department need to be involved in facility business planning.*
- *The environmental statements, assumptions, and constraints frame the entire facility business plan, so the planning team needs to concentrate on them intensely.*
- *A master plan, a lease management system, a capital development plan, facility standards, a comprehensive CAFM system, and facilities condition assessment/reserve studies provide invaluable input for facilities business planning.*

Keywords

Business plan, strategic plan, annual workplan, capital planning, facility business planning, master plan, space plan, CAFM, programmatic planning and budgeting, budgeting, program, programming, planning cycle, hierarchy of plans, annual budget, capital budget

Introduction

We are inclined to say that if you have time to read only one chapter in this book, it should be this one. That may be an overstatement, but it does highlight the importance of *facility business planning*. *For every company business plan, there should be a corresponding facility plan or annex.* That idea may seem self-evident. The fact is, however, that, in our experience, few companies do adequate facility business planning, to their disadvantage and to the detriment of good facility management.

It has always amazed us that, whereas in the military no major initiative would be considered or plan prepared without the facility management staff being there to present the FM impact, private companies over and over again fail to include the FM in business planning and pay the price because facilities are not ready when operational plans need to become reality. When business plans depend upon construction or alterations, as most do, there is a lead time that, if not planned for, will be the Achilles' heel of a new business operation. Bricks and mortar (or a new boiler, chiller, or elevator) cannot be produced overnight—or, if they are, the company pays a premium for them. One of the best examples of this was observed on a visit to a new manufacturing plant in China. There was a huge, rough hole in the floor where, the plant manager told us, a new production machine, of unknown dimensions, was to be placed whenever it arrived, while the plant had been in production for several years already.

Failure to plan is detrimental to the company's business, but it is devastating to the proper functioning of the facility management department, and consequently to the careers of facility managers. One of our favorite stories was related by the facility manager of a prestigious U.S. university. He found his university being overwhelmed with new construction funded by the gifts of wealthy graduates, but he lamented, "No one ever endowed an O&M contract to support the new construction." In other words, failure to plan for the operations and maintenance support along with the capital development was overwhelming the facility management department.

Observing the federal government's struggle to contend with an ever-increasing inventory of aging buildings with documented maintenance and repair needs makes it obvious that there is a wide disconnect between the federal government's capital planning system and its annual planning system. Its failure to plan could lead one to conclude that it has an inventory of facilities that it will never be able to properly operate, maintain, and repair.

A recent copy of a well-known FM journal just arrived with the first of a series of articles on capital planning. The article was excellent, as far as it went. But it totally ignored the fact that whenever a capital asset is put in place, it will have an impact on staffing, operations, maintenance, and logistics, all of which need to be planned simultaneously with the capital asset but never seem to be.

Too often, *capital planning* within our firms involves only providing enough *space* for new initiatives. It is bizarre but true that too often we build a facility with a known life cycle of thirty to seventy years, yet we plan only the original hard and soft costs for construction. Partly this is a function of budgeting processes, but it is a principal cause of the backlog of maintenance and repair that has been documented in study after study of the public sector and is no less the case in the private sector. We have built a capital infrastructure without providing the operational and maintenance resources needed to keep it functional. We facility managers are the unwilling inheritors of this funding shortfall, yet many of us seem unwilling to take the necessary steps to improve that situation. In fact, too many of the facility managers with whom we meet accept a maintenance and repair backlog as just one of the inevitabilities of the job. As a result, they lay themselves open to sanctions (which occasionally include the loss of a job) simply because they have not planned for the full spectrum of FM activities *and have not insisted that their companies consider these in strategic business planning.*

Without being overly dramatic, there is no doubt that, in the FM area, *the greatest opportunity for expense savings and avoidances lies in better business facility planning.*

The Problem

Why, then, is facility business planning done so poorly? Why are there almost legendary tales of cost overruns due to poor planning in the FM area? It is our observation that there are four basic problems:

1. Even facility managers have failed to understand the true nature of facility business planning.
2. There has not been a recognized methodology for facility business planning.
3. Facility managers are not members of the strategic business planning team.
4. Most facility departments use faulty budgeting systems.

We will address all of these issues except the last, which is part and parcel of the other three problems, in the increasing order of difficulty of solving them.

Facility Business Planning

It should be unnecessary to say what facility business planning is not, but you cannot pick up a professional or trade journal or the proceedings of a FM professional conference without seeing planning terms used and abused. First of all, facility business planning is not master planning. A *master plan* is a technical plan for a given piece of real estate that addresses how that land will be developed over a specified time period. Good master plan data, along with good facility condition assessments, provide excellent input data for facility business plans. The U.S. Department of Defense (DoD) has done an excellent job of master planning based on condition assessments. On the other hand, for reasons not fully within its control (it is partly a political problem, partly a problem of poor stewardship, and partly a problem of poor budgeting procedures), DoD's facility business planning is less than ideal. Hence DoD is a classic example of an organization that has capital facilities that are declining because they cannot be maintained properly. DoD has a huge backlog of maintenance and repair, commonly referred to as BMAR.

Second, facility business planning is not space planning. This is the biggest planning fallacy we have observed in the private sector. *Space plans* are very important—space is the *lingua franca* of facility management—but space plans and space forecasts, like master plans, simply provide good input for facility business plans. Space plans capture and quantify only part of future facility needs (not equipment needs, for example), and do not indicate how the requirements will be met or predict the cost of operating or maintaining the new facilities needed to meet those requirements.

For many years, *computer-assisted facility management (CAFM)* vendors advertised their systems as the solution to facility business planning, but they really helped to forecast only one FM resource: space. CAFM systems make facility space planning much easier and more accurate (provided that they are integrated with the financial management information system), but they do not do facility business planning.

Finally, facility business planning is not the formulation of a capital plan. A good capital program is the result of good facility planning and probably addresses the "big ticket" items to be planned, but it fails to address the impact of capital planning on operations, maintenance, personnel, and logistics. Again, we will use DoD as an example. DoD has highly sophisticated systems for gathering capital requirements (although a quirk of federal budgeting does not allow DoD to call this capital budgeting), but its planning horizon is too short. In addition, in its planning it ignores the need to operate, maintain, renovate, and repair those facilities because those items are funded in another budget. This means that the military continues to expand its stock of facilities, always adding to the current inventory despite the fact that it cannot maintain that inventory. It does not plan up front for the necessary operations and maintenance resources when it does its capital planning. The U.S. National Academy of Sciences has convened at least three panels of "gurus" to attempt to solve this problem across the federal government, but thus far it remains unsolvable.[1] This same problem extends to states, counties, and municipalities and to many large private companies. (Using life-cycle costs in facility planning and capital decision making seems more a matter of being *willing* to do so than of being *able* to do so. The General Accounting Office has recommended it,[2] and both the Federal Facilities Council[3] and the ASTM[4] have produced "how to" manuals on the subject.)

> **Authors' Note:** While we will often use examples of failure to exercise good facility financial management from the U.S. federal government,

we must also give the feds credit for taking a hard look at themselves
and publishing some of the best—*and free*—information on proper facility financial management. Why many of these known best practices
are not more widely implemented, even among the agencies that conducted the studies or were studied, is the subject for another, more
political, book. As this book is being written, we see some light at the
end of the tunnel in initiatives that are underway within the Veterans
Administration, NASA, and the Coast Guard.

Good capital, space, and master planning are all elements of good facility
business planning. Companies that have good capital, space, and master plans
(and can integrate them with financial data) have the information they need in
order to prepare excellent facility plans, particularly if they use CAFM properly.
There is no good facility business planning without good data, and a good CAFM
system can be of enormous assistance as a planning tool, provided that the right
data have been kept and can be accessed readily. The critical step, however, is
using those data sources and integrating facility planning into the business plans
of the company or agency. If, as we suggest, your **strategic plan** examines and
lists not only major capital expenditures but the operations and maintenance resources required to field those assets, then life-cycle costing is relatively simple, a
matter of "chug and plug." Conversely, if you have the data for proper life-cycle
costing of major capital investments, those annual costs make facility business
planning much easier.

One final general note on good facility business planning: While space is the
lingua franca of our business, cost (and occasional income) projections need to be
the basis for our facility business planning because these plans are our method
of communicating with our business colleagues and with upper management.
Financials are what these people understand, so we must communicate with them
in their language. Our facility business planning needs to be bottom-line-oriented;
i.e., we need to focus on what effect our business planning will have on corporate
finances. For all of these reasons, it is apparent that *facility and business managers
have failed to understand the true nature of facility business planning.* This is not likely
to change until we facility managers (and our FM professional organizations)
mount a major effort to do so. In order to do this, we need a business planning
method.

Methodology

Your authors certainly have not observed all corporate and government business
planning, but having worked with and for a large number of companies and government agencies, we assert that *there is no recognized methodology for facility business planning.* We will present here a method that is based on linking planning,
programming, and budgeting; this method is very comfortable for most of us in
the building profession because it tracks the plan-design-build process that we all
have used. Its effectiveness depends upon the use of common definitions that will

be presented later in this chapter. This methodology requires that we *budget the way we work* and *plan the way we budget*. The method ties our plans to our budgets to our capital and operational execution over time using the common language of resources (finances and personnel spaces).

We are not presumptive enough to assume that, if the company or agency currently does no business planning, the facility manager is immediately going to convince senior management that this type of planning needs to be done. As mentioned earlier, the popularity of business planning has ebbed and flowed. However, if the company has no business planning, we feel that promoting business planning and the facility manager's place on the business planning team should be one of the facility manager's top priorities. A facility manager who operates without a business plan is a facility manager who is doomed to reaction, failed projects, and ultimate failure. While the facility manager may not be a principal company business planner, he can help the process and improve his stature with upper management by using the facility business planning techniques mentioned here. To establish a platform to accomplish these goals, the facility manager needs to be a player in company business planning.

FM Participation in Business Planning

The final problem is that *facility managers are not on the strategic planning teams in their companies.* In our experience, this occurs for two reasons.

1. Facility managers are placed too low in the organization. We recommend that the FM be no more than two levels below the CEO. Even at that level, it takes a dynamic individual to be involved in the really strategic business decision-making sessions of a private company, although it is less of a problem in the public sector.
2. Some facility managers are unable and/or unwilling, by education, training, or temperament, to participate in company business planning.

Addressing the second reason, we have long advocated that facility managers increase their business skills and education. In Chapter 1, we discussed at length the argument that facility management is a business, not a technical, function. Facility managers need to display business acumen and be able to speak the language of business so that they will be respected by their business colleagues and upper management. Unless the facility manager has the business skills to contribute materially to strategic business planning, she will never be accepted on the strategic business planning team.

FMs may need to devise a strategy (make a suggestion, kick the door off its hinges, or take some other action of their own design) that lets upper management understand the importance of proper facility business planning. Unfortunately, one of the most successful strategies is to build upon a disaster. Show how the failure to have the FM at the table when strategic business decisions were made caused a major problem (for example, the plant opened six months late, and so staff had to be accommodated in inadequate leased space because construction had not been considered in the business plan). We cannot state too strongly that *there can be no good long-term facility management without good facility business planning.*

We firmly believe that the key to achieving that goal is for the facility manager to become a player in the company's strategic planning. Without that standing, facility managers will never be as effective as they should be and will always be in a reactive mode. Because we tend to deal in services that require long lead times, like construction, alterations, or major leasing projects, constant reaction means that we will (1) fail, (2) partially succeed, but always be tainted as not producing on time, or (3) have to throw money at our projects to achieve even suboptimal results. Those types of results cause too many FMs to be judged by management as the "same old facility manager who just never seems to be able to produce for us." Likewise, to force yourself onto the strategic planning team and then not be able to produce is also a recipe for disaster.

A Faulty Budgeting System

Inherent in all three of the problems just discussed is a problem that seems so mundane that it is often totally overlooked. Our budget formats are useless as a management tool. Because we should plan the way we budget and budget the way we work, a proper budget format is the keystone of proper planning. It is the framework upon which we hang our planning and budgeting methodology. Unfortunately, most facility departments and some organizations don't have a proper budget format. As mentioned earlier, this occurs because (1) the facility manager seemingly doesn't understand that it is a problem, (2) such a format is not part of a recognized methodology, and (3) even if the format is recognized as a problem, the FM is not in a position to change it.

Another issue that can complicate planning immensely is chargebacks. We will discuss chargeback budgeting in the next chapter, but having FM funds in the budgets of business units also creates a planning problem. If a company is on a full chargeback system (which few are), there is little planning for the FM to do. In such a case, almost the entire planning effort is devoted to providing business unit managers with cost estimates and rationales/justifications for FM projects in the business units' budgets. Under the more common scenario of partial chargeback, the FM will plan for common services like HVAC. This planning will include recalculating the "rent" to be charged for the common services and the price for specialized services that the FM department will offer the business units.

The remainder of this chapter will outline the policies and procedures for producing an outstanding facility business plan. Once the facility manager has the ability to produce such a plan, it is up to him to sell himself, his methodology, and his plan to his company's business planners. Before we proceed, then, let's look at a few definitions that form the basis of a proper planning and budgeting system.

Definitions

To introduce FMs to a proper methodology for facility business planning, it is necessary to understand the concept of *programs* and *programmatic planning and budgeting*. This concept is premised on planning and budgeting the way we work and maintaining the same planning categories (programs) throughout planning, budgeting, and budget execution.

For the remainder of this book, we will use the following definitions:

- *Planning*. Developing a scheme to carry out the decisions of management. This includes consideration of administration, facilities, communications, and logistics as well as operations.
- *Program*. One of the basic building blocks of facility management. A program is a logical group of work that has *clearly delineated management* and *resources committed to it*. (Plan and budget the way you work. Make the corporate statement of accounts fit your programs, not vice versa.)
- *Programming*. Developing a scheme of actions designed to accomplish defined and measurable objectives, specific in time phasing and resources. Do not confuse this business programming with the programming done by architects and interior designers as they determine user requirements for a project.
- *Budgeting*. The process by which the funds required to carry out programmed objectives and workloads are determined. Budgeting deals with reality because it is where the rubber meets the road. The budget is arranged in a systematic manner by program, account, and subaccount and also indicates the management and control systems to be used during execution.

In general, we will discuss two budgets. In the United States, the *capital budget* is used for large, usually one-time projects (construction, renovation, and major repair are typical), the projects included are largely defined by the tax code, and the money can be spent in multiple years. (While we are not international experts, it is our observation that those same characteristics generally apply internationally as well.) The *annual* (or expense or O&M) *budget* is for operations, maintenance, repair, minor construction/alterations, real estate, and overhead and is allocated on an annual basis (although some companies have two-year budgets). Money that is not spent in a given year is "lost" to the facility manager.

Notice the inclusion of budgeting in this chapter on planning. Until it is executed, a budget is a plan.

In the remainder of this chapter, we will concentrate primarily on the programs that fall into the annual plan and budget. In Chapter 5, we will discuss capital program and budget formulation in detail.

Continuity

Another premise of our planning and budgeting system is that any program can be tracked and studied over time, from concept, through planning, through budgeting, to execution. This approach is critical to the proper management of FM resources. For example, an FM and/or her management should be able to track each FM program as follows:

Strategic facility business plan → annual facility workplan → budget

Once the FM is executing an annual budget, she should be able to track any program, account, or subaccount backward against actual expenses for last year, last quarter, and last month and forward the results to projections for next month, next quarter, and through the end of the fiscal year. This is inherent in some companies' budgeting systems (statement of accounts), but if it is not, then the facility manager needs to set up a financial management information system that provides the capability to track programs and accounts over time. We expect the corporate financial management information system to be able to do this, but many facility managers have to set up, using their CAFM system, a separate FM financial management information system that either runs in parallel or periodically dumps into the corporate system.

Until such rigor and systematic analysis are present, facility planning and budgeting will be less than optimum. We achieve this systematic discipline by programmatic planning and budgeting. This system is sometimes referred to as the PPBS—planning, programming, and budgeting system. We strongly advocate its use in facility business planning and budgeting. As an alternative to programmatic planning and budgeting, facility managers may want to consider the system and set of accounts spelled out in the Institute of Management Accountants statement number 4BB, July 1, 1997.[5] This statement it is conducive to activity-based costing, provides some excellent definitions, and provides a model statement of accounts. Our only reservation is that, in order for this statement to be truly helpful, the facility manager needs to verify that the accounts in this statement reflect the way the facility department works.

Centralization Versus Decentralization

We simply do not have the time or space to discuss the theories of organizing the facility management department, yet organizational theory has a major influence on how the FM plans and budget. There is no purely centralized or purely decentralized FM organization, but we will, in general, tend to use a centralized model in most of our examples because that is the most complex organization. If you are a facility manager in one of the business units of a large but decentralized organization, you can apply these concepts to your situation just as if you were the corporate facility manager. It is interesting to note that the principal factor that determines whether facility management within an organization is primarily centralized or primarily decentralized is where the facility management money is controlled, at the corporate level or with the decentralized business unit. Total chargeback, which is almost never used, is the ultimate in decentralization.

As you analyze an FM department for organizational structure, follow the money!

Business Planning

Before we go into facility business planning specifically, we'll discuss some pertinent issues in business planning in general. Sadly, business planning has been treated almost like a fad (right now it seems to be "in" again). We suspect that the tendency for business planning to have cycles of favor will continue, but we believe that most companies that plan to be around for the long term will commit to business planning. The bigger issue for the facility manager is becoming a member of the planning team.

Why Plan?

Because we deal with bricks and mortar, it is even more important that we join our business colleagues and ask the question, "Why plan?" We have asked that question of facility management students in classes and seminars over the past ten years, and the most frequent responses are given in the following list:

- It provides focus, structure, and sequence.
- It encourages the development of objectives.
- It encourages systematic forward thinking.
- It allows faster response time in execution.
- It increases efficiency and effectiveness.
- It provides a map.
- It avoids financial mistakes.
- The process builds a team.
- It develops goals and objectives.
- It forms the basis for a budget.
- If done properly, it saves time and decreases the workload.
- It averts disaster.[6]

Most of those reasons are self-explanatory, but a few invite comment. First of all, there is merit to building a planning team, policy, and procedures. Part of that comes from forcing people to function outside of their normal responsibilities and to view the company goals and objectives overall. In order to develop a plan, each member of the team has to be a contributor. Those tough decisions that often get swept aside as we perform our daily tasks (Is there outsourcing in our future? Do we really want to spend capital funds on a new headquarters? What about the $267,000 in maintenance and repair backlog?) have to be put on the table in a forum where they can truly be addressed during planning. Proper business planning can be a godsend to the facility manager.

Second, and closely associated with the first concept, is the proper composition of the planning team. It is fine to hire a business planning consultant to help develop the process, but it is a fatal flaw to then turn facility business planning over to the consultant. A consultant is best used to provide structure for the process, to facilitate planning sessions, and to physically pull the plan together. Senior management must spend some time in business planning. At the corporate level, the U.S. Pentagon handles this very well. Each major staff agency represented by a major general has a major/lieutenant colonel "horseholder" who represents that agency in planning. The horseholder is a conduit for input from the manager of that agency, normally a general or senior executive, to the planning group and vice versa. Unless management stays involved, as is assured by scheduled periodic meetings of principals plus their horseholders, the business planning procedure will soon deteriorate into just another bureaucratic exercise and be ignored.

A third concept that needs to be thought out in large organizations is how a plan should be put together. One of the authors frequently teaches seminars on facility financial management and asks the seminar attendees whether it is better to use top-down planning, where top management makes the decisions and mid- and lower-level management and technicians fill in the details, or to use bottom-up planning, where the base plan is prepared by operational managers. When given that choice, seminar attendees, undoubtedly reflecting the fact that most of them are mid-level managers, nearly always promote bottom-up planning. In fact, what works best is the *planning cycle* shown in Figure 3-1.

In order to be successful, the planning cycle needs early guidance from upper management. There is no sense heading down planning avenues where upper management has no intention of taking the company. Consequently, at the start of

Figure 3-1. The Ideal Business Planning Cycle.

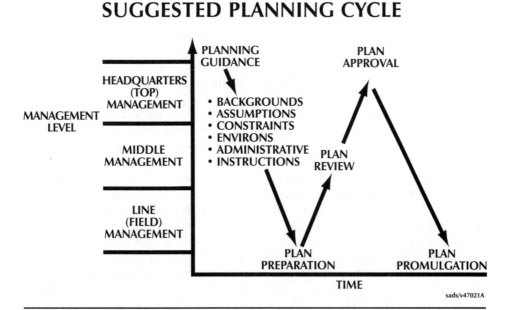

the planning cycle, the consultant should lead upper management in developing guidance for the plan, which might be outlined as follows:

- Background
- Assumptions
- Constraints
- Business environment projections
- Administrative instructions

These elements may well be added to or altered during the development of the business plan. If upper management does not provide guidance in these areas at the start of the process, there will be a lot of wheel spinning, and the final plan will probably not accurately reflect the direction in which management truly plans to take the company. The FM's strategic business plan will contain the listed factors that are applicable to facilities plus facility-specific factors that are necessary to develop this strategic plan. Some of these factors will not be apparent when planning starts; to provide a well-rounded plan, they will need to be added as the plan is developed.

A second point is that the business planning graphic (Figure 3-1) is oversimplified. Planning is an iterative process. In fact, certain parts of the plan and sometimes the entire plan may go back and forth between the line managers and technicians and upper management many times before the plan is finally approved. The graphic also fails to reflect the interior politics, fights, squabbles, and discussions that need to be resolved. (One of your authors was constantly at odds with his IT department during facility planning; financial analysts will always be a necessary damper during planning deliberations.) The importance of proper attention to planning, organization for planning, and the planning cycle cannot be overemphasized. The plan will be suboptimal if the planning process, organization, and commitment by all to the results do not exist.

Effective Planning

Many, many books have been written on business planning, and we don't intend to make this a primer. While we are going to provide a specific format for a facility management business plan, if an FM's company already has a facility management business plan, the FM will, of course, comply with its format. We do not think that it will be that difficult to adapt our format to that of your company.

If a company currently does no business planning, we suggest that the FM scan two or three books on general business planning to pick out the common concepts and formats. Keep in mind that there are certain forms, rules, and practices that are required for good facility business planning. Effective business planning, as we have illustrated in Figure 3-1, needs to be participative, iterative, and continuous. Any facility manager who wishes to become an expert in the tie-in between facility business planning, budgeting, and other aspects of facility financial planning should take the International Facility Management Association's competency-based course "Money Talks." This course was developed by Professor Mike Hoots of the University of Southern Colorado and is based on materials developed by him and one of your authors. Mike is one of the few individuals to bind the skills of financial management to all competencies of facility management and then to teach it to other professionals.

One of our favorite ways to impress upon facility managers the value and relative return on investment from planning is to relate it to project management (which most facility managers readily understand) using Figure 3-2. Mike Hoots says, "Effective planning is often the difference between enjoying facilities management and merely enduring it."[7]

Figure 3-2 illustrates two important points.

1. A relatively modest up-front planning effort can have immense consequences—for example, in terms of having a facility ready on time or saving money.
2. Once construction starts, the return on a planning effort diminishes radically.

In fact, those who are experienced in project management understand that changes made after implementation begins are costly. In some cases, the FM has only limited leverage to determine what the true cost of the change is.

Successful Facility Business Planning

Like most management skills, good facility business planning is a balance between having a plan and planning only to the degree that benefits outweigh the costs. Mike Hoots makes two outstanding points about the proper amount of facility business planning: "Only plan to the degree that benefits outweigh the costs but ALWAYS have a plan" and "An important purpose of longer range planning is to save yourself time, not increase your workload."[8]

The attributes and advantages of good facility business planning are as many and varied as the companies doing the planning, but they generally include those in the following list. Successful facility business planning:

- Correlates and integrates business and facilities planning
- Positions facilities to complement and enhance financial performance
- Helps avoid unwarranted investments
- Accelerates response time
- Improves major capital expenditure coordination
- Highlights the continuity between short- and long-term goals
- Helps manage and control costs
- Helps manage and support change
- Helps facilitate task management
- Minimizes unscheduled work

Figure 3-2. Relative Return on Long-Range Planning Investment.

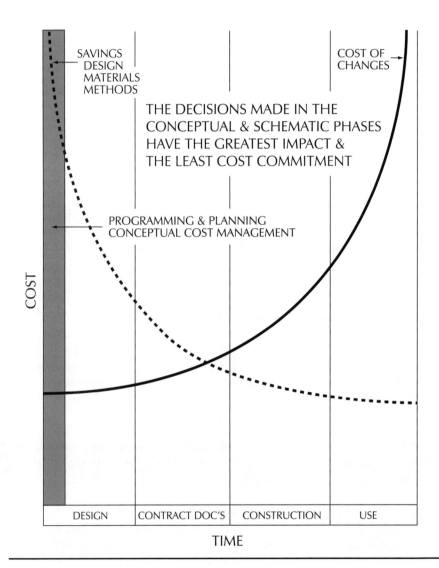

RELATION BETWEEN TIMING OF DECISIONS AND COST SAVINGS

SAVINGS
DESIGN
MATERIALS
METHODS

COST OF
CHANGES

THE DECISIONS MADE IN THE
CONCEPTUAL & SCHEMATIC PHASES
HAVE THE GREATEST IMPACT &
THE LEAST COST COMMITMENT

PROGRAMMING & PLANNING
CONCEPTUAL COST MANAGEMENT

COST

DESIGN | CONTRACT DOC'S | CONSTRUCTION | USE

TIME

- Increases management confidence in the ability to keep everything under control
- Provides focus, structure, and sequence
- Encourages working in teams
- Facilitates the development of goals and objectives

- Provides the base for budgeting
- Uses planning to save time, not to increase your workload[9]

Hierarchy of Plans

How far out to plan and the time frame for plans vary widely, particularly in private industry. Our experience is that few firms' strategic plans extend beyond ten years, and many are capped at five. Some firms actually prepare an intermediate-range plan. For this book, we will use a single ten-year strategic business planning model for illustrative purposes. Figure 3-3 represents a spectrum of facility business plans using that ten-year planning horizon. We think this *hierarchy of plans* both represents the prevalent planning mode among companies that do plan and is the minimum essential.

From the planning model in Figure 3-3, we have provided a strategic facility business plan (Appendix B) that is ten years in length, with the first five years spelled out in detail and years 6 to 10 lumped into a single estimate of resources that will be required. The corresponding annual workplan example (Appendix C) is Year 1 of last year's strategic plan updated to reflect changes since the last planning cycle. It represents a statement of the unconstrained requirements for next year and is your starting position for the budget cycle. The budget is the workplan for any particular year after both internal and external adjustments have been made. It is the financial plan for the next fiscal year.

Figure 3-3 shows that the business planning process is a rolling process. As one year is stripped off to become first the annual workplan and then the budget, another year, ten years out, is added to the strategic plan.

Figure 3-3. Hierarchy of Plans.

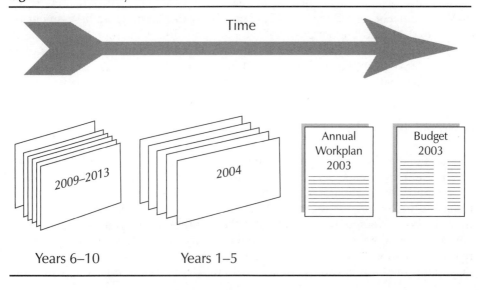

The Plan

We have given a considerable preamble. Now, what does a facility business plan look like? Appendix B is a strategic facilities business plan. This might be a stand-alone document, or, more likely, it might be an attachment to the company's business plan. Next we will briefly discuss the various parts of a facilities business plan. As we mentioned earlier, what we depict is a ten-year plan with years 6 to 10 lumped into a single entry. The plan is organized around programs, and the unit of measure is dollars. In some cases we have shown subaccounts based on our experience of what management and budget departments want to be transparent in reviewing facility budgets and allocating corporate funds. We believe that most of the programs and accounts are self-explanatory to facility managers, and so we have not tried to define them further. Remember again, programs are an indication of how you *work*. You may have another list of programs, but *if your budget exceeds $100,000 annually and you have a capital program to manage, we recommend programs closely aligned with those indicated in Appendix B.* It took one of your authors nine years to convince his finance department to agree to a statement of accounts that reflected these programs. It was worth every minute of that fight because it allowed the unification of operations and finance, CAFM and a financial management information system.

In the following explanation, we plan for building functions only, although we understand that many facility managers have a broader range of administrative functional management, such as security, reprographics, and so on.

Introduction

The introduction to the plan should include any material that will help upper management, budgeters, or anyone who might need to review the strategic facility business plan to understand it better. For instance, the introduction might make statements regarding the challenges faced in planning, an assessment of results to date, and the objectives of the planning. To set the tone for the rest of the plan, keep this section short and material. To make the facility business plan complete, take from the introduction to the company business plan any pertinent information that needs to be repeated to make the facility business plan understandable.

Environmental Statements

This section needs to capture those unique facets of the facility management and business environments that are going to influence the design, construction, renovation, and operation and maintenance of the facilities over the next ten years. Consider the company, the competition, and the market (for instance, lease costs may be above average in the location of the facilities in question). A major item here might be the regulatory environment, particularly if the facilities are sensitive to regulations. The energy availability and pricing environment is another major consideration in some companies. To make the facility business plan complete, take from the company business plan's environmental statements any pertinent information that needs to be repeated.

Assumptions

Again, take from the company business plan all of the assumptions that need to be repeated in order to make the facility plan complete and include them in the facility management business plan. In addition, you will have to make assumptions of your own. In fact, as the planning process develops, even more assumptions absolutely will be added. The importance of these assumptions cannot be overemphasized. "Garbage in, garbage out" applies here. Care must be taken not to assume yourself into widely different scenarios. No part of planning will be more of a challenge than making the proper assumptions and ensuring that all assumptions are recorded. At a minimum, there will probably be assumptions about space growth, inflation, major new facilities, and budget and staffing growth.

Constraints

Again restate from the company business plan all of the external constraints that will be placed upon the department over the ten-year window. In addition, consider posing some constraints from the viewpoint of the FM department—energy constraints to produce cost savings, for example.

The importance of getting the environmental statements, assumptions, and constraints right cannot be overstated. These sections frame the entire facility business plan and require intense attention. Get the FM staff and outside experts involved in determining that these sections of your plan are correct. They will then be more likely to support the plan during implementation. Get agreement on those sections from both immediate management and the company business planning team. Once that is done, if there is an accurate cost database, the rest of the plan will both fall into place and be easily defended to upper management.

Discussion

This section centers around a ten-year estimate of costs (five single years plus years 6 to 10 rolled into a single figure), displayed for each program and account (and subaccount, if desired). In the example given in Appendix B, the display is listed as Annex A. This section of the report is a detailed discussion of the numbers that will allow upper management to understand, in financial terms, your plan for facilities and the facility management department for the next ten years.

Once the FM has developed sophisticated planning skills, we actually favor outlining three scenarios in the discussion section, but, in the interest of brevity, we have limited our example plan financials to one scenario only. Because this is a plan, point estimates (i.e., one scenario) are inherently less accurate than a bracket of choices (three scenarios):

1. Most conservative scenario in terms of financing
2. Most liberal scenario in terms of financing
3. Most likely scenario (which is what you have in Appendix B)

Because the FM has thought through and recorded a range of possible outcomes, the plan will be of more value to him during implementation as situations change. If there is a business downturn during Year 3, for instance, the FM may revert to the conservative scenario for one or two years until the business rights itself.

We have chosen to display "then year" (inflated) dollars in Appendix B. An optional planning technique would be to plan in constant dollars so that any increases or decreases displayed indicate actual program changes. Under this procedure, when the plan for any specific year actually becomes the budget, the CFO indicates during the budget formulation what percent inflation is allowed for each program/account and adjusts the numbers accordingly across the company.

Conclusions

The next two sections are specifically targeted at those who use the facility management business plan, particularly upper management. Using the discussion and Annex A, demonstrate those conclusions that no one should miss because they are imperative to the success of the department in the future. The conclusions should be supported by the facts contained in the plan.

Recommendations

Recommendations should flow from the conclusions. This is the "special pleadings" section of the plan. Recommend those key items that are highlighted in the conclusions, but also recommend actions outside the FM department that, if they are not completed, will affect the department's performance.

Last Words on Strategic Facility Business Planning

It is our experience that, in facility management business planning, the perfect is often the enemy of the good enough. Part of the reason for this may be that because of our technical backgrounds, we are uncomfortable with the fact that planning has a degree of uncertainty. When we try to develop the perfect plan, two things can happen. First, we waste time trying to plan the unplannable or trying to get a degree of accuracy in the out years that is unrealistic. Second, because we do not necessarily have a perfect plan, we lose both faith in the plan and interest in the planning process. Our experience shows that it takes three planning cycles to get the first acceptable facility business plan and five to perfect it to the point where tinkering with the basics becomes counterproductive.

Figure 3-4 demonstrates that planning is an ongoing function that requires some amount of the facility manager's time throughout the year.

Figure 3-4. Annual Planning Activities.

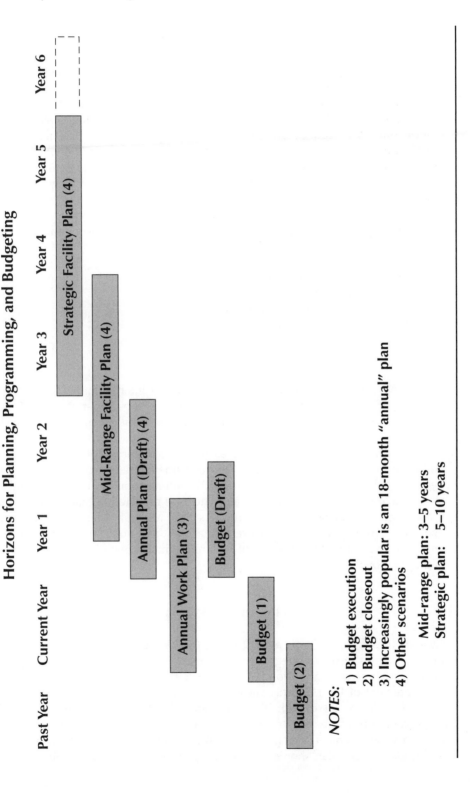

Horizons for Planning, Programming, and Budgeting

Past Year | Current Year | Year 1 | Year 2 | Year 3 | Year 4 | Year 5 | Year 6

Strategic Facility Plan (4)

Mid-Range Facility Plan (4)

Annual Plan (Draft) (4)

Annual Work Plan (3)

Budget (Draft)

Budget (1)

Budget (2)

NOTES:
1) Budget execution
2) Budget closeout
3) Increasingly popular is an 18-month "annual" plan
4) Other scenarios

Mid-range plan: 3–5 years
Strategic plan: 5–10 years

At one point during the year, the facility manager can be closing out last year's budget, developing this year's budget from the annual workplan, and updating and adding another year to the facility management strategic business plan. In our opinion, the most common planning pitfall is failing to commit to planning or treating planning as just another administrative requirement. In the hurly-burly of a facility manager's life, planning can be neglected or sloughed off to a planning team or a consultant. When that happens, the facility manager and the FM department become less involved and the department's operations start to depart more and more from the plan. Soon the facility management business plan is just another document that gathers dust on the shelf, no longer worth the effort that was put into it.

While neglect of the planning process over time is a major reason why facility business planning fails, Mike Hoots notes other common reasons for the failure of facility business planning:

- Ineffective preparation by managers
- Faulty definition of the organization's mission
- Vaguely formulated goals and requirements
- Inadequate information base and analysis
- Poorly handled participation and conflict resolution
- Inadequate linkage with control systems[10]

To these we would add the problems of lack of internal and external buy-in, planning being done by the wrong people, and, perhaps worst of all, no follow-through to ensure that the plan is translated into a budget and ultimately into operations.

These failures have all been addressed earlier in this chapter, but it is important once more to reiterate that the FM department needs a clear mission, well-defined goals and objectives, and supportive information systems and databases to optimize its planning. But what also must be repeated is that failure to have those items should not stop planning. As the FM department plans better, its goals, objectives, policies, procedures, databases, and support systems will likewise improve. The mere presence of a planning mechanism improves operations and operational tools.

The Annual Workplan

As shown in Figure 3-3, the *annual workplan* (Appendix C) is no more than the first year of last year's strategic facility management business plan, upgraded to include any newer information gathered since the last planning cycle. As such, it is a statement of the relatively unconstrained requirements for the next budget year—a wish list, if you will. We recommend that the workplan not exceed 5 to 15 percent of the amount of funds that the department is likely to receive unless the excess represents a capital project that is reasonably certain to get funded. In addition, the workplan should represent a plan that is capable of being executed if it is funded. If the department is given funds and then does not deliver, its credibility will be severely damaged.

About three months before the start of the company's budget cycle, extract and update the annual workplan. Ensure that the rationale for each requirement in the workplan is valid (it has been months since the workplan was originated, and conditions have changed in the interim), add or subtract requirements, and prioritize the requirements within each program. Once that information is available, preparation of the budget should be relatively easy.

The Annual Budget

We will discuss capital budgeting in Chapter 5 and the annual budget in detail in Chapter 4, but we want to stress again that the budget is no more than a one-year plan (some companies are doing two-year budgeting). The annual budget, as indicated in Figure 3-3, is the logical extension of the facility management strategic business and annual work planning efforts, updated with the most recent information and management guidance available. We view the annual budget as the facility manager's most important facility management information tool. Despite the fact that in order to prepare the budget, some assumptions will still need to be made, the budget is the most finite statement of the department's capabilities that management will see. It is the FM department's contract with the company to provide X products and services given Y resources. More facility management careers hinge on the ability to develop and implement a budget than on any other factor. The entire planning process explained in this chapter serves to provide the FM department with the best annual budget year after year. That is its reason for being, and it is the reason we emphasize the need to realize that good facility business planning is the cornerstone of good financial management of facility management resources.

Planning Tools

For facility managers who are at one location, one site, facility business planning can be relatively simple. For an international corporation, it can be extremely complex. As mentioned previously, a *master plan* for each of the major locations can provide excellent information for facility business planning, particularly for major project work. A *lease management system* tracks not only when leases are due, but when escalators kick in, the status of subleases, and other leasing-related factors that are essential for long-range planning. *Facilities condition assessments* or *reserve studies* are invaluable for planning. When done well, these studies show not only a qualitative assessment of the maintenance and repair status of the facilities, but both a profile for probable maintenance and repair costs and an estimate of probable replacement dates for major facility systems.

We have long maintained that the major function of *space, furniture, and equipment standards* is to aid in planning, not to control the workplace environment.

Continuity between how a facility is planned and how it is to be operated is needed. But standards are better used by the facility planner as a planning tool than by the facility operator to try to regulate the issuance of space, furniture, or equipment to customers in the workplace.

We will discuss formulating a *capital program* in Chapter 5. Knowledge of the company's ten-year capital program is essential for the facility management business planner because (1) there may need to be facility capital expenditures to accommodate another department's capital initiatives and (2) there always will be an annual operations and maintenance impact once a capital project is brought on line.

Hopefully, the department has a *CAFM system that is capable of computer-assisted design, project management, space management, work management, and financial management*. This facility management information system (FMIS) should provide the data not only to document past history and assist in tracking current operations, but also to help forecast and plan the future.

Few departments have all of these tools available initially (and not all tools are needed by all departments), so there is plenty of stubby pencil work done in the early iterations of facility business planning. As the planning process becomes more sophisticated, the FM can and should bring more of these tools on line. He may find out, for instance, that he has been keeping the wrong or irrelevant data on space or work management. As the planning process improves, so should the tools, and vice versa. This is one of the reasons that truly effective planning processes take three to five years to implement (it takes a while for the FM to find out what she does not truly know, and then she needs time [and funds] to correct this).

A Different View

Little has actually been written on the mechanics of long- and short-term facility business planning. The emphasis has tended to be on planning space and projects, which, as we have mentioned frequently, is only part of the overall planning responsibility for the facility managers. For another view of forecasting and long- and short-term facility business planning, see pages 113 to 129 of *Facility Management* by Rondeau, Brown, and Lapides.[11]

Think Like a CFO

In this chapter we have tried to give you a methodology and examples of a facility business planning system that anyone can adapt to his or her company or agency. One thing more is necessary, and that is that the FM think like upper management, particularly the CFO. We teach FMs to plan financially and to turn goals and objectives into hard numbers that they can defend both strategically and tactically. For some of us, this will require an initial refocusing. However, as we use better and more powerful tools through successive planning cycles, each cycle becomes better. So, too, as we manage our departments through successive iterations of planning, we will also become more skillful as planners, budgeters, and financial managers.

Summary

Early in its efforts to define the profession of facility management, the IFMA noted that a core competency for facility managers is to be able to develop, maintain, and evaluate long-term, interim, and short-term facility plans.[12] The need for those skills, and their use, was confirmed by a National Academy of Science study group in 1986.[13] Long-range facilities business planning and annual work planning using programmatic planning and budgeting provide the facility manager and the company with the best tools for evaluating the past, forecasting the future, and developing implementable budgets.

In the following chapters we will discuss the development, execution, and evaluation of budgets in detail. Remember, a budget is also a plan and should be thought of as one. Budgeting is the logical extension of a well-developed business planning cycle. Chapter 4 addresses the annual budget, and Chapter 5 outlines proper capital budgeting procedures.

Notes

1. *Committing to the Cost of Ownership* (Washington, D.C.: National Research Council, 1990), *Pay Now or Pay Later* (Washington, D.C.: National Research Council, 1991), and *Stewardship of Federal Facilities* (Washington, D.C.: National Research Council, 1998).

2. *Leading Practices in Capital Decision-Making*, GAO/AIMD-99-32 (Washington, D.C.: General Accounting Office, December 1998).

3. *Sustainable Federal Facilities*, Technical Report No. 142 (Washington, D.C.: Federal Facilities Council, 2001).

4. *ASTM Standards on Building Economics*, 4th ed. (West Conshohocken, Pa.: ASTM, 1999).

5. *Practices and Techniques: The Accounting Classification of Workpoint Costs*, Statement 4BB (Montvale, N.J.: Institute of Management Accountants, 1997).

6. Tom Kvan, Dean of Architecture, University of Hong Kong.

7. Michael Hoots, *Facility Financial Forecasting and Budgeting* (Houston: International Facility Management Association, 1999), p. 24.

8. Ibid., pp. 24–25.

9. Ibid.

10. Ibid., pp. 28–29.

11. Rondeau, Brown, and Lapides, *Facility Management* (New York: Wiley, 1995), pp. 113–129.

12. *Competencies for Facility Management Professionals* (Houston: International Facility Management Association, 1992), pp. 96–100.

13. Building Research Board, *Programming Practices in the Building Process* (Washington, D.C.: National Academy Press, 1986), p. 6.

4

Annual Budgeting

Pulse Points

- *Budget like you work and plan like you budget (programmatic planning and budgeting).*
- *There is merit to having a multiyear "annual" budget.*
- *Capital and annual budgeting require different procedures and tools.*
- *The annual facility budget is unique.*
- *One of the greatest budget challenges is the adequate funding of maintenance and repair.*
- *Good facility budgeting should flow out of good strategic and annual work planning.*
- *When submitting the annual budget, the facility manager should have already considered how and where cuts will be made if they are demanded.*
- *The facility manager must understand how the accounting and purchasing departments affect the FM budget.*
- *The annual budget should be the facility manager's principal information management system and is the most important financial management tool.*
- *The facility manager should be able to manage the FM budget within +/ −¹/₂ percent at year's end.*
- *Zero-base each program every three to five years.*
- *Use a two-signature policy for both authorizing and expensing funds.*
- *Facility managers must have the data and the information system to develop and manage a chargeback system.*
- *The theme for communicating with management regarding the FM budget is "no surprises!"*

Keywords

Programmatic budgeting, expense budget, capital budget, annual budget, zero-based budgeting, chargeback, discretionary costs, nondiscretionary costs, controllable costs, uncontrollable costs, allocate, expense, commitments, fungible, cost of ownership, forecasting, fiscal year, burn rate, accruals, approval levels

Introduction

Whether a cost should be capitalized or expensed will be discussed in Chapter 5. This topic can be extremely complex and can vary from one political jurisdiction to another. In fact, there are tax engineering consultants who will examine a major project to identify aspects of a capital building project that can be expensed. If tax engineering of new facilities is in line with corporate goals, the facility manager should work with the accounting department to ensure that the facility department is not setting company financial policy.

Annual budgeting is a logical extension of the planning process. It is important that we plan like we budget and budget like we work; consequently, our discussion and examples will all be of *programmatic budgeting*, as explained in Chapter 3. The annual budget derives directly from the annual workplan (Figure 3-3). In some companies the annual budget is referred to as the operations and maintenance budget or the operating budget; however, it is most commonly called the *expense budget*. We use the term *annual budget,* since it is the most descriptive. In the interest of providing the broadest understanding of annual budgeting, we discuss an annual budget for only the building-related functions of facility management. In addition, in our examples and discussion, personnel expenses and spaces are budgeted at the FM department level and there is no chargeback or allocation system used within the company. This is perhaps the most complex type of budget that a facility manager will have to manage.

At the end of the chapter, we discuss chargeback in detail, since it is so commonly used in the business world and is increasingly being used in government. Whether or not the FM uses chargeback, it is important that the FM understand centralized annual budgeting.

We acknowledge that some companies' "annual" budgets cover two years. There is some merit to this practice, particularly in reducing budget administration. We also have talked to an FM budget analyst from a high-tech firm who stated that her firm's fiscal year was only six months long. Regardless of the length of the budget year, the policies, procedures, and formats that we present in this chapter are valid. We approve the trend toward multiyear budgeting, but we also understand that business requirements and their associated accounting practices will set the length of the budget period.

There is a scarcity of good material on the development, execution, and evaluation of an annual budget. Two sources that we find particularly helpful are Mike Hoots's *Money Talks* seminar text, published by the IFMA, and the chapter "Managing the Budget" in *The Facility Management Handbook,* 2d ed., from the American Management Association. The former has some particularly helpful definitions and a brief discussion of accounting that are usable by those of us who are not accountants, while the latter has a more in-depth discussion of all aspects of annual budgeting.

As you proceed through this chapter and as you manage your budget, you should base all of your decisions on two principles:

1. Seize funding opportunities that can be justified.
2. When given resources, use them efficiently and productively.

Definition

The annual budget is the budget given to a department in accordance with which it conducts its work programs for the year and administers itself. As mentioned earlier, annual funds are usually for one fiscal year, as opposed to capital funds (Chapter 5), which are multiyear. Funds in the annual budget that are not expended by the end of the fiscal year must be turned back to the company (actually, it takes them) unless they are set aside, i.e., accrued. Both annual and *capital budgets* can be used to fund projects and major replacements, but annual projects will generally be smaller than capital projects. The value of projects or replacements that can be expensed rather than capitalized is a product of tax law and company policy. Some firms prefer to expense as much as they can; others take a longer view and capitalize major projects and replacement. The decision to expense or capitalize may require FM department input, but it should remain in the finance department.

An example of an annual budget is given in Appendix D. For illustrative purposes, this annual budget is one that could have evolved from the workplan in Appendix C, completing the cycle described in Figure 3-3. We want to stress once again that it is important that the FM use a budget format that reflects the way the FM department works rather than just accept a format that has historically been used or was developed by accountants in the finance department.

As the last item of introductory material, facility managers need to understand a bit about costs, the importance of the definition of the varying categories of costs, and how those definitions mesh with operations.

Costs

We will discuss costs at great length in Chapter 6, but it is worthwhile to understand that some costs are discretionary and some are not. *Nondiscretionary costs* are relatively easy to understand. For example, the FM must pay the water bill. What is a *discretionary cost* is less clear. For instance, suppose the boss has told the facility manager that project X must be carried out in the next fiscal year. Are the costs for that project discretionary, since they won't occur unless the project is executed, or are they nondiscretionary, since the FM's job may hang on completing project X? The popular definition of discretionary costs is those costs that can be controlled by the manager without a direct effect upon operations. The annual costs that most often have a large discretionary component are construction; alterations; the purchase of new furniture, furnishings, and equipment; service levels; overtime, travel, and training; staffing; and elements of maintenance.

Costs can also be classified as *controllable costs* or *uncontrollable costs*. The ability to control costs has two components. It is necessary to identify first *who* can control the costs and then the *degree* to which those costs can be controlled. Most costs have both a controllable and an uncontrollable aspect. *Committed costs* (or simply *commitments*) are a subset of uncontrollable costs; these funds may have been committed in an earlier time period but extend into the present or may have been committed by the manager of another department but mandate costs to the FM department. IT departments often do this. Their projects tend to have a large FM component. Signing a long-term lease is an example of taking an action at one point in time with long-term consequences. For example, a long-term lease commits the FM department to a stream of annual costs for the term of the lease, not just for the year in which the lease is signed. FM budgets contain many examples of committed costs.

Don't get hung up on definitions, but realize that it is important generally to understand that a budget is composed of costs that are discretionary, nondiscretionary, controllable, and uncontrollable. In addition, previous management actions will have committed the FM to certain costs in the current fiscal year. While facility managers don't need to be accountants, understanding some of these basic accounting terms will help them do their job better and communicate more effectively with the company finance department.

With these introductory concepts, let's move into budgeting by first looking at its importance to the facility manager and the FM department and then proceeding to the composition of the budget, the budget cycle, and, finally, budget mechanics. Throughout the discussion, the facility manager needs to keep in mind the concept that the budget flows from the workplan, which flows from the facility department strategic business plan. Appendices B, C, and D can be used as concrete examples of this movement from planning to budget.

The Importance of Budgeting to the Facility Manager

For facility managers of all but the smallest departments, budgeting will probably be among the top three consumers of their managerial effort, and the budget will be one of the top three most important managerial topics. Our goal in introducing programmatic budgeting flowing from a business planning cycle and in tying the budget into both managerial responsibility and the work management system is not to diminish the importance of budgeting, but to make sure that the FM department works smarter and more efficiently. The goal of an effective FM business planning system is to produce a meaningful budget. Any manager who is not intimately familiar with his budget is less effective than he could be and is probably doomed to failure. If anything, a budget is even more important in the public sector than in a private company. *Budgeting at every level must strike a balance.* The manager should be provided with enough resources to accomplish the department's mission. At the same time, though facility managers sometimes don't like to admit it, the FM should be sufficiently resource-constrained that she is challenged to provide services and products in the most cost-effective way possible. Too often these simple facts are lost both to the facility manager and to the company's financial analysts.

As indicated by Figure 3-4, budgeting is not a one-time event. If FMs are to be successful in obtaining resources, not only will they be working on multiple budgets, but they also must be in constant communication with the finance department's budget analyst responsible for the budget. If an FM, for example, has a large U.S. federal FM budget, he may have to be fielding questions from the boss, the parent department's budget department, the Office of Management and Budget, Congress, and, if it is conducting a study or audit, the General Accounting Office. At the same time, the facility manager must be dealing with the budget needs of the ultimate users of FM services, his customers. Too many facility managers try to provide all the rationale for the FM budget without outside political help. Instead, the FM must continually gather and understand the customers' requirements, allay their fears, and elicit their support for their projects and services in the budget battle that takes place as budgets are developed within companies. This is why we stress that budgeting is likely to be time-consuming. In the closing days of a fiscal year, the manager will be almost totally consumed with closing out the old budget, managing accruals, and preparing to make the transition to the new budget and fiscal year. One of our goals is to lessen that end-of-the-year crunch by helping the FM manage the budget better during the entire year. But a large amount of annual budget activity at year's end will never be entirely eliminated. We discuss more of the necessary communication involved in budget management later in this chapter, but now let's look at the composition of the facility department's annual budget.

Characteristics of FM Annual Budgets

The following list gives the unique characteristics of annual facility budgets:

- They are large—the facility budget is usually the second or third largest budget even without the personnel costs that we have included in our examples.
- They are diverse, covering a wide range of activities.
- They have both long- and short-term aspects.
- They are partly responsive to regulation.
- They are partly reactionary.
- They contain both discretionary and nondiscretionary elements.
- They contain both controllable and uncontrollable elements.

Because the FM budget is both large and unique, it is often the target of more than its share of scrutiny. One of our colleagues once said that one reason for this is that everyone who owns a house thinks that that fact automatically makes him or her a facility management expert. An estimate we budgeted for an office renovation was once challenged by our vice president as "more than I paid for my house." That was true, but his house was not in a fifty-year-old building in the downtown business district, nor did it need to accommodate the latest in information technology.

The diversity of the FM budget, which covers everything from providing janitorial services, to ensuring that snow is plowed in the winter, to providing access to all facilities for the handicapped, to historic renovation, requires that the FM have a tremendous range of knowledge. At the same time, the FM must also have the ability to forecast costs over that range of products and services. No other department director faces a demand for as broad a range of knowledge and skills in preparing the budget.

While this is particularly true of the capital budget, even the annual budget can have downstream consequences. That means that the facility manager, while budgeting adequate funds for functions like snow removal and custodial services, must also realize that the annual construction/renovation/alteration/replacement programs will have long-term effects on future budgets. In general, new construction or the installation of new equipment releases a chain of downstream costs, commonly called the *cost of ownership*, as indicated in Figure 4-1.

Those downstream costs make subsequent budgets less discretionary and controllable. In actuality, the U.S. Congress, state legislatures, and local city councils have often chosen to simply ignore some of those uncontrollable costs, such as maintenance and repair. Even though they are ignored, however, these costs are still there. As we often hear, "You can pay me now or pay me later." When

Figure 4-1. The Cost of Ownership.

THE COST OF OWNERSHIP

- Acquisition
    Site costs
    Design
    Construction or purchase

- Operations
    Utilities
    Custodial

- Maintenance and repair

- Replacement of components

- Alterations and improvements

- Rehabilitation/Replacement

- Disposal

---

these costs are ignored, they limit the options of subsequent budgeters. What would have been a relatively minor maintenance and repair cost has, when ignored, caused a facility to deteriorate to the point where a costly major renovation or replacement is necessary.

Another factor that characterizes facility management department budgets is our current regulatory environment. Regulation often hits FM budgets particularly hard because the facility manager must often translate broadly written laws into bricks and mortar facility implementation. In the United States during the 1980s, facility budgets were pummeled by the need to make physical changes to comply with new OSHA, EPA, and Americans with Disabilities Act regulations and legislation, much of which defied understanding, let alone budgeting. Gradually standards evolved and accommodations were made, but in some FM departments (school districts come to mind) the impact of these federal regulations on annual budgets was profound.

Traditional Problems in Annual Budgeting

In our experience, the overwhelmingly most serious annual budgeting problem is the lack of valid data. We point out this same problem throughout our discussion of financial management and budgeting, but it is particularly true here. When people fail to budget the way they work, they cannot forecast future work from past work data. Many facility departments cannot calculate even the simplest unit costs without manipulating information from a variety of sources for both the denominator and the numerator of the unit cost. Finally, few work management systems are closely tied into the budget and the company financial management system, with the result that once the FM has developed factors to be used in planning, they cannot be replicated by the company's financial analysts. In our opinion, designing and implementing a work management system that produces usable unit costs easily is perhaps the greatest IT challenge facing facility managers today.

Budget politics are a problem because most facility managers do not play politics well and because they often try to communicate their solutions to facility problems in technical rather than business language. For each initiative in your budget, except for those initiatives that affect only the FM department, you should seek out one of the affected customers and provide information that will enable that customer to be the advocate for that initiative. A new initiative will be much more acceptable if it is supported by the director of marketing or the dean or the human resources vice president. This is normally obvious for a renovation project, but it can be just as important for the replacement of a faulty air handler needed to provide adequate ventilation to department X. Get the manager of that department involved. IT department heads have always been very good at selling the latest technological widget as the *business* solution to the company's problem. We must become as adroit in using the language of business to show that FM initiatives are vital to business solutions.

Since there are good reasons for management to have a short-term focus, one of the greatest challenges facing facility managers is trying to obtain resources for long-term projects. This is perhaps less of a problem for a government FM because government financials do not undergo quarterly scrutiny to assess costs and profit. Because of this focus on quarterly returns in publicly owned companies, management is naturally antagonistic to substantial long-term commitments of capital. This means that FMs either must be particularly good in their arguments or must search for alternative solutions—e.g., lease rather than build. Realistically, the facility manager will sometimes win this challenge and sometimes lose it.

The greatest challenge of all is the fact that facility management, particularly in the area of maintenance and repair, continues to be underfunded. The facility manager of a prestigious East Coast university once said, "Everyone wants their name on a building and is all too willing to fund the construction of a new academic building, but no one ever endowed an operations and maintenance contract." He found himself with an ever-increasing inventory of buildings and an annual budget that increased only modestly, if at all. At least three committees of the National Academy of Sciences have concluded, over a ten-year period, that the backlog of federal building maintenance and repair is continuing to grow. The U.S. Congress, despite having formulae to anticipate maintenance and repair costs, continues to provide inadequate maintenance and repair funds to federal facility managers. From examining this continuing situation, we can state two conclusions:

1. Most states, localities, and the federal government have more infrastructure than they will ever be willing to adequately maintain and repair.
2. Public-sector facility managers and many private facility managers need to be comfortable with reactive management and with dealing with inadequate resources.

These conclusions have major budget implications for the public-sector facility manager.

A Good Budget

There has been little research done or material written concerning FM budgeting. We have had the opportunity to discuss the characteristics of good FM budgets with a variety of facility managers in seminars and classes. A summary of their responses is given in the following list:

- It contains the categories that the FM and others need to manage.
- It is workplan driven—i.e., the programs it contains are the units of work managed.
- It is structured in the way the department operates and ties together resource management and management responsibility.
- It provides easily identifiable or calculable total costs, comparative costs, and unit costs.

• It provides easily identifiable management responsibilities.

A review of most FM annual budgets reveals that distressingly few of them have any of these characteristics. This remains a quandary and is one of the reasons that we have written this book. Facility managers have plenty of room for improvement in their budgets' contents and formats.

Having looked at the challenges and characteristics of annual budgeting, we would now like to discuss budget mechanics, starting with budget preparation.

Budget Preparation

If the company and the facility manager have a well-developed FM business planning process, budget preparation should be relatively easy because the annual workplan will provide 70 to 80 percent of the budget input. If an FM doesn't have an annual workplan, the process remains the same, but the FM needs to construct the budget in toto rather than revising a baseline document. (See the comments on zero-based budgeting later in the chapter.)

Serious budget preparation in most large organizations starts three to six months before the start of the fiscal year. At the beginning of the process, the finance department issues budget procedures, such as format and timing, and budget guidance, such as targets and limits. One common piece of guidance is how inflation should be handled. The FM must be told whether inflation should be factored into the budget figures submitted or whether the finance department will adjust for inflation across the whole company. Inflation adjustment can be a major issue for the FM because in recent years the rate of inflation for construction and maintenance supplies and services has tended to be higher than the increase in the Consumer Price Index, a commonly used index of inflation.

If the facility manager is working from an annual workplan during budget preparation, she should consult with her subordinate managers, technical staff, and customers to validate existing requirements and to gather any new requirements that may have been generated since the workplan was developed. If there is no workplan, the emphasis is on gathering the requirements, quantifying them, and ensuring that they are valid.

Realistically, even in those companies that do not have a workplan, probably 80 to 90 percent of the budget will be based on the previous year's budget, adjusted for known new requirements. For that reason, we recommend to facility managers that they zero-base one-third of their accounts every year, meaning that all of them are done over three years (or one-fifth of their accounts every year in large organizations). Annual budgeting that is totally zero-based is a worthy goal but is probably unrealistic. It failed in the U.S. federal government back in the 1970s.

To forecast new requirements, a facility manager should consider one or more of the following:

• Like requirements in past budgets
• Industry benchmarks from sources like Means or the professional organizations

• The experience of other facility managers in the vicinity
• Estimates by managers, supervisors, and contractors with experience in the locality

A technique that FMs can use when *forecasting* new requirements is to get three or four knowledgeable individuals together in a room and ask them to forecast for each requirement their most optimistic estimate, most pessimistic estimate, and most likely estimate. Alternatively, the FM can have them vote on data that he has gathered from the sources in the preceding list as most likely, least likely on the high end, and least likely on the low end. From this process and the ensuing discussion, the facility manager can make an informed forecast and have excellent results in estimating. For a more sophisticated estimating technique, see Mike Hoots's explanation of calculating estimated value (EV), which is more often used on individual projects such as capital budget line items than on annual budget accounts.[1] Some of the sources and techniques that FMs have found useful in projecting budget data are included in Figure 4-2.

Early in the budget process, FM budget requirements will typically be greater than the budget guidance provided by the finance department. We prefer to go forward with our first budget submission 2 to 5 percent in excess of budget guidance, using the rationale that the finance department probably has a small contingency fund to be handed out as the total company budget is developed and that the FM department's requirements have as much right to those funds as other departments' requirements. In support of this practice, the facility manager should prepare a decrement list and prioritize within each program so that, if cuts have to be made, the FM is prepared to take them. One step in preparing to take cuts is for the FM to notify a customer if the customer's project or service is "on the bubble" for elimination. Often customers are in a better position to pressure the finance department than the FM is.

If cuts have to be made, it is the best policy to make them rationally and according to a predeveloped decrement list. Some facility managers favor submitting for elimination those projects that they know the finance department cannot or will not eliminate—renovation of the CEO's office or funds to pay the water bill, for example. We have used this technique, but we believe that the FM is better off being honest with the finance department and working with it rather than playing budget games. Likely legitimate targets for decrements are cosmetic items, discretionary items, and postponable items. Invisible items and items for which there are no advocates are easy targets, but the FM must analyze them carefully because they could be critical to the organization.

In closing this section on budget preparation, we repeat what we said when we started: By using a systematic planning, programming, and budget system, the facility manager will largely eliminate the administrivia of budget preparation. That allows the FM to allot more managerial time to the substantial issues of prioritization and allocation of resources among those projects and services that will most benefit the company.

Once the budget has been prepared and approved, the facility manager then must manage it during its execution.

Figure 4-2. Projecting Budget Data.

Category	How Projected	Source
Capital	Gather discrete projects annually	Call for projects; estimate concepts
Utilities	Estimate discrete new requirements	In-house records
	Project annual growth from 3- to 5-year curve	Utility companies
Operations	Arithmetic projection	Unit cost indicators
Nondiscretionary mainte- nance and repair	Arithmetic projection (projects can be gath- ered discretely)	Unit cost indicators (esti- mate projects from concept design)
Custodial	Arithmetic projection	Unit cost indicators
Nonproject moving	Arithmetic projection	Unit cost indicators
Discretionary projects	Gather discrete projects annually	Call for projects; estimate concept
Lease costs and income	Review leases	Leases
Personnel costs	Arithmetic projections	Use actual salaries and benefits or standard salaries and benefits
Training and travel costs	Gather requirements	Actual costs for training and standard costs for travel
Office equipment and vehicles	Gather requirements for purchases; arithmetic calculation of opera- tional costs	Call for requirements; cost data on vehicles/ equipment
Nonprojects design and engineering	Guesstimate	Historical data

David Cotts, *The Facility Management Handbook,* 2d ed. (New York: AMACOM, 1999), p. 312.

Fiscal Years

As mentioned previously, how a company designates its *fiscal year* is important. Most private companies tend to use the calendar year (probably because it is also the tax year). Most governments have fiscal years that run from July through June. When the U.S federal government went to an October through September fiscal year, the claim was that this would ease the budget deadlock in Washington. This adjustment may have been an improvement for the "budget bunnies" and "fiscal mavens" who had to administer the budget, since the end-of-year activities no longer occurred during peak vacation time. It is clear that fiscal gridlock has not ended because that is primarily a product of politics. If anything, the U.S. govern- ment has relied more on continuing resolutions since the change of fiscal years than it did before. The average facility manager should play with the hand that she is dealt regarding the fiscal year. Personally, we find it discouraging to be conducting end-of-year activities in the office on Christmas Eve, a possible result of the January–December fiscal year.

Getting the Word Out

In large organizations, as soon as the budget is approved, an important FM function is getting the word out to all sites and locations that have budgeting and accounting responsibilities. Every facility manager within the organization needs to know what was approved in the fiscal plan, the budget. Too often, headquarters does not understand that there has been a lack of communication until the first quarter's (month's) reports come in and it is evident that not everyone is operating off the same sheet of music. This is particularly true in a centralized FM organization if the approved budget is a radical departure from (1) what was done in the previous year or (2) what was submitted by those sites and locations. The need to communicate seems so basic, but often it is allowed to slide, leaving the FM organization trying to catch up after one-quarter of the fiscal year has gone by.

Before we move into a discussion of executing the budget and accounting for the funds entrusted to the FM, it is necessary to understand some terms.

Some Important Financial Terms

Facility managers do not need to be accountants, but they need to understand accounting terms that have a major effect on how they manage their department and how they relate to the accounting department. When we **allocate** funds, we set them aside for a specific purpose, but control of those funds remains within the organization (hopefully with the FM). If those funds are *fungible* at the facility manager's level, that means that the FM has the authority to move them among accounts to meet managerial needs. When we *commit* funds, we obligate them outside the organization, by signing a contract or a purchase order. When our contractor or vendor provides its services or goods satisfactorily, we must pay that vendor or contractor, so we cannot use those funds for another purpose.

When those goods and services are verified as acceptable, the funds are paid out or **expensed**. When looking at budget reports, facility managers need to understand that the figures shown indicate expenses clearly but also may contain funds that have been committed but appear as available. The time lag that leads to misleading figures on a report can continue for thirty to ninety days. As the fiscal year moves along, knowing the exact status of each account becomes increasingly important.

The contracting vehicle that a FM uses in her work and the way each procurement device obligates funds has a profound effect on how we manage budget implementation. Let us give you examples through a series of questions and answers.

- When a facility manager sets aside and justifies money for a project and gets it approved as part of his budget, what has he done? (He has allocated those funds.)

- When a facility manager signs a contract with Jones and Smith, Inc., to build out an interiors project, what has she done? (She has committed those funds, so she can't touch them unless she cancels the contract.)
- When the facility manager signs a purchase order with Capital Furniture for furniture for that interiors project once it is built out, what has he done? (He has committed those funds, so, again, he can't touch them.)
- When the facility manager signs a blanket purchase order with Joe and Mary's Maintenance Company for on-call carpet cleaning, indicating that she plans to spend up to $20,000 with Joe and Mary's during the fiscal year, what has she done to the funds? (Be careful; this one is tricky—which is why we love blanket purchase orders for services.)

Blanket purchase orders (BPOs) are a special breed of purchasing document. If written properly, the BPO has obligated nothing to Joe and Mary's—the facility manager is not even obligated to use that firm for carpet cleaning. Thus, the FM has committed no funds until she executes the first job order with Joe and Mary's. Executing an individual job order commits the FM department to paying for that specific service and no other. Some facility managers insist on writing maximums and a minimum guarantee into their blanket purchase orders, which we find defeats the entire purpose of using this highly flexible purchasing document. Obviously when the vendor presents a valid invoice and the work is validated, the FM department then expends the funds.

These financial terms represent the linkages, which the facility manager must be expert in managing, between the purchasing, accounting, and facility management departments. An FM can't manage either of the other two departments, but, especially with the emphasis on outsourcing, no facility manager will be successful unless he maintains the proper relationship with the accounting and purchasing departments and understands how each of these departments affects his operations and his budget. For example, if the accounting department is more than ninety days late in posting expenses, corporate budget reports will give a seriously flawed picture of the status of FM department finances to both the facility manager and corporate executives. And it happens! For self-preservation, the facility manager must not be totally dependent upon the accounting department for the accuracy of his accounts.

Another aspect of this same issue is the necessity for large facility departments with a full range of accounts to have a facility management accountant. The preferred approach would be to have an accountant from the accounting department colocated with the facility manager. Another approach would be to have an accountant funded by the FM department tracking the FM budget and then translating it to the accounting department. The latter technique will almost always be used for large capital projects and will be discussed in the next chapter. One of the authors experienced so many accounting problems that affected operations that he finally used a precious personnel space to hire an FM accountant to help manage the entire FM budget. It was money well spent, but it should have been unnecessary. Ideally, as we discuss throughout this book, the work management system will be so integrated with the corporate financial system that the former will feed the latter. Since that does not occur in many facility management departments, an individual doing facility management accounting is necessary.

Accounting is not the only factor that affects budget execution. Closely aligned with accounting is transaction flow, the flow of orders, invoices, and products within the corporation or government agency. A typical flow of transactions for goods or services within a company is depicted in Figure 4-3.

Because they are such prolific users of the procurement system, facility managers should understand exactly how this system works within their company. At least two points in the process can have a major impact on FM budget execution. The first of these choke points occurs in the controller's office, where some clerk must match a purchase order (3) with an invoice (5) and pay the vendor *correctly* (6). Experienced facility managers understand that the process does not always happen correctly and expeditiously. The effect on the FM budget is over-payment, underpayment, or incorrect information on periodic reports. Whether because of policy or inefficiency, it is common for vendor payments to be held in the accounting department for thirty days, with sixty to ninety days not uncommon. This is a serious problem, particularly at the end of the fiscal year, when it is important that expenses get recorded against the appropriate fiscal year.

Another trouble point depicted in Figure 4-3 can be the loading dock. Most FMs don't tend to employ the highest-quality personnel there. Yet, if loading dock personnel do not pull the shipping documents from delivered goods and route them correctly, invoices will not be paid promptly and budget reports will not be correct. This problem is widespread, yet many facility managers have never educated themselves about the flow of documentation that affects their accounting and budget execution.

Contrary to popular wisdom, we contend that more budget problems occur because of poor procurement processing than because of operational cost over-runs, yet few facility managers that we have taught and observed have even looked at those processes. One of the reasons for a facility management accountant is that this individual has the time, knowledge, and responsibility to manage processes to ensure that vendors are paid on a timely basis and that charges to the FM accounts are both timely and accurate.

Burn Rate

When we have asked facility managers to draw a profile of how they spend their funds, we have been perplexed to find that most of them have never thought about it. This is borne out by the fact that on their budget reports, the anticipated expense column is divided equally throughout the year for each account, whereas we know that we expend funds at dramatically different rates during the year. For example, we don't do much heating in summertime. Lack of understanding of how FM funds should be expended within a fiscal year means that our budget reports are not as valuable a management tool as they could be.

Figure 4-4 represents a typical annual expense profile for one year, a profile that is more desirable in that it reduces the peaks and valleys of spending. Tradi-tionally, at the start of a fiscal year, there are leftover requirements from the last

Figure 4-3. Transaction Flow.

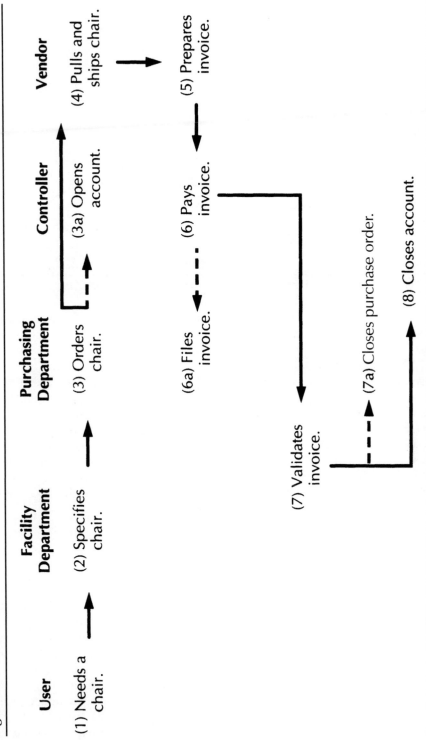

David Cotts, *The Facility Management Handbook*, 2d ed. (New York: AMACOM, 1999), p. 312.

Figure 4-4. Annual Expense Profiles.

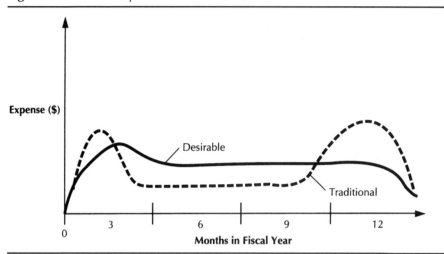

David Cotts, *The Facility Management Handbook,* 2d ed. (New York: AMACOM, 1999), p. 312.

fiscal year that the facility department tries to meet in the first three months. Using this catch-up technique causes the expense reports to management to show a *burn rate* of expenses that will break the budget if expenses continue at that rate. The inexperienced facility manager, acting on incorrectly structured expenses, puts on the brakes and radically reduces spending until after the midyear review. At that point, because no one wants to lose any funds, many departments go on a year-end spending binge. The more desirable profile recognizes in advance both the pent-up demand early in the year and the end-of-year spending. That is the profile that should be in the "target" column of budget reports. Through good planning, financial management, and procurement management, the facility manager smoothes the hills and valleys and ensures that funds are used for priority work, not just what can be pushed out the door the fastest at the last minute.

Periodic Review

How often the FM budget is reviewed will be a matter of company policy and personal preference. Most companies conduct at least a quarterly budget review, with the midyear review being a major one at which a major reallocation of resources can occur. We prefer a fairly cursory first-quarter review within the department, a major midyear review with the boss, and a final review at the end of the third quarter to make any last-minute tweaks of the workplan and resources. Within the department, we recommend a review at the end of the month for fiscal months ten and eleven and weekly reviews during month twelve. In fact, during the last week of the fiscal year, we urge daily budget reviews to ensure that all billing is up to date and that the FM department receives and uses effectively any company resources that become available at the last minute. The smart, aggressive facility manager will have in place ways to commit funds (contracts, purchase orders, etc.) expeditiously.

We do not advocate spending money recklessly, but we have always prided ourselves on our ability to use effectively all the funds allocated to us plus any additional funds that might become available in the last days of a fiscal year. An FM gets no gold star for leaving money on the table, just as he gets none for spending money on worthless purchases or projects just so that he can say he used up all of his funding. The success of end-of-fiscal-year activities often distinguishes the excellent facility manager from the average one.

Reviewing the Budget

We believe that a certain amount of review should be built into the budget format. Appendix D reflects the practice of regular review, as it provides monthly comparisons of actual expenditures per account (and subaccount in certain cases) with:

- The budgeted expenditures for that month
- The variance between actual and anticipated expenditures
- The actual expenditure for the same month last year
- The budgeted amount at year end

Two other comparisons that we find helpful starting at midyear are (1) the actual expenditures last month and (2) the actual expenditures last quarter. Note that between the annual workplan (Appendix C) and the annual budget (Appendix D), FM resources were reduced approximately 2 percent by Corporate Finance.

As we discuss at some length in Chapter 6, the budget report should allow the facility manager to easily calculate unit costs and to hold individuals responsible for their fiscal performance. This requires a proper budget format and integration of the work management and corporate financial management systems to ensure that unit costs, which can be used as benchmarks, can be easily calculated. Unless systems are set up to accomplish this, it will not occur. It is perhaps the principal reason that so many benchmarking exercises fail.

At least annually, the facility manager should use the budget reports to make comparisons such as the percentage of the budget devoted to maintenance and repair versus new work. What is that figure for this year? What is the trend historically? Is that ratio what you want it to be? Also, how do unit costs compare to generalized benchmarks, such as the IFMA benchmark study, the BOMA Experience Report, and the General Services Administration standard for this location(s)? This type of internal analysis will enable the facility manager to understand how well the department is running and where improvement is needed. Used in this way, *the budget is the most important financial management tool.*

Challenges During Budget Execution

One of the reasons that budget management is so time-consuming is that challenges never cease. The following list, developed by a focus group, gives some of the challenges that occur during budget execution:

- Monitoring
- Projecting
- Reviewing and reallocation
- Reprioritizing and taking cuts
- Managing floors and ceilings
- Handling new requirements

We have discussed the first four already, but we would like to address the subjects of floors, ceilings, and how to handle new requirements before we talk about budget closeout.

Management, or the political overseers in the public sector, is delineating a floor when it says that the FM department must spend X amount of allocated funds for a specific purpose Y. It is designating a ceiling when it says that the FM department may not spend more than A amount of funds for purpose B. An example of the latter is the U.S. Congress's setting a ceiling on the amount of O&M funds that could be used for new work, alterations, and minor construction within the Defense Department budget. That was probably a wise decision in a multimillion-dollar budget, but for most companies, this situation can be better handled by using specific accounts and subaccounts.

Unfortunately, new requirements occur during the budget year, but they can be minimized if there is a good planning system in place within the company. Faced with an unexpected requirement during the budget year, the facility manager should proceed through the following sequence of actions:

- Understand, analyze, and estimate the cost of the new requirement.
- Submit the cost of the new requirement to management with a request for funding.
- Simultaneously, within the FM department, conduct an analysis of how the new requirement, if not funded by management, will be funded internally and what the impacts will be.
- If the requirement is funded, prepare and submit to management a plan to fit the extra work into the workplan.
- If told to eat the requirement, submit an impact statement showing the effect on other accounts, request reconsideration, and notify the affected customers that their projects or needs will be delayed or not funded.

Because of their size, facility management department budgets are often viewed as a source of funding for other company initiatives, particularly at midyear reviews, and the FM must be constantly alert to defend against both the

reallocation of funds to other departments and the imposition of new requirements without the needed funds.

The final accounting practice that facility managers must understand in order
to properly manage budget execution is accruals.

Accruals

Good accrual management at year end is a necessary skill for facility managers.
Accruals are funds estimated to be expended by a certain date as a result of obligations made before that date. Usually accruals are critical at the end of the fiscal
year. The accruals reported by the facility manager to the finance department are
those funds that the FM estimates that she can obligate by the end of the fiscal
year, although they may well not be expensed until the first quarter of the next
fiscal year. Accruing funds is as much an art as a science. There is a penalty for
accruing incorrectly. If a FM accrues funds for a particular need but miscalculates
what he can commit, and the requirement is valid, he can lose the money in the
current fiscal year but still have to pay for it as an unbudgeted requirement in the
next fiscal year. He will have been double-dipped by the accrual system. There is
a parallel set of problems for underaccruing.

Often the finance department simply sets aside all corporate accruals in one
accrual pot and pays the bills when they come in without careful attention to who
is paid how much. A really astute facility manager can capitalize on that process
by slightly overcommitting funds beyond those accrued and using some of that
corporate float for FM requirements.

Budget Closeout

A good facility manager should be able to manage his budget within plus or
minus $1/2$ percent. It is interesting that groups of FMs tend to say that managing
within 5 percent is good performance. We think that opinion demonstrates that
these facility managers do not have the tools and the will to truly manage their
budget. Good budget management is a learned skill. It starts with having a budget
format that makes the budget the principal FM financial management system. In
addition, it is important to have the proper corporate FM accounts and subaccounts, and either to have the FM work management system feed directly and
accurately into the corporate financial management system or to have an FM accountant. Using the analogy of the budget as a map, the FM must know at all
times where he is in order to get to his destination.

Zero-Based Budgeting

Zero-based budgeting is a process that requires every dollar in the budget to be
justified each year. One of the authors participated in the preparation of a zero-
based budgeting exercise within the U.S. federal government. It was never fully

implemented, and it soon joined the file containing great ideas that just didn't work. Zero-based budgeting is a great idea in theory. It forces managers to justify every program every year, so that program creep does not occur and programs that have not worked or that have reached the end of their usefulness are eliminated. We have heard of one facility manager, from Silicon Valley, who claimed to zero-base the FM budget every budget cycle. Realistically, for medium and large FM departments, zero-based budgeting is an administrative nightmare because neither the program managers nor the budget analysts at the corporate level truly have the time to devote to examining every budget account in detail in every budget cycle. We do, however, recommend a compromise: Zero-base each program every three to five years. This minimizes creep while making the analytical load manageable and doable.

Budget Evaluation

Perhaps because they are so overwhelmed with the end-of-budget-year activities or the activities associated with the new fiscal year, we have found that few FMs actually evaluate how well they managed their budget. We have no interest in making work, but we think each FM should ask himself one question at the conclusion of each budget year: *"Did I do what I said I was going to do with the resources that the company provided to me in my original budget?"* If the answer is yes, then it was a successful year. If the answer is no, another question must be asked and answered: "If the budget was not followed, was the reason that our budget estimates were bad, that we did not manage operations well, or that we had either requirements added or resources removed?"

Facility managers who are in a position to really reshape both their budget and their operations in the upcoming fiscal year should also answer the following questions as part of a comprehensive evaluation:

- What lessons did we learn in executing last year's budget and how can we apply them to this year's?
- Are our budgets, capital and annual, in balance and supportive?
- Do we have more capital assets than we are willing to maintain? (Answering this question may take analysis over several years' budgets.)
- Is the amortization of previous capital projects having a serious effect on our annual budget?
- What did our expenditure profile, the burn rate, look like? Was it what we wanted it to be?
- What percentage of our total budget is administrative? New work? Maintenance and repair? Is that good or bad? What are the trends? (This is another question that will require multi-year analysis to answer.)
- Was the fact that we were on or off target good or bad? Could we have influenced that more?
- Is our budget structure conducive to good management? If not, how should we change it?[2]

Instead, the question that is usually asked is, "Was I on target?" which is really meaningless. This begs the question of whether the target was correct. One of our management colleagues was always on target at year end, but it was because he ran his department in a very risk-averse manner, even at times when management needed more innovation and greater customer service than he provided. In our practice, we always were on target, as mentioned previously, but our budget management was much better in some years than in others. It is always easy to fool others, but it should not be easy to fool yourself. Self-analysis is an important part of good management, and simple budget evaluation is a valuable part of that introspection.

Additional Budget Control Issues

Budgeting for Personnel

There are three other issues that we feel are important in a discussion of budgeting. The first of these is the control of personnel positions. Budget time is the most logical time for staffing increases or decreases based on the work program for the upcoming year. Most federal government FM departments have specifically authorized personnel positions (control of spaces), giving the facility manager little freedom to increase or decrease staffing. Some government agencies may allow a facility manager to fill a government vacancy with a temporary hire, consultant, or contractor by controlling the total amount of funds that can be expended on personnel of all types (control of faces). In rare cases, the government FM may, in fact, have a small authorization to hire staff over and above the authorized spaces. Most companies allocate, from the human resources department, a standardized personnel authorization (pay and benefits), based on the projected slots required to run the FM department. The FM then has limited flexibility to use those funds to pay the staff. The private sector is more likely to estimate the personnel costs of new initiatives, so an FM who takes on more work is compensated with additional staffing to help her manage the additional budget for the new initiative. We don't want to imply that private-sector facility managers have a completely free hand in budgeting for staff, however. We have witnessed only one company where the funding for human resources was absolutely fungible and the FM was free to use it to staff as he saw best.

Two-Signature Policy

Internal approvals are important within an FM organization. We highly recommend that the FM department use two signatures to validate both requirements (yes, we do need a new boiler at a cost of $78,300) and payments (yes, Acme Mechanical installed and trained us on the new boiler and presented a proper invoice, for which we should pay it $78,300). FM departments handle a large volume of requests with high dollar values.

We like the two-signature system, with one of the people who sign being the manager directly involved, to keep honest folks honest and to ensure that mistakes, which can often happen in high-volume work such as ours, are minimized. We have always felt that two signatures protect both of the signers, plus the facility manager if he happens not to be one of them.

Approval Levels

We also believe that realistic funding *approval levels* need to be set in each department and then rigidly enforced. Approval guidelines may be company policy. There are no generally accepted guidelines for funding approval levels, but it is our observation that departments tend to set them too low. The facility manager should look at approvals occasionally to see if they (1) make sense and (2) really hold the responsible manager primarily responsible. In a large department, it is realistic to have the facility manager approve all requirements over $5,000 and payments exceeding $10,000. For capital projects, the facility manager will normally be the initiating signature. There will always be special guidelines, such as that the facility manager will approve all leases regardless of dollar value.

Others with an Interest in the Budget

Managing a budget has a high communications component. The type and depth of communication varies widely between, say, the office manager of a law firm and the facility manager of an international corporation. In all cases, however, during budget preparation, the facility manager has to communicate constantly with three individuals and their organizations: her boss, the finance department, and her customers.

The theme for communicating with your boss is "no surprises." Ideas for new initiatives will not survive the first cut without management support, so the FM needs to bring the boss along every step of the way. That includes every significant hiccup during budget execution. Advise the boss as soon as the facts are straight so that (1) he doesn't get blindsided and (2) he can help solve the problem.

As we stress particularly in Chapter 5, the FM needs to play it straight with the finance department. In the best situation, the FM will have a budget analyst located in the FM department with whom she works consistently. Keeping this person informed and on the team can go a long way toward getting favorable treatment from the finance department. Remember that the finance department sets the rules for financial management. The FM deviates from those rules at his own considerable risk.

Finally, keep the customers aware of the financial status of their projects and of ongoing financial actions that will affect them. If they are given the correct information and rationale, customers often can keep a project on track with corporate management and the finance department when the FM would not be able to do so. A successful technique is to schedule a quarterly update with each operating manager who has an active project or issue merely to keep these managers updated and to develop strategies that allow both the customer and the FM department to win.

Chargeback Budgeting

Up to this point, we have discussed centralized budgeting, in which all accounts are developed, defended, and implemented by the facility manager. Now we want to discuss the budget system that is more likely to be found in the private sector, chargebacks/allocations. Chargebacks are much less likely to occur in the public sector, but they do happen.

Chargebacks involve giving, wholly or in part, those funds that are normally provided to the FM department for FM tasks to the company's operating managers. The operating managers then purchase FM goods and services from the FM department or, in some cases, from outside contractors, or they may decide to use the funds for some other purpose. There are as many rules for administering chargebacks and allocations as there are companies. In actual practice, in most types of chargeback system, the facility department still budgets and controls funds for building services like HVAC, elevator services, and custodial and grounds maintenance. The facility department charges each operating division a rent for those services, the terms of which are spelled out in a service agreement. Discretionary FM goods and services, like alterations and furniture purchases, must be purchased from the FM department, in most cases, to ensure that they meet any standard that exists. Another level of goods and services—providing picture framing, for example—can be obtained at cost from the FM department or can be purchased from an outside vendor.

The main advantage of chargebacks is that they require operating division managers to be cost-conscious in their use of FM services and give them total control over their budget. Chargebacks also make FM costs more transparent and understandable to line managers, and, particularly in manufacturing situations, they allow the FM costs to be more readily tied to a product. From the customers' point of view, chargebacks give them options. The FM must earn their business. In our experience, customers are willing to use the in-house FM services if they are not more than 10 percent over market price.

The downside of a generalized chargeback system is that it requires often unrealistic allocation rules and can be a burden to administer. For example, what is the rationalization for charging the same rent to two operational managers, one of whom occupies space in a Class B rental that is twenty years old, while the other occupies space in a brand new owned office building? In addition, a generalized system fails to recognize that some items are best funded through the FM budget (e.g., utilities). We agree that the facility manager needs to have some discretionary budget, but chargebacks severely reduce his flexibility.

Within the past ten years, chargebacks and allocations have become a way of life for most private-sector facility managers. The chargeback system seems to function most effectively when the FM service or product cost can be directly measured, when the costs are above a norm or a standard, and when the cost must be allocated to a product.

Given the broad utilization of chargebacks, it is important that the facility manager have the skill to develop a chargeback system or evaluate an existing one. In addition, the FM must ensure that the department has the hardware and software to administer a chargeback budget, which may or may not be possible with the existing work management system. Here we are illustrating another area where it is important that the financial management and work management systems are integrated. Finally, the FM must ensure that the necessary customer contact is maintained throughout the budget year. The costs of a department using chargebacks are constantly being challenged, and the FM must prepare many more estimates annually for customers than she would for internal use. Since the funds are in the customers' hands, the FM must convince his customers that he is the vendor of choice at an acceptable cost. It cannot be overemphasized that chargebacks must reflect the true costs of the services and space provided.

Project Accounting

Project accounting will be covered in Chapter 7, but two issues need to be addressed here. First, annual budgets must not, as too many do, consist of nothing but a list of projects. Second, the facility manager and the supporting accounting staff must make special efforts to ensure that project costs are appropriately entered into the annual or capital budget in both the facility department and the corporate financial management system.

Conclusion

Remember two things from this chapter. First, the FM department is a major consumer of corporate resources, and consequently it will always be under scrutiny. Second, with a good planning system, a good budget format, and integration of the FM work management and corporate financial management systems, the facility manager should be in an excellent position not only to answer any resource questions and to defend the department's use of resources, but also to conduct meaningful internal review and to show management that, by using resources effectively and efficiently, the FM department is contributing to the corporate bottom line in financial terms.

Notes

1. Michael Hoots, *Money Talks* (Houston: International Facility Management Association, 2000), pp. 79–80.
2. David Cotts, *The Facility Management Handbook*, 2d ed. (New York, AMACOM, 1999), p. 315.

5

Capital Budgeting

Pulse Points

- *Every facility manager of a midsized or larger company or agency should be able to manage a capital development program.*
- *The finance department should make the rules for capital program development and budgeting.*
- *Capital budgeting is planning the expenditure of funds for assets that will return benefits beyond one year and are a product of both tax law and company policy.*
- *In order for a project to be capital funded, the economic benefits that accrue to the company should exceed the cost of the capital used to produce the project.*
- *Companies with significant annual capital requirements should have a capital review board and a policy for gathering, reviewing, and prioritizing capital projects.*
- *All nonemergency projects should be subject to the same prioritization analysis and scrutiny using life-cycle costing and considering the time value of money.*

Keywords

Capital, capital project, capital program, depreciation, hurdle rate, capital review board, payback, net present value, internal rate of return, benefit/cost ratio

Introduction

In 2001, U.S companies invested $1.1 trillion in *capital projects*. Of this, $748 billion was expended on new equipment and $362 billion on new facilities.[1] Our experience is that most facility managers glory in the planning, design, and execution of capital projects. There is good reason for this. A capital project is often a

81

chance for the facility management department to work on a new business initiative. Such a project may provide some needed exposure for the facility department. This high interest in capital projects is so common that it has tended to skew the management of facilities. Too many facility managers think of themselves principally as project managers. Their budgets then reflect only project management rather than complete facility management principles. Those FM budgets are simply a listing of projects.

Capital program development, budgeting, and execution are important. However, not all companies have large *capital* requirements. If the facility manager's company is small or is still occupying leased space, its construction, major equipment purchase, renovation, replacement, and major repair needs do not require a separate capital budget.

The principal drivers for facility programs are new or expanding business, the need to recapitalize existing buildings or systems, and the necessity for meeting new regulations. Some companies purposely stay away from capitalizing expenses. As they grow, however, most companies will want to develop policies and procedures for a capital program. Every facility manager of a midsized or larger company or agency should be able to manage a capital development program.

Most public-sector facility managers will have a capital budgeting function, although, unbelievably, the U.S. federal government and many state governments do not acknowledge capital budgets.* Instead, money to meet capital needs is appropriated as part of the annual budgeting process. This can lead to bizarre peaks and valleys in the annual budget if a megaproject must be funded in one year. A 1999 study of U.S. federal budgeting all but recommended the establishment of an official capital budget, and the co-chair and two other members of the commission actually recommended its establishment.[2] This is not the first time this recommendation has been made, but there does not seem to be any significant movement in that direction. The reality is that most of the major U.S. federal agencies operate some type of capital program development process. They merely call it something else.

Capital Budget Rulemaking

In those companies and agencies that had a capital budget, for many years the facility manager had 70 to 80 percent of the capital requirements. That has changed somewhat with the Information Age, to the point that, in some companies, facility management and information technology annually compete equally for the capital dollars. Nevertheless, the facility manager is such a major player in capital program development that facility managers have sometimes overstepped

*While the U.S. government does not have a capital budget, it is obvious that the topic of capital budgeting is under consideration. Within the last five years, there has been a presidential commission on the topic (1999) and a GAO Executive Guide, *Leading Practices in Capital Decision-Making* (December 1998) has been issued. The latter is an excellent macro-level discussion of putting together a capital budget, particularly in the public sector.

the bounds in capital budget decision making. It is important to understand that the *finance department (CFO, controller, etc.) makes the rules for capital program development and budgeting.* The facility manager needs to understand the policies, procedures, and rules for capital budgeting and to follow them implicitly. In our personal experience, we have seen that the facility manager can assist the finance department in developing procedures for gathering capital requirements, for prioritizing among competing requirements, for setting policies and procedures to be used during execution, and for recommending the methods for reporting progress and expenditures. Many facility managers have prior experience and training in those functions. The facility manager can assist, but the making of policy and rules for capital budgeting needs to reside with the chief financial officer, and the FM department needs to follow the capital program's policies and rules.

There are several good reasons for the finance department to oversee the development and budgeting of the capital program and to be responsible for the policies and procedures used. Facility managers have sometimes gone astray, particularly in the two areas of determining the suitability of a project for capitalization and controlling project costs, when they have overstepped their bounds, ignored the rules, and even become policy makers rather than project executors.* This risk is prevalent in rapidly growing companies whose capital requirements grow over time from the occasional purchase of computer equipment to the construction of major facilities, capital leasing, and the major renovation of existing office space. The managers in those companies that are just growing into the need for a capital budget initially have neither the experience nor the financial knowledge to manage a capital program effectively. Often the facility manager has stepped in to fill the policy and procedures gap as the need for a capital program became obvious. It is then difficult for the FM to step back when the finance department rightfully takes ownership of capital program development.

There are other reasons that the finance department needs to be in charge of the capital development program. *Capital budgeting involves the allocation of major amounts of company resources.* The success or failure of a particular capital project can have a significant effect on the success or failure of the business. Policy decision making on projects of such business import should remain in the finance department!

Another reason that it is important for the finance department to manage the capital program is that capital projects often are multidisciplinary. For example, the decision to build a new call center involves investment in facilities, communications, human resources, and information technology. No one operational department manager should be setting the policies for such a project's budgeting and execution. Finally, because of the nature of the expenditures, capital budget decisions tend to be long-lasting. For example, it is a significant decision when a

---

*A case that is often given as an example is the Fort Lee airfield case, where a facility that should have been approved for "capital" funding because of its total cost was built, over a period of years, by diverting incremental annual operations and maintenance funds. The airfield was built piecemeal. While the facility manager was not the initiator of this action, he knew it was wrong and did not blow the whistle.

company goes from leasing workspace to building its own. That decision, be it good or bad, will be with the company for as long as the company holds the asset. Such legal and financial decisions should be corporate and not within the purview of a single department such as the facility management department.

With some large government agencies, such as transportation departments, state university systems, and the Department of Defense, the political body simply votes to give the agency a specific amount of capital money each year to accomplish projects X, Y, and Z without much direct involvement in that allocation. Even in that case, however, the policies for capitalization, prioritization of projects, and accounting should remain with the financial department rather than the agency's facility management department. Because the number and amount of capital projects for these large agencies (transportation departments, for example) so overwhelm the remainder of the capital needs of the other agencies, these agencies are given broader powers in the areas of capital program development, budgeting, and execution within overall guidelines. This is a compromise, a concession to reality. It may reflect a historical political situation, but that is another story for another time.

In the remainder of this chapter, we will discuss a model in which all business units, including the facility department and other departments such as information technology, submit their capital requirements annually to the finance department. Once submitted, these requirements are assessed, prioritized, programmed, budgeted, and then released back to the submitting department for execution, which takes place over multiple years in many cases.

Where Capital Programs Go Astray

Our observation is that when companies or agencies struggle with the development, budgeting, and execution of their capital program, they do not have a rigorous system for gathering capital requirements. Nor are they adept at costing those requirements and prioritizing them, including the making of go/no-go decisions. Finally, companies often fail to have a system to feed back capital project costs into the corporate accounting system.

Dramatic changes in the economy can also have dramatic effects on the capital program. First of all, the requirement can go away. Second, the funding can dry up. For example, as this book is written, the Virginia Department of Transportation has stopped or delayed 183 highway projects with a value of $210 million.[3]

In the remainder of this chapter, we will address those weaknesses in a capital development program. The actual implementation of capital projects is addressed in Chapter 7.

Definition

Interestingly, there does not seem to be any consistent definition of capital costs. We can look at two different definitions of capital costs that point to some important facility management considerations. *The Facility Management Handbook,* 2d ed., defines capital costs as:

> the costs of acquiring, substantially improving, expanding, changing the functional use of, or replacing a building or building system. Capitalization rules are driven by tax laws so they vary between locations.[4]

The Institute of Management Accountants defines capital costs as those that:

> include the normal cost of capital used to provide the organization or business unit with the assets used in the work activity. These charges include interest expense on borrowed funds as well as use of internal funds provided. Charges for the cost of capital on internal funds should be at the organization's normal calculation of opportunity costs, return on equity or weighted average cost of capital.[5]

We add yet two more concepts to help you understand capital budgeting. Capital budgeting is planning the expenditure of funds on assets that will return benefits beyond one year. In addition, capital costs are a product of both tax law (it varies quite widely between the United States and Canada, for example) and company policy. All of these concepts need to be kept in mind as we discuss what a company capitalizes and how a capital program is put together. Explicit and implicit in capital projects are some characteristics that differentiate them from projects that can be expensed:

- Capital projects are large and can influence the balance sheet in a significant way.
- They are often multiyear in costing and execution.
- They are defined by both the tax code and company rules.
- They are depreciable.
- They are often highly visible, with high stakeholder interest.
- They often indicate a new business initiative.

Capitalize Versus Expense

To the accountant, capitalization has an accounting impact. When a project is capitalized, the cost of the asset produced or purchased (and the associated taxes) is placed on the balance sheet and allocated to the income statement over several years (*depreciation*). That means that it has less impact on current income. Some companies want to expense costs to the extent permissible by law. This is where facility management and financial management interface. Within the law, the corporate CFO will determine whether an item will be capitalized or expensed. An entirely new field of law, tax engineering, has been developed to assist building owners in assigning costs, particularly building costs, to capital or expense accounts to meet corporate financial goals. An excellent summary of tax engineering is contained in the July/August 1992 edition of *Corporate Management*.[6] Whether a cost can be capitalized and depreciated is a matter of law. How to depreciate that cost is yet another economic consideration.

Depreciation

The simplest form of depreciation complies with the matching principle. In this accounting concept, if the expected life of the asset is, for example, twenty years, then the asset will be depreciated evenly over twenty years. That is referred to as straight-line depreciation. However, political entities often want to encourage economic activity or to simplify the tax code by accelerating depreciation. For example, part of this book is being written on a computer that the state of Virginia allowed to be written off in one year by a small business. Accelerated depreciation has led to a number of different types of depreciation calculation. Some common types are:

- Sum-of-the-years'-digits method
- Declining-balance method
- Units of production method

While we think it is important that facility managers understand this much about depreciation, they should leave the rules for and the actual calculation of depreciation and the replacement value of assets to the finance department. They simply should know that depreciation exists and understand its impact on the balance sheet and the income statement for any individual year.

The Cost of Capital

It is simplistic to say this, but it is helpful for the facility manager who is preparing a project for submission to the corporate capital program to consider the following statement: *In order to get the project into the program, the economic benefits that accrue to the company should exceed the cost of the capital used for the project.* The CFO could say, "O.K., Mr. Facility Manager, why should I invest in your project, which you estimate will return 6 percent annually, when it costs me 7.5 percent to borrow in the capital markets, plus I must cover my administrative costs?" This situation leads to the concept of a *hurdle rate*, the threshold that the CFO sets for accepting capital projects at any point in time. This rate is normally the rate at which the company can borrow money in the market plus an administrative fee, perhaps 8 percent in the example used here. With those definitions in place, we turn to the process of developing a capital program.

Form and Format

In the remainder of this chapter, it may seem that we are placing too much stress on form and format. We will present a system for developing, considering, prioritizing, and accepting or rejecting capital projects. Capital projects tend to be large, sometimes politically charged, and multiyear. If a company ensures that all projects are developed and considered uniformly (use the same format and procedure), that will go far to ensure that the process is both efficient and effective. If it does not, the process can get sticky, even ugly!

Though we are using the example of a medium-sized, U.S.-based company in the remainder of this chapter, the procedures are easily adaptable to a department's specific needs. For public-sector agencies, there will be one additional step after agency approval: approval by the Congress, legislature, or local council.

Project Identification and Feasibility

Any single year's capital program submission is likely to be a mix of projects that have previously been considered and new requirements. The basis for any year's capital development program is the applicable portion of the strategic facilities business plan. However, you can expect some additions and deletions. Some companies may even include projects that have already been approved but have not yet been executed. We recommend a once-a-year call for projects, with all projects to reach headquarters by a specified date. Where appropriate, the facility manager may want to sit down with certain department heads to assist them in the development of their facility capital project requests. The timing of the call for projects depends upon the fiscal year used and the degree of staffing/review of the projects needed after the projects reach headquarters and prior to the actual decision-making and prioritization meeting. Once projects have been identified as appropriate for a particular year, they are submitted to a review board.

Capital Review Board

We have had success using a *capital review board* composed of a small number of managers and chaired by the CFO. The purpose of the board is to make go/no-go decisions on the project submissions and to prioritize those projects that are accepted for funding. It is counterintuitive, but we believe that it is advantageous to have those managers who have significant projects before the board on the board. It is our experience that the senior procurement manager should be on the board so that the purchasing department is involved in the process up front. Human resources input is also often helpful. In a manufacturing company, you may want the vice president of manufacturing on the board. The marketing vice president can also add perspective. The more of the major business unit managers there are on the board, the better. A principal manager within the finance department should be the board's executive.

The board should meet once a year to consider new projects. In large organizations, a midyear review to work in any emergency new projects or to reprioritize projects based on their ability to be executed may be helpful. Some boards will consider all submissions in competition with all other submissions. Others will set up project classifications, such as maintenance of business, securing new business, facilities, information technology, safety, and environmental enhancement. Projects will compete for assigned funds only within their classification.

Normally the board's executive will have prescreened the projects before the meeting and prepared a draft program for the board to use in its deliberations. The executive will also ensure that all *t*'s are crossed and *i*'s dotted—in particular, that all project submissions are as complete as possible and the cost estimates as accurate as possible. That same executive will determine the hurdle rate, the rate of return required of each project before company funds will be committed to that project.

It is our experience that this board organization works very well. Two problem areas can develop, however. First, the capital system can become clogged. Each year the board should accept a small number of projects beyond the probable funding level, because some projects will drop out or will not be executable in a reasonable period of time, but the board will seldom be able to even consider all requirements. Good capital program discipline depends upon good project execution (see Chapter 7), so that the program input and output are reasonably the same, or the system will become clogged. This will lead to petty disputes among the board members if the members think that the only way to get their project executed is to lobby it up the priority list.

Second, with the exception of the occasional absolute emergency project, all projects should be subject to the same prioritization analysis and scrutiny. If the internal rate of return (IRR) is the desired prioritization vehicle, then an IRR should be calculated for each project by neutral analysts. No system is perfect, but the system must be consistent.

Project Submissions

Project submissions are very important. They need to be in a common format. Most boards accept submissions that add up to slightly more than the expected capital budget to allow for project hiccups during the year.[7] All submissions should include the following information:

- Fiscal year
- Location and sponsoring department
- Project title
- Program and category code (if applicable)
- Project number
- Project cost estimate (by phase if applicable)
- Project description
- Project justification
- Calculation of decision device (NPV, IRR, benefit/cost ratio, etc.)
- Concept drawing or rendering[8]

An advocate for each project should appear before the board with a fixed amount of time to present and justify that project. Most departments will use an experienced briefer to present their project(s), but the board may want to require a fixed format to eliminate the beauty pageant effect.

This is not a factor for equipment purchases, but for construction, renovation, and major repair projects, the forwarding department will have to have done a feasibility study and enough design (we recommend 30 to 35 percent design development) to get an accurate cost estimate before the project can even be submitted to the board. Approving a project based on a gross or notional cost estimate almost guarantees a continuing problem with that project through project execution. In fact, a major misestimated project can affect your entire facility program because, in our experience, notional costs are normally understated, and the board will find that the project eats up more and more of the firm's capital resources as it moves through design and construction. As Virginia's transportation secretary said recently when viewing his capital program, which was filled with notional estimates, "The six year plan is so out of whack . . . it's quite clear there'll be a major downward adjustment [in the entire program]."[9] For the facility management department, the funds for these studies and 30 percent design efforts* are funded from an annual budget, but, if the project is accepted and executed, the costs may be transferred to the capital project.

Cost Justification

As a company puts together a capital program or engages in an individual capital project, a myriad of questions arise and research must be done. The fact remains that in our experience, among all of the details that must be considered, concerns over costs predominates. So, what the board is really doing is determining one of the following:

- How best to allocate company financial resources effectively and efficiently
- How to prioritize projects competing for limited resources
- Which project has the highest potential for reward
- Which project minimizes financial risk

We advocate the use of life-cycle costing in all cost justifications (see Chapter 6), but regardless of whether the board considers life-cycle costs or initial costs only, it should use one of the following cost evaluation tools:

- Average payback
- Actual payback
- *Net present value* (NPV)
- *Internal rate of return* (IRR)
- *Benefit/cost ratio*

---

*These are the funds for studies, design, and engineering contained under overhead in the annual budget model shown in Appendix D.

The calculation of each of these cost evaluation tools is outlined in Appendix E, along with an evaluation of each. The examples given are simplified. In actuality, the calculation of the value of tools such as NPV or IRR should be done by qualified analysts in the finance department, using costs and benefits identified by the facility management department.

The best explanation for facility managers of the accounting and financial management terms and principles needed to calculate the exact value of these cost evaluation tools is contained in Chapter 18 of Mike Hoots's *Money Talks*. We also applaud Professor Hoots for being one of the pioneers in explaining the interface between facility management and financial management, a subject that was too long overlooked.

Of the tools presented, we strongly favor the use of the internal rate of return (IRR) because it can be compared directly with the hurdle rate. Over 70 percent of managers responding to an academic survey since the 1950s indicated that they used the IRR to make capital decisions. NPV is popular, but it trails the IRR by 3:1.[10] The *payback* methods are overly simplistic and overused for evaluating capital projects because they do not fully consider the time value of money. The benefit/cost ratio is appropriate for large, complex projects, but it requires a sophisticated staff to calculate the wide-ranging costs and benefits.

Conclusion

Any facility manager who does not understand the preceding section but who manages a substantial capital program should seek training. Both the International Facility Management Association (IFMA) and the American Society for Testing and Materials (ASTM) provide training in building economics. Or, the facility manager can train him- or herself using *ASTM Standards on Building Economics*.

A system for gathering, analyzing, and prioritizing competing capital requirements is essential to the effectiveness and efficiency of capital program implementation, which we will cover in depth in Chapter 7.

Superior development and management of the capital program can be an excellent way for the facility manager to "earn her spurs" within the upper management of the company or agency. Mike Hoots and Jeff Hamer, one of the first proponents of business expertise within the IFMA, conclude that the financial analysis involved in capital program development and management:

- Is not just for Harvard MBA types.
- Doesn't have to consume untold hours.
- Can greatly enhance the marketability of FM proposals.
- Helps the FM become a player.
- Must be coordinated with the financial department.
- Needs only be as complex as the situation requires.
- Need only be as accurate as the situation demands.
- Must be tailored to the needs of the decision makers.

• Should be of presentation quality.[11]

For an excellent supplemental overview of the entirety of the capital budgeting process read Barry Lynch's article "Tactics to Improve Your Capital Budgeting Process."[12] Barry Lynch is one of the "thinkers" in our profession, and he offers some great suggestions for upgrading a corporate capital development system once it is in operation.

Each company will need to adapt our system to its unique situation, but it is important that the system allocate funds properly and consider both reward and risk. Without a system, capital budget development will easily regress to office politics, which will only be exacerbated during project implementation. Combine a good facility capital development program with a good strategic facility business planning system, and the facility manager will be well on the way to fiscal stability and success.

Notes

1. U.S. Census Bureau press release, January 29, 2003.
2. *Report of the President's Commission to Study Capital Budgeting,* February 1, 1999, p. 4.
3. Peter Bacque, "VDOT Hits Roadblock," *Richmond (Va.) Times-Dispatch* online, January 26, 2002.
4. David Cotts, *The Facility Management Handbook,* 2d ed. (New York: AMACOM, 1999), p. 415.
5. *Practices and Techniques: The Accounting Classification of Workplace Costs,* Statement 4BB (Montvale, N.J.: Institute of Management Accountants, 1997), p. 19.
6. Richard R. Swarts, "Tax Engineering: Designing Corporate Facilities to Maximize Tax Savings," *Corporate Management,* July/August 1992, pp. 13–17.
7. Cotts, p. 80.
8. Ibid.
9. Whittington W. Clement, as quoted in Bacque.
10. Michael Hoots and Jeffrey Hamer, *Facility Financial Forecasting and Budgeting* (Houston: International Facility Management Association, 1998), p. 202.
11. Michael Hoots and Jeffrey Hamer, *Facility Forecasting and Budgeting Course* (Houston: International Facility Management Association, 1998), p. 4.
12. Barry Lynch, "Tactics to Improve Your Capital Budgeting Process," *FMJ,* November/December 2001, pp. 50–53.

6

Costs and Cost Controls

Pulse Points

- *Facility managers manage a cost center, a large cost center. This means FM costs will be constantly under scrutiny.*
- *Facility managers must understand their costs of doing business and have systems in place that calculate and update them effortlessly.*
- *Good facility business planning offers the greatest opportunity for cost savings.*
- *Facility management investment decisions are driven both by opportunity costs and by the costs of not doing business.*
- *FM unit costs should be instantly and automatically available from our work management and financial management systems and should be easily calculable without a lot of manipulation.*
- *The FM work management system should be compatible with the corporate financial reporting system.*
- *For large facility management departments an accountant is needed.*
- *Cost containment is so important that the facility manager must perform cost analysis, constantly get employee input to better cost containment, and should consider forming a cost containment committee.*
- *Facility managers should set the example for cost containment.*
- *Facility managers should use life-cycle costing for all major investment decisions.*
- *Benchmarking should be the start of the continuous improvement process. It does no good to benchmark processes that you already know are inefficient.*

Keywords

cost center, chargebacks, unit costs, service agreements, activity-based accounting, life-cycle costs, benchmarking, project accounting, cost containment, cost reduction, cost avoidance, controllable costs, engineered costs, non-discretionary costs, discretionary costs, committed costs, capital costs, operations costs, ownership costs, fixed costs, variable costs, unit costs, soft costs, sunk costs, price book, job order contracting, break-even analyses

Introduction

How Much Do I Cost?

While cost savings and cost reductions do involve financial considerations, they are not financial management issues; they are simply management issues. At the same time, they cannot be handled separately. As we teach, speak to, and write for facility managers, they always and soon ask, "How can we reduce costs?" We reiterate here that facility managers manage a cost center, a large cost center. We must focus on costs like a laser, and any facility manager who is not comfortable with that constant pressure is in the wrong business. To stress its importance, we will directly address the topic of cost containment in this chapter.

One of our all-time favorite facility management articles appeared in a 1996 issue of *FM Journal*. The article was "How Much Do I Cost?" by Jim Whiteside, a Madison, Wisconsin, facility manager.[1] Those five words articulate an extremely important aspect of the life of a facility manager and present a question that FMs should constantly ask. The answer to that question determines whether a facility manager will be viewed within the company as successful or not, whether the FM department will be contracted out, and even what the future direction of FM within that company will be.

Costs are the most scrutinized aspect of an FM's performance, so they cannot be ignored. Whether that is a good thing is discussed later in this chapter. The theme of Whitehead's article is that costs are important in the evaluation of job performance, but that few FMs really know their actual costs to their companies and agencies, and we concur. In Chapters 1 and 2, we assert that facility managers are making decisions for the department or are recommending decisions to upper management without good data and without the benefit of appropriate financial tools. This is an invitation to disaster.

In this regard, we envy facility managers who are in a manufacturing environment. They are more likely to have calculated the costs of their services, since product managers in these firms need to know that cost so that it can be assigned to the products that the company manufactures. We consulted two accounting textbooks, and both of them used a manufacturing environment for their examples of cost accounting. Unfortunately, in the real world, facility managers, even those within the manufacturing sector, do not consistently make exact calculations of the cost of FM services. Most often, poor cost definitions, the lack of programmatic budgeting, and the failure of the CAFM system to capture costs accurately contribute to this failure. It is clear that we should join Jim Whiteside in trying to determine how much we cost. One of our recurrent themes in this book is the importance of setting up effective and fully automated cost accounting. To the extent that FMs do not accomplish this, they ensure that service agreements, chargebacks, activity-based accounting, life-cycle cost, and benchmarking will be highly suspect.

Costs and Budgeting

Another way of thinking about costs is in the context of budgeting, which is merely projecting costs for the next fiscal period. Most budgeting is classified as cost budgeting. It is important that we be able to define and accurately project those costs if our budgets are to be meaningful, relevant, and credible. The sad truth is that we are too seldom able to do this, for some of the reasons mentioned earlier. Once we have made the corporate case for treating facilities as assets, our companies depend on us to be able to make proper financial analyses and recommendations to management. Either we project those costs that are necessary if we are to protect company assets through our budget or we recommend disposing of an asset because our cost analysis indicates that retaining it is no longer economically wise. These decisions must be based on accurate costs, and we have to be sure that we can calculate these costs.

In general, we account for our costs over time by FM function, by process/product supported, or by business activity (activity-based costing). For the remainder of this book, when we discuss accounting, we will be talking about accounting by FM function unless we mention otherwise.

Project Accounting

Project accounting is another skill that facility managers must have, but it is conducted slightly differently. Costs are accumulated according to one of three different standard formats that reflect the organization of the specifications. Consequently, project costs often have to be "translated" by a knowledgeable individual before they can be entered into a corporate or government financial reporting system, and frequently the entire project is entered as a single cost line at the conclusion of the project.

Corporate Decision Making

Especially in the absence of good financial data and without the use of accepted financial analyses, our decision making defaults to politics. It is our opinion that most facility managers would do better to rely on accurate data and good financial analysis skills than on their political ability. Since corporate investment decisions are made by skilled business managers, it is a no-brainer that we would be better off communicating with them in business terms and using financial decision-making tools.

The issue, at its most basic, is how to get accurate data, particularly costs, easily and consistently, and then how to use the decision-making tools that management understands.

Two Views of the Same Costs

There are some complicating factors even if accurate costs are calculated. BOMI, as quoted in *Today's Facility Manager,* highlights the difference between facility managers' and property managers' approach to costs, despite the fact that the two groups' technical job descriptions are almost identical. The facility manager manages facilities to support the business, whereas for the property manager, the facilities *are* the business. People in both groups can be business-focused, but their view of the business is substantially different, and they view the costs of facilities differently even if the costs are accurately calculated.[2]

Best Practices

Our experience has been that the best way to reduce costs is to practice facility management effectively and efficiently. That means putting in place *best practices* that have been developed by other facility managers or through research. Promoting best practices is one of the most important roles of the professional associations. The government manages large facilities where innovative ideas for cost reduction and containment can be developed and perfected and should be another incubator for and promoter of best practices. We are disappointed that neither the professional associations nor the government is the force for broad knowledge and technology transfer that it could be. For example, IFMA's Best Practices Seminars were terrific, but they have been discontinued. The National Academy of Sciences' Federal Facilities Council produces great seminars and workshops, but these are restricted to members only. Finally, as facility managers, we have not turned to academia to produce new concepts, policies, and procedures for cost reduction in facility management. We have not funded FM university research adequately. Every university FM program with which we are acquainted is short of research funds. When academic institutions do produce best practices, these practices are often ignored.

We believe that cost containment best practices are particularly important, and we have included our favorite best practices as Appendix G.

The Department as a Cost Center

One final point about costs should be made here in the introduction to this chapter. About fifteen years ago, a number of individuals started to discuss operating a facility department as a profit center. While we applaud the concept that facility managers need to think of themselves as businesspeople and to run their departments in a businesslike way, a corporate or government FM department is a *cost center* and a very large one. To view it any other way is self-delusional and can lead to bad management decisions. We know of several cases where entrepreneurial facility managers have formed FM service companies (we tried to do it ourselves) from an existing corporate FM department and have also sought business from other corporate clients. But that is not running a department as a profit center; it is a form of outsourcing. It is extremely important that facility managers understand that their departments are cost centers and that the pressure on them to reduce those costs will never stop. Facility managers must focus on costs and always seek ways to reduce those costs while retaining the quantity, quality, and response of services.

In the remainder of the chapter, we define costs, explore some of the principal management cost concepts encountered in FM, discuss cost containment, examine life-cycle costing and benchmarking in detail, and provide a listing of FM best practices that, when implemented, will affect either short- or long-term FM costs. We continue to believe that facility managers should learn from others and implement best practices, and we have gathered a number of cost savings/cost containment best practices for your use (Appendix G).

Cost Containment

Definitions

Costs are a measurement of the resources necessary to produce a product or service. Since a firm's profit is its total revenue minus its costs, a company cannot remain viable in the long run unless it controls its costs.* Unfortunately, there are construction companies that are paying the bills from the last job out of the revenues from this job because they did not properly estimate and control their costs. Unstable companies cannot be counted on to provide best-value services because, by their nature, they must have a short-term business outlook. That affects us in several ways. The quality of the work may suffer as the contractor tries to reduce costs, or the contractor may try to flood us with change orders. Yet few of us ever look at the financial health of our contractors prior to entering into an agreement with them.

Unfortunately, sometimes an inability to truly understand costs can be found in corporate and agency facility managers. We repeat that facility managers must be able to understand their costs, to calculate them accurately, and to function in an environment in which upper management is constantly pressing for cost reduction. In both the public and the private sectors, costs are important. Every dollar that the FM spends means that the FM's boss must add an additional dollar to the budget or a salesperson must sell an additional dollar's worth of product. Always keep that in mind.

It is possible to avoid or reduce costs. Figure 6-1 is a previously published list of facility management functions. We believe that an FM department that has put no special emphasis on cost reduction or avoidance can make improvements by employing these methods. We again assert that it is our belief that good strategic facility planning offers the greatest opportunity for cost savings.

---

*Remember the joke about the merchant who lost a quarter on every item he sold, but explained that he made up for it in volume?

Figure 6-1. Opportunities for Cost Savings and Avoidances.

	Cost Savings (%)[1]			
Function	*Capital*	*Annual*	*Avoidances*[2]	*Areas Affected*
Facility planning and forecasting strategic and mid-term planning	5–15	10–20	15–25	Construction costs, O&M costs, leasing costs, financing costs
Lease administration	–	5–10	5–10	Utility costs, build-out costs, shared costs, property management costs
Space planning, allocation, and management	–	3–5	–	Rents and space-related costs
Architectural-engineering planning and design	8–12	10–30	20–30	Maintenance costs, energy costs, operating costs, construction costs
Workplace planning, design, and specification	–	–	3–7	Employee efficiency
Budgeting, accounting, and economic justification	1–2	2–3	–	Accuracy of accounts, better budget utilization
Real estate acquisition and disposal	2–5	2–5	5–7	Operational costs, acquisition costs, disposal price
Construction project management	7–10	7–10	10–15	Construction and alteration costs
Alterations, renovations, and workplace installation	–	2–3	7–10	Project costs, staff disruption costs
Operations, maintenance, and repair	–	7–10	15–20	Energy costs, maintenance costs, capital costs, insurance costs, and major repairs
Communications and security	2–3	2–3	7–10	Avoid insurance costs and increase productivity, save communications costs

1. Percentage of funds in current-year program.
2. Average mutual percentage over lifetime—capital and annual.

Types of Costs

In accounting and economics books, costs are sliced, diced, and defined in enough ways to make one's head spin. For that reason, we employ the definitions used by Mike Hoots in his financial management course *Money Talks*,[3] which is specifically designed for facility managers. We have added selected others that we believe are really necessary if you are to have a working understanding of the types of costs that you will encounter in facility management. One of the purposes of this book is to bring some degree of standardization to the definition of terms, of which costs are just one group. The problems that the lack of definitions and accounting standards causes for upper management and legislative bodies that must appropriate funds for us is outlined in the Federal Facilities Council's Report, *Deferred Maintenance Reporting for Federal Facilities*.[4] One of our strongest hopes is for agreement on planning and budgeting formats, facility management terms, and means and methods of calculating the proper funding for facility maintenance and repair. We have contributed to this effort over the past twenty years, but the field is so fractionalized that at present there is no effective way to set standards. One of the purposes of this book is to make converts to standardization, one reader at a time. As you will notice, none of these definitions are exclusive. For instance, a direct cost can also be a soft cost. An expense can also be an engineered cost. In some cases the definitions will overlap. Often these definitions represent different ways of looking at the same costs for a different management purpose.

Mike Hoots, in his text *Money Talks*, characterizes five categories of costs that he says are important for facility managers to understand in order (1) to structure their budgets, (2) to understand budgets in the context of their company's or agency's budgets, and (3) to be able to converse knowledgeably with their business counterparts outside the department.

- **Controllable costs.** Can be significantly affected by the actions of the responsibility center manager. The keys to identifying controllable costs are:
  - They are assigned to a responsibility center manager.
  - They can be significantly influenced by that manager.
- **Engineered costs.** Can be precisely determined and measured and are directly related to the outputs of responsibility centers. Changes in engineered costs typically have a direct impact on the ability to fund operational activities.
- **Non-discretionary costs.** Cannot be varied at the discretion of the manager. Cuts in non-discretionary cost items *would* result in some impact (typically a degradation) on operations.
- **Discretionary costs.** Can be varied at the discretion of the manager without a direct impact on operations. This is not to imply that changes in discretionary costs will not some day affect operations, just that a direct correlation is not immediately apparent.
- **Committed costs.** Result from obligations previously entered into that have not been completely paid for or otherwise reconciled. Committed costs are controllable only to the extent that a firm can renege on its commitments.

But the penalties are typically so severe that this is not an option unless bankruptcy is imminent.[5]

To these we add our own previously published definitions of costs.

- **Capital costs.** Used to acquire, substantially improve, expand, change the functional use of, or replace a building or building system. Capitalization rules are driven by tax laws, so they vary between locations.
- **Operations costs.** Associated with the day-to-day operation of a facility. Includes all maintenance and repair (both fixed and variable); administrative costs; labor costs; janitorial, housekeeping, and other cleaning costs; all utility costs; management fees; and all costs associated with roadways and grounds.
- **Ownership costs.** Result from ownership of the building, servicing existing debt, and receiving a return on equity. Also includes costs of capital improvements, repair, and upkeep that would not be considered standard operating costs.
- **Life-cycle costs.** Incident to the planning, design, construction, operation, and maintenance of a structure over time.[6]

Finally, we use these additional definitions in teaching and consulting:

- **Fixed costs.** Costs not related directly to the level of production; sometimes referred to as sunk costs.
- **Variable costs.** Costs that vary directly with the level of production.
- **Unit cost.** The cost for one unit of a good or service. These costs are commonly used in benchmarking.
- **Soft costs.** Costs not directly attributable to construction, renovation, maintenance, and repair in facility management, especially project management.
- **Sunk costs.** Costs that have already been expended and therefore are not considered in financial decisions concerning future work.

Economic Cost Concepts

Finally, it is important to also understand two more definitions of cost concepts. We include these because they are so important to us. Economists view *opportunity costs* generally as the costs of goods, services, or interest forgone by investing money one way rather than another. "Why," asks your CFO, "should I invest in your new chiller, Mr. FM, when it has a life-cycle IRR of 3.2 percent? I can take the same money and invest it in the market and get a return of 11.9 percent over the same period." There may be a reason, but the FM had better be able to explain convincingly to the CFO, the CEO, and the executive committee what it is.

Alan Whitson deals with another aspect of the same concept: the consequences of delaying a project after it has been cost-justified. In this situation, the department has justified a project on the basis of its cost savings, but for some reason a glitch in the capital budgeting process delayed the start of the project.

Particularly if that project was approved over a high internal hurdle rate, the loss of planned savings as a result of a one-year delay (typically capital projects are considered once a year) can be substantial when it is projected over the life of the project. Since the planned savings were lost, there is no longer the possibility of reinvesting them.[7] Time is money!

A counterpart concept is *the cost of not doing business.* In a mall, temporarily unused space gets built out at astonishing rates by crews working day and night in a manner that appears wasteful of resources. Why is there such a hurry? Because there is a cost of not doing business, and a retail business makes no money until the store is open. Facility managers see this cost in many ways. Imagine what happens if there is a disruption of electricity in a trading room of a financial institution or a 24/7 business call center. The responsible facility and operational managers soon discover the cost of not doing business. The average hourly cost of system failure for a brokerage firm in 2000 was $6,450,000.[8] Such factors may demand that the facility manager expend resources heavily in areas like security, alternative sites, and backup systems, to an extent that would appear excessive to a facility manager in a school system, for example. An FM must keep in mind the cost of not doing business.

Managing Costs and Cost Containment

Costs at the Micro Level

For many reasons (estimating, benchmarking, and the pricing of job orders are some), a facility manager may want to compare a cost that he has calculated or one that has been submitted to him against a standard. Our favorite comparator is an in-house price database, but it is our experience that few facility departments have one, and if they do, they fail to keep it updated. Others that we have seen used are listed here, although not all of the sources listed contain parallel or even complete cost data for comparison:

Sources of FM Cost Data and Micro-Pricing

- R.S. Means Facility Cost Data
- Whitestone Research
- BOMA Experience Report
- IFMA Benchmark Study
- *Engineering News Record*
- Bureau of Labor Statistics (hourly labor rates)

At least one private FM service provider, Johnson Controls, has both a national and an international office cost database. Some benchmarking consultants have compiled their own databases of FM costs. In this age of Web-based databases, we are sure that there are databases available on the Web of which we are not even aware. Each of these sources has its strengths and weaknesses, and some are better in one application than in another. For example, many departments use R.S. Means for their "price book" during their initial attempt at job-order contracting (JOC). Some then develop their own price book, while others continue to use Means. There are even JOC consultants who will help an FM develop a department-specific price book because the success of this highly effective method of contracting is dependent upon good cost data.

Again, each department has unique needs, but for most large, innovative facility departments, the facility manager will probably be a regular subscriber to the data contained in both Means and the BOMA Experience Report. As the facility manager is developing unit costs for all services and a database of departmental costs for internal and external benchmarking purposes, those two references provide accepted and easy comparisons for departmental costs.

Before using any of these sources, the FM may need to determine some way to update the data to the year in question through indexing. Most of the data are at least a year old when they are published. Many of the sources in the preceding list are available online, and most require a purchase of the data in order to access them. Historically, increases in facility costs have been greater than the increases in the Consumer Price Index, particularly in large metropolitan areas. It is necessary to choose the method of indexing wisely.

We cannot overemphasize the importance of these micro-costs because they form the basis for unit costs, benchmarking, project estimating, chargebacks, service-level agreements, budget projections, and operational evaluations. They are key to the measurement of the department's performance, both internally and by upper management. They should be instantly and automatically available from our work management and financial management systems, which should be in sync, and unit costs derived from the micro-costs should be easily calculable without a lot of manipulation. Yet more than half of facility managers report that they cannot properly allocate space costs because their cost data are inaccurate and require a manual, error-prone collection process. In addition, 40 percent of FMs say that they do not charge back for space because they cannot accurately calculate what they should be charging their customers.[9] Our experience is that the degrees of inaccuracy are *understated* because facility managers have not

- Used programmatic budgeting with a proper statement of accounts
- Established procedures to ensure that accurate information is entered into their work management systems (particularly costs like overheads and travel time)
- Ensured that the work management and financial management systems are compatible
- Decided what are critical unit costs and ensured that those costs are easily calculable

Until those practices are in place, the facility manager needs to spend time personally ensuring that operational and work management personnel focus on establishing them.

The FM Accountant

In addition, in our experience, a facility management accountant is needed for a medium or large facility department. This individual may work for the facility department or for the finance department, but she or he needs to be colocated with the facility manager until the financial reporting goals listed here are achieved.

Cost Containment

In this section, we will draw heavily on the writing of Professor Michael Hoots of the University of Southern Colorado because he has observed and written most extensively on financial management for the facility manager. We emphasize that cost containment is more a management than a financial management function. "The most powerful method of showing the facility function's efficiency is through *documented* cost savings and avoidance," according to Hoots. He noted the following as ways in which costs could be contained or saved:

- Time is money and can be minimized through proper, prior planning and proactive management.
- Fast-tracking high productivity projects can cost more up front but yield bigger returns after completion.
- The proper mix of in-house and contract labor will minimize personnel costs.
- Space is money and must be judiciously allocated.
- Long-term operating costs can be reduced by facility life-cycle management and value engineering.
- Proper accounting, economic analysis, and procurement techniques and controls can show quick results.
- A strong preventive maintenance program must be balanced against a sensible repair policy (cost efficiency curve).[10]

We concur in all of these observations. Another good source of advice for us has been facility management students. Over the past ten years we have asked our students to list the areas where they had been the most successful at either cost savings or cost avoidance. Of those mentioned, the following were the most frequently designated:

- Energy management
- Implementation of standards
- Auditing by specialized auditors (particularly of energy and communications costs)
- Chargebacks to operating units
- Outsourcing
- Rightsizing
- Risk sharing with vendors

- Risk avoidance/insurance analysis
- Changing customer expectations
- Quality management
- National sales contracts
- Challenging real estate assessments
- Better asset management
- Recycling
- Lease management/renegotiation
- Better space utilization
- Better planning

Comments on Cost Containment Initiatives

Most of the initiatives in this list are self-explanatory, but we would like to comment briefly on five of them. We are convinced that facility managers need to revisit energy management. Since the strong emphasis on this area in the mid-1970s, many FMs have gotten fat in their thinking and in their practices regarding energy use. Utilities continue to be 30 to 40 percent of the average facility's operations costs. While there is no longer any low-hanging fruit in energy management in most companies or any large energy-saving incentives from utility companies, the costs are so large that the FM simply must address them.

Regarding specialized audits, we are somehow repulsed (call it hubris) by the idea of consultants coming onto our turf and finding mistakes in our billings for telecommunications, utilities, and real estate assessments in return for a percentage of the savings. But we know from talking to other facility managers that this has often worked. For a fee of 30 to 40 percent of the cost savings discovered, it is obvious that these consultants can actually be quite cost-effective.

We are less convinced that chargebacks and allocations really save money. The selling point for chargebacks was that under centralized budgeting, too many operational managers viewed their space and facility services as free and consequently had little incentive to economize and save the company or agency money. Now that the practice of chargebacks has matured, our observation is that except when there is a sudden increase in the terms of their internal "rent," operations managers generally ignore facility costs. Because they are focused on managing their business unit, they view the internal rent as just another cost of doing business and don't really try to reduce those costs by economizing on the space or amenities requested. The principal advantage of chargebacks is that they have led many facility managers to become more adept at computing their actual costs of doing business so that they can accurately calculate the "rent" for space and charges for "over and above" services.

We observe that facility managers who implement total quality management also contain costs well because some of the skills and procedures required for quality management and for cost containment are very similar. The FM cannot, for example, arbitrarily cut costs that are going to affect the services provided to the customer. Proper service is a trade-off between the wants of an organization and its ability to pay the bill, but decisions need to be made in conjunction with customers. Organizations that have the means to communicate openly and regularly with their customers tend to also be the most cost-effective because the goals and objectives of the service provider and the customer are in sync.

Finally, we want to reiterate our belief that *better planning will save more than all of the other measures put together.*

Organizing for Cost Containment

We have noticed how haphazardly facility managers approach cost containment, while at the same time telling us how much pressure is being put on them to reduce costs. That contradiction is troubling. Being serious about cost containment means organizing to manage it effectively. Hoots provides three ideas to assure cost consciousness: use either internal or consultant cost analysts, get employee input, and form a committee or create some other management mechanism to decide among cost reduction ideas.[11]

Cost Containment Implementation

In addition to encouraging FMs to organize appropriately, Hoots also suggests good procedures for effective cost containment. What follows is a combination of his ideas and ours from our practice:

- Identify areas with high cost containment potential (the low-hanging fruit), and begin there.
- Generate specific savings ideas. Focus on these areas:
  - Increasing output
  - Improving operational methods
  - Regulating or leveling the work flow
  - Minimizing waste
  - Reducing overhead
  - Analyzing control points and changing them, if necessary
  - Ensuring adequate and well-positioned storage space
  - Minimizing downtime and travel time
  - Investing in employee training, whether the workforce is in-house or contracted out
- Provide a format for cost containment suggestions.
- Develop a uniform way to measure actual savings and to ensure that the rate of investment that "sold" a project is actually achieved.
- Include cost containment as a part of departmental objectives, job descriptions, and performance reviews.
- Provide incentives for meaningful and *accepted* cost containment suggestions.
- Establish a procedure that ensures that accepted cost containment suggestions become part of the normal routine of business.
- Celebrate success and communicate your results.

- Involve your management in the program through frequent reviews and updates.
- *Set the example!*

Many of us who work in medium or large organizations have access to cost analysts and industrial engineers who service the business units. Consider using them to analyze FM operations and to suggest ways in which the department can become more cost-effective and efficient.[12]

Cost Analyses

Breakeven Analysis

We need to be able to sell our specific ideas and projects using methods with which our management is familiar and comfortable. Often FMs think that this is beyond them. In this section, we hope to show you that, given a good cost database, the FM is able to perform both simple and reasonably sophisticated cost analyses.

An always contentious cost issue in our FM departments was recycling. We would often have noneconomic reasons to recycle pointed out to us by some of our customers who were devoted to recycling. The costs and benefits of recycling have fluctuated wildly in changing economic situations. In any event, since management was feeling the same type of pressure that we were, we felt that we owed upper management a business case for supporting or rejecting recycling. We created a breakeven analysis of recycling white paper, cardboard, and cans. In the example, revenues and avoided cost exceeded the cost of the recycling program, so not only was it good to recycle, but it was good business.

In some cases, and recycling is a good example, breakeven analyses need to be recalculated as often as annually.

A breakeven analysis is pretty simple, but it can be very effective. Let's now turn to a more sophisticated cost analysis.

Life-Cycle Costing

We sometimes wonder just why life-cycle costing is talked about so much but used so seldom by facility managers. Many of the reasons go back to those given in Chapter 1: It just is not in our education, our natures, or our tool bag to use this widely accepted method of analysis for making go/no-go decisions on projects or for rank-ordering competing projects. Maybe we are afraid of the answers we will get if we do a life-cycle cost (LCC) analysis. On the other hand, it might be that the methodology or the unavailability of data scares us.

Whatever the reason, the failure to use life-cycle costing is disappointing. The definitive study of maintenance and repair of public buildings, *Committing to the Cost of Ownership,* could not exactly quantify the amount of deferred maintenance and repair needed for those buildings but determined that it was substantial.[13]

One of the reasons for the backlog of deferred maintenance is that governments continue to build more public buildings even though they don't fund the maintenance and repair of the current inventory and don't have a clue as to what impact the additional buildings will have on future annual operating budgets because they don't use LCC. From observation, this same problem exists in the private sector as well. It is as if managers realize that they have a problem, a serious problem, but refuse to recognize that they are making the problem worse when they fail to calculate life-cycle costs when new work is being considered.

We want to convince FMs that life-cycle costing is certainly within the capability of most managers. We used it in our practice. Many FMs have access to budget analysts or economists who can help them do LCC analyses if they are needed. Our experience has been that, with the level of instruction we provide in this chapter, the reader should feel confident of being able to do a life-cycle cost analysis of most of the facility management projects that might be competing for company funds. An excellent guide to LCC is the National Research Council's *Pay Now or Pay Later*. It presents the pros and cons of calculating life-cycle costing, the obstacles to doing so, and the benefits that can result, as well as showing how to implement life-cycle costing within the facility management financial system.[14] The facility manager who is willing to try an LCC analysis on his own should do one and have it checked by both another facility manager and a budget analyst to see that both the FM and the budgetary reasoning are sound. We guarantee that once you have done one LCC analysis, future ones will be easier. Remember, too, to make the analysis fit the situation. There is no need to consider peripheral issues in order to determine the true life-cycle costs. Stick to the essential costs that will be understood by management and are pertinent to the decision.

Another source of life-cycle cost analysis that can save time is to require competing vendors or contractors to submit life-cycle cost analyses as part of their proposals. We have seen some excellent ones. The FM must set down the parameters for the study and then analyze the costs and benefits presented. What does the CFO or the capital planning board really need to know? The FM can pick up some very good information that she otherwise might well have missed by comparing one life-cycle costing analysis against another for the same project or product.

Life-cycle costing depends upon two concepts. Life-cycle costs are all of the present and future costs associated with a facility investment objective. Also, it is critical that you understand the time value of money in order to clearly compare the life-cycle costs of alternative facility resource investments by taking into account both inflation/deflation and the earning potential of money.[15] With those concepts in mind, let's take a look at a methodical approach to life-cycle costing and set down some general rules.

Stanton Lindquist and Steve Margulis offer facility managers the following seven-step guide to conducting an LCC analysis:[16]

- Decide which projects to compare. Use LCC for projects that have the same performance objectives. Use a net present value or internal rate of return to prioritize projects with different performance objectives.

- Ensure that projects are both technically acceptable and comparable.
- Specify the parameters and study values, such as base date, discount rate, escalation rate, service date, and the study period.
- Decide what input data should be used. Examples are acquisition data (including design cost, purchase cost, installation cost, and construction cost); operating, maintenance, and repair costs; and residual value.
- Collect the needed data (easy to state, but often the most difficult part of the study).
- Decide how to actually calculate costs (a budget analyst can be helpful here).
- Integrate the LCC results into the management decision.

The last point is an important one. Seldom will the LCC be the only factor in a management decision. It is, however, an important factor, so we want it to be understandable and appropriate to the particular project we are analyzing.

Appendix F is the best example of an LCC analysis for facility management beginners. Professor Preston goes through a simple LCC step by step and also reintroduces the concepts of the time value of money and the internal rate of return, which were described in the discussion of making capital program decisions in Chapter 5. This analysis has helped our understanding of the concepts of LCC, net present value, and internal rate of return. We hope it will help others to understand these basic concepts and to decide to use them in their practice.

Two other examples for facility managers who are just learning LCC are contained in the Lindquist and Margulis article and in Thomas Rozman's presentation on this topic, contained in the proceedings of World Workplace 2001.[17] A software program, Building Life Cycle Cost Program, version 4.3, is available from the National Institute of Science and Technology at *www.nist.gov*. This software program is reasonably sophisticated and will be more helpful to those FMs who are already using LCC but would like to improve the quality of their analyses.

Benchmarking

Benchmarking swept through the management world coincidentally with total quality management (TQM). One of the tenets of TQM is that we should measure performance and expect to be measured. Benchmarking was one way of doing that. While we sense that much of TQM is viewed by our fellow facility managers as the "flavor of last month (year?) (decade?)," benchmarking seems to have survived, although we find that there is still a lot of confusion about how best to use it. The bible for benchmarking remains Robert C. Camp's 1989 management classic, *Benchmarking*. In this section, however, we would like to relate benchmarking to better facility management. We will stress benchmarking *costs* in this section because that is what this book focuses on, but benchmarking should cover response and customer evaluations as well as costs.

Benchmarking starts with the calculation of unit costs. Remember, you need to calculate unit costs in order to arrive at the cost of doing business, not just to benchmark. These unit costs

- Tell the true cost of each product and service
- Can be compared to a standard
- Become the basis for benchmarking
- Are invaluable in estimating and planning
- Become management aids
- Need to be systematically but easily calculated and updated

Once unit costs have been calculated—there could be up to a hundred for a complex FM organization—you need to analyze them to see which ones are the "drivers," i.e., the ones that are eating up significant parts of the budget. Concentrate on those costs that are particularly important to management or on the costs of areas where you feel the department is not performing well. Those are the costs to benchmark initially. Ultimately, we like to benchmark each of our services every three to five years on a rotating basis.

We want to reiterate the importance of calculating unit costs whether or not there is a plan to benchmark. Furthermore, if the department is benchmarking, it should include response and customer service as well as costs. From this point forward, however, we will deal with the limited subject of benchmarking costs only.

Most facility managers who initiate benchmarking take their first efforts to the level of overkill. It is much better to start small, identify the budget drivers, and then decide on the methodology.

- Compare the department's unit costs with aggregated benchmark data, such as the BOMA Experience Report (published annually) or the latest IFMA Benchmarking Report. The Association of Higher Education Facilities Officers (APPA) publishes benchmarking data biannually for colleges and universities.
- Participate in industrywide benchmarking. Several of IFMA's councils have sponsored industry-specific benchmarking efforts in the past.
- Join a blind benchmarking study. There is usually a cost, and it will be run by a consultant. You may want to benchmark against like organizations (perhaps competitors) or against best-in-class organizations.
- Hire a benchmarking consultant. Such a consultant normally has a database of benchmarking data that may or may not be applicable to your industry.
- Use some combination of these alternatives.

We have sought good, reliable, nonproprietary FM cost databases on the Internet, but we have been unsuccessful. They may be there, but be sure to use any databases that you find subject to the procedures that we offer here.

Compare apples to apples. No two organizations perform exactly the same way, so there will always be some degree of lack of comparability. Reduce this discrepancy as much as possible by defining functions and work processes the same way as the benchmarking partner does. It is invalid, for example, for you to compare your maintenance costs with those of your benchmarking partner if theirs include janitorial maintenance and yours don't. If you hire a consultant, ensuring that apples are compared to apples will be one of the consultant's duties. To make a comparison using a standard database such as the BOMA Experience Report, ensure that what the two sets of data call "operations" is the same. Often this requires that we pick through the line items in our budget, taking 40 percent of line A and adding it to 17 percent of line B and then dividing by 50 percent of our owned space database plus 13.3 percent of our leased space inventory. This can bog facility managers down during benchmarking. Yet few seem to be willing to make the effort to address the problem, the solution to which is to use programmatic budgeting and a CAFM system that is set up to capture the costs in the way that you want to compare them.

(As an aside here, we return to the theme that the profession needs to standardize definitions and budget formats so that unit costs can be easily calculated and easily compared. Many of our budgets make the identification of "operations" costs, for example, very difficult because they are not properly formatted. Standardized budget formats and definitions would increase the effectiveness of benchmarking immeasurably. If it is organized properly, and if data inputs are accurate, the automated work management system will produce the numerator for most unit costs effortlessly, both in aggregate and for individual buildings and sites.)

A consultant can perhaps help here, but, as the saying goes, "you can't make a silk purse out of a sow's ear." If the facility manager is serious about benchmarking, he must do the necessary up-front work to ensure that he is using standardized definitions of work and that his budget is organized to reflect his work program using those definitions.

For quick lessons on the benchmarking process and FM benchmarking, two of the best sources are an article by Theodore Kinni that emphasizes the classic "Plan, Do, Check, Act" of continuous process improvement[18] and Jack Balderston's introduction to FM benchmarking,[19] both of which we have found immensely helpful in our own practice. Two lessons to be learned from these articles are that it is nonproductive to benchmark work processes that are already known to be inefficient and that benchmarks are not the end of a continuous improvement process, they are the beginning. It is extremely important that the manager use benchmarks as a tool. In the category of janitorial costs, for instance, the goal might be to be in the top 5 percent in performance, in which case the services will probably cost more and unit costs will be higher than those of a benchmarking partner who has lesser expectations. Remember, benchmarking is a tool that helps in making the trade-offs between value and cost.

Final Words on Benchmarking

We believe strongly in benchmarking, because it can provide focus and clues to breakthrough improvements during a continuous improvement process, but we want to emphasize that the most important benefit of benchmarking is that it can lead to the accurate calculation of unit costs. Benchmarking data lead to the opportunity to identify to the bosses *in terms that they understand* both areas that are working well and areas that need improvement. While the results cannot always be guaranteed, Sam Johnson, the former facility manager for Cinergy Corp. in Cincinnati, points out another value of already having calculated unit costs. "My boss went out and requested RFP's from facility management outsourcers and even gave them all my numbers," said Johnson. "All those firms came back and said, 'We can't do it as cheaply as you are doing it internally.'"[20]

The point is that Sam Johnson was ready to defend his department in terms that were used by and important to his bosses. Learn from his example and use business arguments to persuade management of the effectiveness and efficiency of the FM department.

Conclusion

Best Practices to Use (a Reprise)

Every policy, procedure, and practice has some cost implications. Appendix G is a list that we have compiled of best practices that either are innovative or stand to produce significant cost savings or avoidances. For each, we indicate the functional area to which it is applicable, give a short description, and provide the contact information that can be used to get additional information. Several of the best practices are contained in documents that unfortunately are not widely distributed. In such cases, we have tried to give you the best contact information. As we compiled this appendix, we realized that there are many more best practices in the cost containment area than we could possibly include in one appendix. That is why we feel that it is important to re-energize best practices seminars. We want to give special thanks to our fellow facility managers and academicians who have developed these best practices. When we mention specific vendors or commercial systems, we are not endorsing them, but instead are acknowledging that the firm provides a product or service that we believe would be helpful for cost containment and better practice in the field of FM when properly applied. Know that these best practices can be helpful in the practice of facility management. Take the time to scan Appendix G now in order to be familiar with the best practices that are available.

No one will ever be comfortable as a facility manager unless he understands that his department's costs will be constantly scrutinized. For that reason, it is important that we ask ourselves, as Jim Whitehead did, "What do I cost?" Once you have calculated your costs accurately, you need to be able to present the results to management in a way that helps managers to understand the true costs of doing business. Cost containment must be a high-priority mission of the department. There should be a cost containment plan developed annually and for each major capital project. Managers, supervisors, and contractors should be held accountable and rewarded for their ability to control costs.

Notes

1. Jim Whiteside, "How Much Do I Cost?" *FM Journal*, March/April 1996, pp. 6–14.

2. "The Finances of FM," *Today's Facility Manager*, April 2000, p. 69.

3. Michael Hoots, *Money Talks* (Houston: International Facility Management Association, 2000).

4. *Deferred Maintenance Reporting for Federal Facilities* (Washington, D.C.: National Academy Press, 2001).

5. Hoots, pp. 88–89.

6. David G. Cotts, *The Facility Management Handbook*, 2d ed. (New York: AMA-COM, 1999), pp. 415, 420.

7. "Time Is Money," *Capital News*, August–September 2000, p. 1.

8. "24/7 Support," *Facilities Design & Management*, March 2000, p. 44.

9. "Managing Space as a Strategic Asset (Executive Summary)," *Facilities Design & Management*, August 2000, p. 6.

10. Michael Hoots, *Facility Financial Forecasting and Budgeting* (Houston: International Facility Management Association, 1998), p. 73.

11. Ibid., pp. 74–75.

12. Ibid., unnumbered page.

13. *Committing to the Cost of Ownership* (Washington, D.C.: National Academy Press, 1990), p. 13.

14. *Pay Now or Pay Later* (Washington, D.C.: National Academy Press, 1991).

15. Stephen T. Margulis and Stanton C. Lindquist, "Beware of the Short-Sighted Bottom Line," *FM Journal*, March/April 1994, p. 7.

16. Ibid, pp. 8–10.

17. Thomas P. Rozman, "Building Maintenance: Pay Me Now or Pay Me (Much More) Later," *Proceedings of World Workplace 2001* (Houston: International Facility Management Association, 2001), pp. 109–118.

18. Theodore B. Kinni, "Benchmarking," *Quality Digest*, November 1993, pp. 24–29.

19. Jack Balderston, "Facilities Benchmarking: Why, What and How," *FM Journal*, September/October 1992, pp. 6–8.

20. Linda K. Monroe, "Benchmarking for Success," *Buildings*, May 2000, p. 46.

7

Project Accounting

Pulse Points

- *The facility manager's role during any project is to ensure that the customer's plans and requirements are constructed, installed, and completed on time and within budget.*
- *Standard corporate accounting systems generally cannot provide the project budget management control, information, and reports that facility managers and their customers need.*
- *A Web-based/Web-enabled system should be able to provide the facility manager and staff with a process that permits an integrated, consistent methodology for creating and managing projects.*
- *The facility manager should have the ability to access and read information or reports on the computer screen or to print hard copy reports from anywhere.*
- *Facility managers rely on their project management training and knowledge to understand and evaluate the success of their projects.*
- *The development or acquisition and implementation of a Project Financial and Accounting System is an important part of the project financial process.*

Keywords

Project accounting, System, project description, project approval process, project number, preliminary and approved budgets, purchase orders, change orders, invoices, payments, facility manager–friendly, against time, contingency, automated reports, outstanding purchase orders and payments

Introduction

The facility manager's role during any project is to ensure that the customer's plans and requirements are constructed, installed, and completed on time and within budget. During this same time period, the management of the organization is measuring the facility manager's performance and ability to complete projects on time and on or under budget. To do this, facility managers must manage a project using their understanding and knowledge of project budgets, what commitments have been made, what purchase orders and related change orders have been issued, what invoices have been processed, what funds have been released in payment, and what funds remain unspent. The facility manager must also be very familiar with *project accounting* and the demonstrable audit trail that must be developed for each project.

We often find that standard corporate accounting systems cannot provide the budget management control, information, and reports on projects that facility managers need for the consistent management of their project budgets and expenditures. If such a project financial and accounting system (*System*) is not currently available, we recommend that it be developed or acquired. This will help the facility manager, with assistance from the organization's finance and accounting departments, to provide specific project management financial control, information, and reports at any point in time for each unique project.

Where possible, a Web-based/Web-enabled System should be available to the facility manager and staff to allow a process that provides an integrated, consistent methodology for creating and managing projects. Whether from the organization's internal intranet platform or from the organization's Internet Web site through a password-protected firewall, the facility manager should be able, through a networked computer system, to access all project-related information, including the status of the project budget approval process, preliminary budgets and approved funding, purchase and change orders, invoices, payments, and project close-out information, all in accordance with the facility manager's corporate project budget policies and procedural requirements.

The System should provide *facility manager–friendly* features and give the facility manager a large degree of flexibility to work within the existing purchase requisition/purchase order/change order process, project financial procedures, and accounting procedures. The System should provide a straightforward, organized process to help the facility manager to manage project financial responsibilities on a departmental level and to track such functions as:

- The *project approval process*
- *Preliminary and approved budgets*
- *Purchase orders*
- *Change orders*
- *Invoices*
- *Payments*

The System's facility manager–friendly database design should permit the facility manager to generate reports via the intranet or the Internet at any time throughout the life of a proposed or approved project. It should also provide a method of ensuring that *only* approved expenditures are charged against a specific project, permitting only authorized personnel to charge expenses against a specific project via specific invoices, and providing specific reports for the facility manager, staff, and management to use in tracking and documenting departmental performance. In addition, the System should provide a very specific project or departmental expenditure audit trail while providing follow-up information for facility management services during and after the project is complete. All project information should be retained for future reference, and a place for electronic and hard copy information should be arranged, with the means of accessing this information known to all who need to know.

The System should rely on the facility manager's familiarity with project and budget tracking, his or her ability to organize and provide the correct information, and his or her ability to use the System as a management tool, not as an end product. Ideally, a separate person (i.e., the facility manager's cost analyst or department administrative assistant—not the facility manager) will receive and review all project information to ensure that it follows the System format and is entered into the System correctly. The facility manager should have the ability to access and *read* information or reports on the computer screen or to print hard copy reports on a regular basis or when needed from anywhere.

Against Budget

Projects have a specific purpose; they have a beginning, a completion time period, and a cost in capital or expense funds. Funds are provided by an organization to accomplish projects. Before projects are approved, organizations require the development of budgets based on the scope of the projects. Approved budgets should include all expense categories, including freight, taxes, and staff time for capital projects, that can be charged to the project, a brief description of the project, and the signatures of the person who prepared the budgets and those in management who have the authority to approve the budget, similar to what is shown in Figure 7.1. Approved budgets become the basis for all project expenditures.

Project costs are subject to the same supply and demand and inflationary pressures that all businesses face. There are no guarantees in bidding a project. The prudent facility manager and his or her customer will ensure that the project budget includes *contingency* funds (between 5 and 10 percent, depending on your risk aversion and company policy) for unexpectedly high bids and for undetectable items that are discovered during construction (e.g., rock, springs, environmental hazards, unknown utilities and structural members in areas being demolished, or changes or revisions in the building code and/or occupancy requirements). The contingency funds may or may not be a separate line item in the budget, depending on organization policy. Many organizations spread the contingency funds over the various line items in the budget. If the contingency amount is a separate approved budget line item, its use must be carefully managed and recorded by the facility manager.

Figure 7-1. Budget Approval Report.

	BUDGET APPROVAL REPORT		PAGE: 1 of 1

ABC CORPORATION—PROJECT FINANCIAL & ACCOUNTING SYSTEM
CP01-0001   RENOVATIONS TO SUITE 410, XYZ BUILDING,
234 BURROUGHS STREET, CHICAGO, IL 60339
FEBRUARY 25, 2001

Company Code: ABC
Category: RENOVATION

UCIC	DESCRIPTION	INITIAL BUDGET	APPROVED BUDGET
00300	CONSULTING FEES	3,500.00	3,500.00
00301	CONSULTING REIMBURSABLE EXPENSES	350.00	350.00
DIVISION TOTAL:		3,850.00	3,850.00
0200	GENERAL CONTRACTOR	105,000.00	105,000.00
0209	ASBESTOS REMOVAL	70,000.00	70,000.00
DIVISION TOTAL:		175,000.00	175,000.00
06400	ARCHITECTURAL WOODWORK	1,500.00	1,500.00
DIVISION TOTAL:		1,500.00	1,500.00
09682	CARPET	50,000.00	50,000.00
DIVISION TOTAL:		50,000.00	50,000.00
12220	MOVING EXPENSES	4,500.00	4,500.00
12600	FURNITURE AND ACCESSORIES	30,000.00	32,000.00
DIVISION TOTAL:		34,500.00	36,500.00
Project SUBTOTAL:		266,850.00	266,850.00
TAX:		0.00	0.00
FREIGHT:		2,000.00	3,000.00
Project TOTAL:		$268,850.00	$269,850.00

THIS RENOVATION WORK WILL UPGRADE THE EXISTING OFFICE SPACE
FINISHES, PROVIDE FOR THE RELOCATION OF EXISTING WORK
STATIONS AND PROVIDE POWER, TELEPHONE AND CABLING FOR EIGHT
NEW WORK STATIONS.

THE PROJECT IS SCHEDULED TO BEGIN ON JUNE 29 AND BE
COMPLETED BY SEPTEMBER 17, 2001.

Prepared by:
_____ 02/25/2001
SAM JONES, FACILITY MANAGER

Approved by:

_____ __/__/__   _____ __/__/__   _____ __/__/__
Russ Abbott, DIRECTOR   RANDAL FLEMING, V.P   JIM MOSS, SR. V.P.

Against Time

Two components of any project that must be considered and managed in the planning and budgeting process are time and cost. Experience has shown that an adequate amount of high-quality planning time is essential to the development of a detailed project program with sufficient budget information to provide the foundation for a realistic schedule and budget. This would ultimately help the facility manager to complete the project on time and within budget. The graph in Figure 7-2 shows that when a project's costs (Cost 1) are well defined and budgeted, the corresponding time (Time 1) requirements should remain within the schedule. When an appropriate amount of time is devoted to programming and budgeting before the construction documents are bid, the project should remain within the approved budget (subject to last-minute changes requested by your customer). If sufficient time is not provided up front, the resulting opportunity for poor planning and poor decisions can lead to change orders to cover increased project time (Time 2) and cost (Cost 2) requirements, thus delaying the operational use of the project.

As the work progresses toward completion, the facility manager should continue to ensure that all construction and nonconstruction items and work are being installed and completed as required. Following the work process in this way gives the facility manager the ability to check that the invoices that have been received match the work that is in place and has been completed to date. During this time and throughout the project, it is *vital* that the customer remain involved in project review, decisions, payment, and any required changes to the schedule and/or the project budget.

Figure 7-2. Project Control of Expenses—Time and Cost.

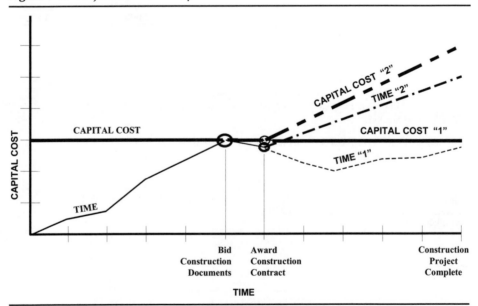

Recording Changes

Proposed change-order work that affects the budget and/or the completion date must be carefully considered, managed, approved or not approved, and documented in a timely manner. No change-order work should begin unless it has been approved by the facility manager as required by the organization. If the change-order work requires a change in the budget (a specific line item amount and subsequently the total budgeted amount) and/or a change in completion time, the requisite approvals must be requested, documented, and obtained before any change-order work begins.

With the approval of the change order, the facility manager must issue a revised project budget, similar to that shown in Figure 7-3. The affected purchase order(s) will then need to be revised via change order(s), which must be issued through the facility manager and distributed to all concerned. Again, this change-order procedure provides a documented audit trail for your customer and for management.

One of the greatest causes of failure during the project cycle is the facility manager's not staying on top of proposed and actual changes in the scope of the work, the approval of revisions to the budget, and the issuance of meaningful and timely change-order documents to complete the audit trail. Many facility managers have found that their careers have ended because at the end of a project, the contractor and/or a vendor has provided them with change-order invoices that put the project dramatically over budget, and it came as a surprise to them. The tracking and approval or disapproval of change orders is an extremely important process that the facility manager must understand and manage.

Payment to Vendors

The project preconstruction conference provides an opportunity to review your organization's payment process with all major project vendors. It is very important that all parties have a clear understanding of the requirements that must be met if you and your finance and accounting department are to process requests for payment or invoices. Contracts must be completed and signed by all parties and insurance certificates must be provided before any work is started on site. General contractor payment requests (which may or may not need to be notarized) must be provided in a form that is acceptable to your organization and may require subcontractor lien waivers, estimates of material stored on site or in a bonded warehouse, the amount of agreed-upon retainage, and other such information.

Project progress payments must be in accordance with the budget and based on approved purchase orders, actual costs of work in place, materials stored on the site, and properly developed invoices from contractors, vendors, or service providers. The facility manager, through regular project progress meetings, will require a candid review of progress, cost to date, change-order items and costs,

Figure 7-3. Project Budget Report.

PROJECT BUDGET REPORT   PAGE: 1 of 1

CP01-0001   RANDOLPH ST./7TH FL. OFFICE RENOVATIONS; CHICAGO, IL.
(R.E. FILE# I-32-0566-01)
August 19, 2001

Company Code: 1STG
Region: Piedmont
Category: BRANCH RELATED Renovation

UCIC	DESCRIPTION	BUDGET TO DATE	CURRENT ESTIMATED COSTS
00300	CONSULTING FEES	30,000.00	30,000.00
	DIVISION TOTAL:	30,000.00	30,000.00
01001	CONSTRUCTION	190,000.00	190,000.00
	DIVISION TOTAL:	190,000.00	190,000.00
02480	LANDSCAPING	4,000.00	4,000.00
	DIVISION TOTAL:	4,000.00	4,000.00
09682	CARPET	400.00	400.00
09690	CARPET TILE	200.00	200.00
	DIVISION TOTAL:	600.00	600.00
10001	SIGNAGE	24,000.00	24,000.00
	DIVISION TOTAL:	24,000.00	24,000.00
11020	SECURITY AND VAULT EQUIPMENT	50,000.00	50,000.00
11111	CLEANING EQUIPMENT	150.00	150.00
11800	TELECOMMUNICATION EQUIPMENT	2,000.00	2,000.00
	DIVISION TOTAL:	52,150.00	52,150.00
12525	CURTAINS	800.00	800.00
12600	FURNITURE AND ACCESSORIES	63,000.00	63,000.00
	DIVISION TOTAL:	64,650.00	64,650.00
16001	ELECTRICAL	600.00	600.00
	DIVISION TOTAL:	600.00	600.00
	PROJECT SUBTOTAL:	366,000.00	366,000.00
	TAX:	25,620.00	25,620.00
	FREIGHT:	0.00	0.00
	PROJECT TOTAL:	391,620.00	391,620.00

THIS PROJECT SHALL RENOVATE THE ENTIRE 7TH FLOOR OF THE XYZ
COMPANY HEADQUARTERS IN CHICAGO. THE PROJECT IS SCHEDULED
TO BEGIN ON MAY I, 2001 AND IS SCHEDULED FOR COMPLETION BY
SEPTEMBER 15, 2001. THE WORK WILL PROVIDE NEW FURNISHINGS,
SIGNAGE, CARPET AND PAINTING FOR THE EXECUTIVE STAFF AND
SENIOR MANAGEMENT. THE PROJECT WILL ALSO PROVIDE EXTENSIVE
RENOVATIONS TO THE MECHANICAL SYSTEMS FOR THE FLOOR AND
INCLUDE THE REMOVAL OF ASBESTOS FROM THE STRUCTURE.

schedule adjustments, and plans to keep the project on schedule and within budget.

The System should assist the facility manager in documenting invoices submitted for payment, using a disbursement approval report similar to that shown in Figure 7-4. This process ensures that no payment is made unless the invoice is tagged with a specific project number and a specific purchase order. It also provides a list of previous invoices and payments, including this payment, against the budget. When the final payment is made, there should be a zero balance and the purchase order should be closed out as completed. Using this report, which includes the check number, the amount paid, and when it was paid, the facility staff can provide information to a vendor regarding payments made. This information becomes an important part of the audit trail.

Managing a Program of Small Projects

When the facility manager is working on a number of small projects, the project accounting aspects of her work are best viewed on a project-by-project basis. Each project should have its own approved budget, scope of work, project number, related purchase and change orders (if required), and paid invoices, all in its own unique database and paper file. This ensures that the facility manager or anyone who looks at the information can easily and readily see the management process being used.

Facility managers rely on their project management training and knowledge to understand and evaluate the success of their projects. Project management tools should include the project financial and accounting system previously discussed (the System). Without a computerized System, the facility manager must rely on a manual paper or spreadsheet system to know where he or she is with the project budget, payments, and expense balance. Experience has shown that one main problem with a manual or spreadsheet system in the management of a number of small projects is that neither type of system allows the facility manager, staff, management, and/or the internal auditor to query the information and quickly develop reports. Furthermore, manually kept project accounting information can be lost or misfiled and is certainly not available through the organization's Web site. Spreadsheet reports are difficult to develop and to use, and may or may not be retrievable through the Web site. No matter what System the facility manager uses, it should include a number of basic components that we have found to be important to successful project accounting.

Each project should always have a unique *project number* that the facility manager can use to track budgets, purchase orders, change orders, and expenses related to that project. The System should employ a project financial process that is based upon good business practice and is familiar to the facility manager, the FM staff, the finance and accounting departments, and management. The System should follow the project budgeting and project management sequence, which might be the following:

Figure 7-4. Disbursement Approval Report.

08/19/01
Page 1 of 1

DISBURSEMENT APPROVAL REPORT

ID: CP01-0001   PO: 0003   INVOICE: ARGA-01-23456   DATE: 08/02/01

VENDOR: ASBESTOS REMOVAL OF IL

Purchase Order TOTAL:	$	70000.00
Previous payments:	$	63000.00
Previous balance:	$	7000.00
TOTAL Invoice (less tax and freight):	$	7000.00
Less Deposits: —	$	0.00
TOTAL Tax:	$	0.00
TOTAL Freight:	$	0.00
TOTAL AMOUNT:	$	7000.00

AMOUNT PAID THIS INVOICE: $ 7000.00
Check Number: 9876567898

Check Date: 08/27/01

BALANCE REMAINING: $ 0.00

INVOICE APPROVED AS SUBMITTED
There is retainage held on this P.O.

THIS P.O. HAS BEEN CLOSED

        UCIC: 0209   Asset code: Title: ASBESTOS REMOVAL
        Ordered: $ 70000.00
        Received: $ 70000.00
        Reference: P.O.s 0003/000
                     Invs.   ARGA-01-12315   ARGA-01-12324   ARGA-01-23456

Comments:
THE REMOVAL OF ASBESTOS WAS COMPLETED ON 08/01/01 AND ALL
APPROVALS AND FINAL INSPECTIONS WERE OBTAINED ON 08/23/01.
FINAL PAYMENT IS BEING MADE AS THE CITY AND OTHER INSPECTION
AUTHORITIES HAVE APPROVED THE WORK AND HAVE INSURED A
CERTIFICATE OF OCCUPANCY TO ABC ORGANIZATION IN CONJUNCTION WITH
THE GENERAL CONTRACTORS WORK.

Approved for payment: _____   8/20/01
                      SAM JONES   Date

• *Project description and project number.* To begin the project process, each project should have a unique **project description** and project number. This is often assigned by the finance department. For example, while working on the development of a project's scope of work and budget *before* the project and its budget are approved, the facility manager might use a numbering system such as PP01-0001 (PP01 for a proposed project in 2001, and -0001 for the first project of the year). If the project is not approved, the facility manager has an audit trail of projects that were not approved in 2001.

When the facility manager receives the approved and signed project budget approval report (Figure 7-1), the project number would be revised to CP01-0001 (CP01 for a capital project approved in 2001, and *-0001* for the first project of the year). This is the first step in the project number cycle for the facility manager's project financial and accounting system. The approved budget would then be posted to the System database (usually by the finance and accounting departments), and the facility manager could then begin to commit and spend project funds.

• *UCIC number(s).* Each line item of work, product, or services in the proposed and approved budget should be listed using a Uniform Construction Index Code (UCIC) number. The UCIC numbers were developed by the American Institute of Architects. This five-number coding system is used by the construction industry in specification and invoice coding for progress payments. The facility manager's assistant or the System manager should ensure that the project data and budget data are entered into the project budget database using the unique project number that has been assigned and the appropriate UCIC number(s) (see Figure 7-1).

• *Vendor(s).* Most finance and accounting departments track and pay invoices by vendor name and/or vendor number established for each vendor. This information should be accessible and included as a part of your System database. After the project is awarded to a general contractor and/or service provider(s), the facility manager should oversee the development of the appropriate purchase requisitions or purchase orders, using the finance and accounting departments' vendor database. During the facility manager's preconstruction conference, contractors and/or service providers should be instructed to include the purchase order number on invoices, for without the purchase order number, no payments can be made.

• *Purchase order(s)* The purchase requisition(s) or purchase order(s) should include the assigned project number, the vendor name and number, all UCIC number(s), the contract amount for each UCIC number, a total purchase order amount, a written description of the services or product(s) to be provided by the vendor, and any and all project, organizational, and legal requirements.

Each purchase requisition or purchase order should have a unique number that is tied to the project number (for example: CP01-0001-001, where *001* would be the next sequential purchase order number). The System manager should ensure that this information is entered into the project database file using the unique project number assigned to this specific project. This purchase order number process ensures that only invoices with the proper number and vendor information will be processed and paid.

• *Change order(s)* When a change order is approved, the facility manager should oversee the completion of a change-order requisition or change order to the previously issued purchase order. The System manager should review the completed change-order requisition or change order and see that the information is entered into the System project database using the unique project number and purchase order number (for example, CP01-0001-001-01, where *01* would be the next sequential change-order number). The vendor should receive a copy of the change order and should include the change-order number on the corresponding invoice.

• *Invoice(s).* Before any invoice is processed, the facility manager's staff should ensure that it includes the proper reference to the assigned purchase order number (and change-order number when applicable). The System manager then sees that the information is entered into the System, generates a disbursement approval report (see Figure 7-4), and attaches this report to the invoice for the facility manager's review and approval. Once the facility manager signs off on the disbursement approval report and the invoice, the approved invoice is then sent to the accounting department for processing and payment. The signed disbursement approval report is filed with a copy of the invoice in the project purchase order/invoice file as part of the audit trail.

After the invoice has been processed and paid by the accounting department, the check number, check date, and amount paid are posted to the System using the project number. The facility manager and staff will then be able to view any related project information and/or reports through the System using the Internet or the organization's internal intranet connection.

• *Project financial and accounting system reports.* With the system Web-enabled, the facility manager and staff should be able to access any and all project reports and information at any time and from any password-protected networked or modem-capable computer in the organization. Only those reports that must be printed should be printed. The System may permit the facility manager to allow some or all project contractors, service providers, and vendors to see some selected parts of the information or to print reports and payment information on their specific project purchase orders and invoices. System reports may include the following:

- *Budget approval report* (Figure 7-1) This report provides the project's initial approved budget by line item.
- *Project budget report* (Figure 7-3). This report provides the project's current approved budget by line item.
- *Disbursement approval report* (Figure 7-4). This report provides information on the current invoice, previous invoices and payments against a purchase order, the amount previously paid, and the balance amount.
- *Project cost distribution by vendor report* (Figure 7-5). This report tracks funds that have been committed, whether paid or not yet paid to vendors.

Figure 7-5. Project Cost Distribution by Vendor Report.

					CHARGES	COMMITTED
	VEND				FUNDS	APPROVED	BUT NOT
VENDOR NAME	ID	P.O.	UCIC	DESCRIPTION	COMMITTED	AND PAID	PAID

PROJECT COST DISTRIBUTION BY VENDOR REPORT   PAGE: 1 of 3

Project Financial & Accounting System
CP01-0001   RANDOLPH ST./7TH FL. OFFICE
ABC Organization—Facility and Real Estate Department
August 19, 2001

VENDOR NAME	VEND ID	P.O.	UCIC	DESCRIPTION	FUNDS COMMITTED	CHARGES APPROVED AND PAID	COMMITTED BUT NOT PAID
Barner/Rummers/ Pitzel, Interior Design	0001	0001	00300	CONSULTING FEES	25,784.26	25,742.38	41.88
				PO TOTAL	25,784.26	25,742.38	41.88
				VENDOR TOTAL	25,784.26	25,742.38	41.88
Jan Lorenc Design, Inc.	0002	0019			0.00	0.00	0.00
Jan Lorenc Design, Inc.	0002	0020	00300	CONSULTING FEES	985.25	985.25	0.00
				PO TOTAL	985.25	985.25	0.00
				VENDOR TOTAL	985.25	985.25	0.00
LeFebure	0003	0003	11020	SECURITY AND VAULT EQUIPMENT	29,055.52	29,055.52	0.00
				ADVANCE PAYMENTS		(8,694.81)	
				PO TOTAL	29,055.52	37,750.33	−8,694.81
				VENDOR TOTAL	29,055.52	37,750.33	−8,694.81
Diebold, Inc.	0004	0004	11020	SECURITY AND VAULT EQUIPMENT	23,275.91	23,275.91	0.00
				TAX TOTAL	0.00	18.92	−18.92
				ADVANCE PAYMENTS		(6,519.60)	
				PO TOTAL	23,275.91	29,814.43	−6,538.52
				VENDOR TOTAL	23,275.91	29,814.43	−6,538.52
State Neon Co., Inc.	0005	0005	10001	SIGNAGE	25,213.76	19,233.17	5,980.59
				TAX TOTAL	0.00	251.69	−251.69
				FREIGHT TOTAL	0.00	337.32	−337.32
				ADVANCE PAYMENTS		(5,585.56)	
				PO TOTAL	25,213.76	25,407.74	−193.98
				VENDOR TOTAL	25,213.76	25,407.74	−193.98
Abrams Construction, Inc.	0006	0006	01001	CONSTRUCTION	101,110.00	101,110.00	0.00
				PO TOTAL	101,110.00	101,110.00	0.00
Vaults of Illinois	0021	0023	11020	SECURITY AND VAULT EQUIPMENT	2,000.00	1,800.00	200.00
				TAX TOTAL	1.00	1.00	0.00
				ADVANCE PAYMENTS		(150.00)	
				PO TOTAL	2,001.00	1,011.00	50.00
				VENDOR TOTAL	197,111.00	197,061.00	50.00

(continues)

Figure 7-5. (Continued).

PROJECT COST DISTRIBUTION BY VENDOR REPORT   PAGE: 2 OF 3

Project Financial & Accounting System
CP01-0001   RANDOLPH ST./7TH FL. OFFICE
ABC Organization—Facility and Real Estate Department
August 19, 2001

VENDOR NAME	VEND ID	P.O.	UCIC	DESCRIPTION	FUNDS COMMITTED	CHARGES APPROVED AND PAID	COMMITTED BUT NOT PAID
Barner/Rummers/ PITZEL, INTERIOR DESIGN	0007	0007	12600	FURNITURE AND ACCESSORIES	18,925.09	18,766.02	159.07
				TAX TOTAL	0.00	142.48	−142.48
				FREIGHT TOTAL	0.00	5.00	−5.00
				PO TOTAL	18,925.09	18,913.50	11.59
				VENDOR TOTAL	18,925.09	18,913.50	11.59
BILL Allen Company	0008	0008	12600	FURNITURE AND ACCESSORIES	45,756.24	45,756.24	0.00
				PO TOTAL	45,756.24	45,756.24	0.00
				VENDOR TOTAL	45,756.24	45,756.24	0.00
Easterwood Landscape Service	0009	0009	02480	LANDSCAPING	4,572.00	0.00	
				4,572.00			
				PO TOTAL	4,572.00	4,572.00	0.00
				VENDOR TOTAL	4,572.00	4,572.00	0.00
Danny Stanford, Masonry Contractor	0010	0010	01001	CONSTRUCTION	1,050.00	1,050.00	0.00
				PO TOTAL	1,050.00	1,050.00	0.00
				VENDOR TOTAL	1,050.00	1,050.00	0.00
City Lumber Company	0011	0011	01001	CONSTRUCTION	1,000.00	1,000.00	0.00
				PO TOTAL	1,000.00	1,000.00	0.00
				VENDOR TOTAL	1,000.00	1,000.00	0.00
Roberds Blades & Associates, Elect. Engr	0012	0012	00300	CONSULTING FEES	374.02	0.98	
				375.00			
				PO TOTAL	375.00	374.02	0.98
				VENDOR TOTAL	375.00	374.02	0.98
Country Fresh	0013	0013	09682	CARPET	240.00	144.00	96.00
	0013	0013	09690	CARPET TILE	200.00	200.00	0.00
				TAX TOTAL	0.00	10.32	−10.32
				FREIGHT TOTAL	−37.00	48.68	−85.68
				PO TOTAL	403.00	403.00	0.00
				VENDOR TOTAL	403.00	403.00	0.00
DCG Electrical	0014	0014	16001	ELECTRICAL	2,726.11	2,726.11	0.00
				PO TOTAL	2,726.11	2,726.11	0.00
				VENDOR TOTAL	2,726.11	2,726.11	0.00

PROJECT COST DISTRIBUTION BY VENDOR REPORT   PAGE: 3 OF 3

Project Financial & Accounting System
CP01-0001   RANDOLPH ST./7TH FL. OFFICE
ABC Organization—Facility and Real Estate Department
August 19, 2001

VENDOR NAME	VEND ID	P.O.	UCIC	DESCRIPTION	FUNDS COMMITTED	CHARGES APPROVED AND PAID	COMMITTED BUT NOT PAID
AT&T Information Systems	0015	0015	11800	TELECOMMUNICATION EQUIPMENT	2,040.00	2,040.00	0.00
				PO TOTAL	2,040.00	2,040.00	0.00
				VENDOR TOTAL	2,040.00	2,040.00	0.00
Truck & Equipment Refurbishing	0016	0016	12600	FURNITURE AND ACCESSORIES	375.00	375.00	0.00
				PO TOTAL	375.00	375.00	0.00
				VENDOR TOTAL	375.00	375.00	0.00
Denny Upholstery & Restoration Shop	0017	0017	12600	FURNITURE AND ACCESSORIES	72.00	72.00	0.00
				PO TOTAL	72.00	72.00	0.00
				VENDOR TOTAL	72.00	72.00	0.00
Action Vacuum Corp.	0018	0018	11111	CLEANING EQUIPMENT	197.55	197.55	0.00
				PO TOTAL	197.55	197.55	0.00
				VENDOR TOTAL	197.55	197.55	0.00
Mark-III Signs, Inc.	0020	0021	10001	SIGNAGE	757.12	757.12	0.00
				PO TOTAL	757.12	757.12	0.00
				VENDOR TOTAL	757.12	757.12	0.00
PROJECT TOTAL					$379,674.81	$394,997.67	−$15,322.86

Last approved budget: $391,620.00   05/27/01

- *Project cost history report* (Figure 7-6). This report tracks all purchase orders (POs), invoices, and checks issued for a project.
- *Project financial status report—detailed (Figure 7-7).* This report tracks budget per item, total spent, and whether each item is under or over the approved budget amount.
- *Purchase order cost distribution report* (Figure 7-8). This report tracks funds committed, paid and not yet paid, by purchase order.
- *Project financial status—summary report (Figure 7-9).* This report tracks the budget for each project, the total spent, and whether the amount spent is under or over the approved budget amount.
- *Outstanding purchase orders report.* This report lists all purchase orders that have not yet been paid and allows tracking of cash flows by project.

Conclusion

There is no one correct way to manage your project accounting requirements, but the management process described in this chapter provides a time-tested and

Figure 7-6. Project Cost History Report.

PROJECT COST HISTORY REPORT   PAGE: 1 of 4

Project Financial & Accounting System
CP01-0001   RANDOLPH ST./7TH FL. OFFICE
Facility Manager: SAM JONES
ABC Organization—Facility and Real Estate Department
August 19, 2001

P.O.	VENDOR	P.O./ INVOICE DATE	INVOICE	CHECK	DATE PAID	FUNDS COMMITTED	CHARGES APPROVED AND PAID	COMMITTED BUT NOT PAID
0001/000	Barner/Rummers/ Pitzel, Interior Design	11/15/00				24,000.00	0.00	
0001/001		03/29/01				984.26	0.00	
0001/002		10/15/01				800.00	0.00	
0001		01/20/01	1184	000000010410	01/23/01		8,904.10	
0001		01/10/01	1280	000000819224	01/10/01		8,192.24	
0001		02/15/01	1346	000000452512	02/15/01		4,525.12	
0001		04/05/01	1531	000000146470	04/05/01		1,464.70	
0001		05/20/01	1803	000000066900	06/01/01		669.00	
0001		06/01/01	101810	000000101810	06/02/01		1,018.10	
0001		06/02/01	1937	000000000112	06/05/01		01.12	
PO TOTAL						25,784.26	25,742.38	41.88
0002/000	Jan Lorenc Design, Inc.	11/15/00				2,600.00	0.00	
0002		01/05/01	0065-01	000000165744	01/05/01		1,657.44	
0002		02/05/01	0065-02	000000001283	02/05/01		012.83	
PO TOTAL						2,600.00	2,520.27	79.73
0003/000	LeFebure	11/30/00		222222019481	11/30/01	29,055.52	8,694.81	20,360.71
			1st Billing #64213A					
0003		01/24/01	642103	222222874662	01/24/01		8,746.62	
0003		11/15/00	642103 B	222222870004	11/20/00		8,708.54	
0003		01/25/01	643103C	916220105	09/22/01		2,905.55	
PO TOTAL						29,055.52	29,055.52	0.00
0004/000	Diebold, Inc.	11/30/00		222222651960	11/30/00	21,732.00	6,519.60	15,212.40
			30% #00221099 & 00221100					
0004/001		03/26/01			11/30/00	1,543.91	0.00	
0004		01/05/01	00224475	000000334800	01/05/01		3,348.00	
0004		01/05/01	00224476	000000317160	01/05/01		3,171.60	
0004		03/15/01	00231516	000000334800	03/15/01		3,348.00	
0004		09/26/01	00231517	000000317160	03/15/01		3,171.60	
0004		04/20/01	00235188	000000138124	04/20/01		1,381.24	
0004		05/10/01	00237879	000000142236	05/10/01		1,422.36	
0004		09/26/01	50282436	000000093243	04/05/01		932.43	
PO TOTAL						23,275.91	23,294.83	−18.92
0005/000	State Neon Co., Inc.	11/30/00		222222550056	11/30/00	25,213.76	5,500.56	19,628.20
			Inv#015.05665 & 015.02014					
0005		02/25/01	015.02012-0	000000401022	02/25/01		4,010.22	
0005		01/08/01	015.02014-0	222222037849	01/09/01		378.49	
0005		01/09/01	015.02015-0	000000279256	01/11/01		2,792.56	

PROJECT COST HISTORY REPORT

Project Financial & Accounting System
CP01-0001 RANDOLPH ST./7TH FL. OFFICE
Facility Manager: SAM JONES
ABC Organization—Facility and Real Estate Department
August 19, 2001

P.O.	VENDOR	P.O./INVOICE DATE	INVOICE	CHECK	DATE PAID	FUNDS COMMITTED	CHARGES APPROVED AND PAID	COMMITTED BUT NOT PAID
0005		03/31/01	015.02942-0	000000193380	03/31/01		1,933.80	
0005		10/15/01	015.02961-0	000000094318	10/15/01		943.18	
0005		11/26/00	015.28817-0	222222012750	11/30/00		127.50	
0005		11/30/00	015.28884-0	222222209360	12/03/00		93.60	
0005		12/30/00	015.20199-0	222220290000	01/05/01		290.00	
0005		02/26/01	015.29003-0	000000013242	02/26/01		137.42	
0005		02/15/01	015.29101-0	000000050045	02/15/01		500.45	
0005		04/15/01	015.29254-0	000000206440	04/15/01		2,064.40	
PO TOTAL						25,213.76	19,822.18	5,391.58
0006/000	Abrams Construction, Inc.	12/01/00				101,110.00	0.00	
0006/001		02/26/01				5,015.00	0.00	
0006/002		04/15/01				−5,015.00	0.00	
0006		01/07/01	1-5382900	222205382900	01/07/01		53,829.00	
0006		02/09/01	2-5455200	222205455200	04/09/01		54,552.00	
0006		04/04/01	2074700	222202074700	04/04/01		20,747.00	
0006		03/07/01	4533900	222204533900	03/07/01		45,339.00	
0006		04/15/01	5-2064300	222202064300	04/15/01		20,643.00	
0006		04/15/01	501500	000000501500	04/15/01		−5,015.00	
0006		04/30/01	6-501500	222220501500	04/30/01		5,015.00	
PO TOTAL						101,110.00	101,110.00	0.00
0007/000	Barner, Rummers, Pitzel, Interior Design	12/15/00				12,270.00	0.00	
0007/001		03/01/01				5,805.09	0.00	
0007/002		10/01/01			10/01/01	0.00	0.00	
				VOID				
0007/003		10/15/01			10/01/01	800.00	0.00	
0007/004		10/15/01			10/01/01	50.00	0.00	
0007		11/05/00	1114	000000122000	11/05/00		1,220.00	
0007		04/05/01	1592	000000184400	04/05/01		1,844.00	
0007		04/05/01	162/00035	000000593775	04/05/01		5,937.75	
0007		05/05/01	171/00035	000000617082	05/05/01		6,170.82	
0007		06/20/01	187	000000069093	06/25/01		690.93	
0007		11/05/00	305000	000000305000	11/05/00		3,050.00	
PO TOTAL						18,925.09	18,913.50	11.59
0008/000	Bill Allen Company	12/15/00				47,000.00	0.00	
0008/001		04/15/01				−1,243.76	0.00	
0008		01/05/01	571876	000001824321	01/05/01		18,243.21	
0008		02/05/01	597966	000001075476	02/05/01		10,754.76	
0008		04/05/01	652749	000001675827	04/05/01		16,758.27	
PO TOTAL						45,756.24	45,756.24	0.00

(continues)

Figure 7-6. (Continued).

Project Financial & Accounting System
CP01-0001 RANDOLPH ST./7TH FL. OFFICE
Facility Manager: SAM JONES
ABC Organization—Facility and Real Estate Department
August 19, 2001

P.O.	VENDOR	P.O./ INVOICE DATE	INVOICE	CHECK	DATE PAID	FUNDS COMMITTED	CHARGES APPROVED AND PAID	COMMITTED BUT NOT PAID
0009/000	Easterwood Landscape Service	02/01/01				4,572.00	0.00	
0009		09/25/01	457200	222220457200	04/30/01		4,572.00	
PO TOTAL						4,572.00	4,572.00	0.00
0010/000	Danny Stanford, Masonry Contractor	03/20/01				1,050.00	0.00	
0010		04/25/01	105000	222220105000	04/25/01		1,050.00	
PO TOTAL						1,050.00	1,050.00	0.00
0011/000	City Lumber Company	03/15/01				1,000.00	0.00	
0011		01/02/01	13355	000000100000	01/02/01		1,000.00	
PO TOTAL						1,000.00	1,000.00	0.00
0012/000	Roberds Blades & Associates, Elect. Engr	11/15/00				375.00	0.00	
0012		01/02/01	00221-01	000000037402	01/02/01		374.02	
PO TOTAL						375.00	374.02	0.98
0013/000	Country Fresh	03/11/01				440.00	0.00	
0013/001		04/29/01				− 37.00	0.00	
0013		04/29/01	0259	222222220403	04/29/01		403.00	
PO TOTAL						403.00	403.00	0.00
0014/000	DCG Electrical	03/15/01				327.31	0.00	
0014/001		02/05/01				2,398.80	0.00	
0014		03/05/01	1905	000000239880	03/05/01		2,398.80	
0014		03/31/01	2100	222222032731	03/31/01		327.31	
PO TOTAL						2,726.11	2,726.11	0.00
0015/000	AT&T Information Systems	03/11/01				2,000.00	0.00	
0015/001		03/05/01				40.00	0.00	
0015		04/05/01	2040	222222202040	04/05/01		2,040.00	
PO TOTAL						2,040.00	2,040.00	0.00

Project Financial & Accounting System
CP01-0001 RANDOLPH ST./7TH FL. OFFICE
Facility Manager: SAM JONES
ABC Organization—Facility and Real Estate Department
August 19, 2001

P.O.	VENDOR	P.O./INVOICE DATE	INVOICE	CHECK	DATE PAID	FUNDS COMMITTED	CHARGES APPROVED AND PAID	COMMITTED BUT NOT PAID
0016/000	Truck & Equipment Refurbishing	03/11/01				375.00	0.00	
0016		12/15/00	37500	000000037500	12/15/00		375.00	
PO TOTAL						375.00	375.00	0.00
0017/000	Denny Upholstery & Restoration Shop	03/11/01				750.00	0.00	
0017/001		04/18/01				−678.00	0.00	
0017		04/18/01	7200	222222207200	04/18/01		72.00	
PO TOTAL						72.00	72.00	0.00
0018/000	Action Vacuum Corp.	04/10/01				197.55	0.00	
0018		04/01/01	19755	222222019755	04/01/01		197.55	
PO TOTAL						197.55	197.55	0.00
0019/000	Jan Lorenc Design, Inc.	10/07/01	VOID		10/07/01	0.00	0.00	
PO TOTAL						0.00	0.00	0.00
0020/000	Jan Lorenc Design, Inc.	04/15/01				1,000.00	0.00	
0020/001		05/30/01				−14.75	0.00	
0020		05/10/01	900.25	123456701525	05/17/01		900.25	
PO TOTAL						900.25	900.25	0.00
0021/000	Mark-III Signs, Inc.	10/15/01				757.12	0.00	
0021		08/05/01	1027	000000075712	08/05/01		757.12	
PO TOTAL						757.12	757.12	0.00
0022/000	HUGHES FLOOR COVERING	09/06/90				0.00	0.00	
PO TOTAL						0.00	0.00	0.00
0023/000	VAULTS OF ILLINOIS	11/29/90				2,001.00	150.00	1,001.00
0023		11/29/90	2323	345	11/29/90		1,651.00	
PO TOTAL						2,001.00	1,801.00	200.00
PROJECT TOTAL						$382,274.81	$376,567.97	$5,706.84

Last approved budget: $391,620.00   05/27/01

Figure 7-7. Project Financial Status Report—Detailed.

PROJECT FINANCIAL STATUS REPORT—DETAILED   PAGE: 1 of 1
Project Financial & Accounting System
ABC Organization—Facility and Real Estate Department
August 19, 2001
Project ID:CP01-0001
RANDOLPH ST./7TH FL. OFFICE
Facility Manager: SAM JONES
Region: P

UCIC	DESCRIPTION	BUDGET: CURRENT/ ORIGINAL	FUNDS COMMITTED	EST COSTS: CURRENT ORIGINAL	AMOUNT SPENT: THIS YEAR/ PRIOR YEARS	TOTAL SPENT/ OVER-UNDER BUDGET
00300	CONSULTING FEES	30,000.00	27,144.51	30,000.00	0.00	0.00
		30,000.00		30,000.00	0.00	−2,855.49
01001	CONSTRUCTION	190,000.00	197,160.00	190,000.00	0.00	0.00
		190,000.00		190,000.00	0.00	7,160.00
02480	LANDSCAPING	4,000.00	4,572.00	4,000.00	0.00	0.00
		4,000.00		4,000.00	0.00	572.00
09682	CARPET	400.00	240.00	400.00	0.00	0.00
		400.00		400.00	0.00	−160.00
09690	CARPET TILE	200.00	200.00	200.00	0.00	0.00
		200.00		200.00	0.00	0.00
10001	SIGNAGE	24,000.00	25,970.88	24,000.00	0.00	0.00
		24,000.00		24,000.00	0.00	1,970.88
11020	SECURITY AND VAULT	50,000.00	54,331.43	50,000.00	0.00	0.00
	EQUIPMENT	50,000.00		50,000.00	0.00	4,331.43
11111	CLEANING EQUIPMENT	150.00	197.55	150.00	0.00	0.00
		150.00		150.00	0.00	47.55
11800	TELECOMMUNICATION	2,000.00	2,040.00	2,000.00	0.00	0.00
	EQUIPMENT	2,000.00		2,000.00	0.00	40.00
12525	CURTAINS	800.00	0.00	800.00	0.00	0.00
		800.00		800.00	0.00	−800.00
12600	FURNITURE AND	63,850.00	65,128.33	63,850.00	0.00	0.00
	ACCESSORIES	63,850.00		63,850.00	0.00	1,278.33
16001	ELECTRICAL	600.00	2,726.11	600.00	0.00	0.00
		600.00	600.00	0.00	2,126.11	
FREIGHT		0.00	0.00	0.00	0.00	0.00
		0.00		0.00	0.00	0.00
TAX		25,620.00	0.00	25,620.00	0.00	0.00
		25,620.00		25,620.00	0.00	−25,620.00
ADVANCE PAYMENTS/DEPOSITS:					0.00	20,949.97
					150.00	
TAX:		25,620.00	1.00	25,620.00	0.00	0.00
					0.00	−1.00
FREIGHT:		0.00	−37.00	0.00	0.00	0.00
					0.00	37.00
PROJECT TOTAL:		417,240.00	379,674.81	417,240.00	0.00	20,949.97
		$417,240.00		$417,240.00	$150.00	−$37,565.19

*** Conflict in budgets entered for each UCIC and actual approved budget:
Current Actual Approved Budget: $391,620.00
                          Tax: $25,620.00
TOTAL Actual Approved Budget: $417,240.00
          Over/Under Budget: −$37,565.19

						37.00
TOTAL PROJECT :		$417,240.00	$379,674.81	$417,240.00	$ 0.00	$20,949.97
		$417,240.00		$417,240.00	$150.00	−$37,565.19

Figure 7-8. Purchase Order Cost Distribution Report.

PURCHASE ORDER COST DISTRIBUTION REPORT   PAGE: 1 of 3

Project Financial & Accounting System
CP01-0001 RANDOLPH ST./7TH FL. OFFICE
ABC Organization—Facility and Real Estate Dept.
August 19, 2001

P.O.	VEND ID	UCIC	DESCRIPTION	VENDOR NAME	FUNDS COMMITTED	CHARGES APPROVED AND PAID	COMMITTED BUT NOT PAID
0001/000	0001	00300	CONSULTING FEES	Warner/Summers/ Ditzel, Architects	25,784.26	25,742.38	41.88
P.O. TOTAL					25,784.26	25,742.38	41.88
0002/000			VOID				
P.O. TOTAL					0.00	0.00	0.00
0003/000	0003	11020	SECURITY AND VAULT EQUIPMENT	LeFebure	29,055.52	29,055.52	0.00
(ADVANCE PAYMENTS:						8,694.81)	
P.O. TOTAL					29,055.52	37,750.33	−8,694.81
0004/000	0004	11020	SECURITY AND VAULT EQUIPMENT	Diebold, Inc.	23,275.91	23,275.91	0.00
(ADVANCE PAYMENTS:						6,519.60)	
TAX:					0.00	18.92	−18.92
P.O. TOTAL					23,275.91	29,814.43	−6,538.52
0005/000	0005	10001	SIGNAGE	State Neon Co., Inc.	25,213.76	19,233.17	5,980.59
(ADVANCE PAYMENTS:						5,500.56)	
TAX:					0.00	251.69	−251.69
FREIGHT:					0.00	337.32	−337.32
P.O. TOTAL					25,213.76	25,407.74	−193.98
0006/000	0006	01001	CONSTRUCTION	Abrams Construction, Inc.	101,110.00	101,110.00	0.00
P.O. TOTAL					101,110.00	101,110.00	0.00
0007/000	0007	12600	FURNITURE AND ACCESSORIES	Barner/Rummers/ Pitzel, Interior Design	18,925.09	18,766.02	159.07
TAX:					0.00	142.48	−142.48
FREIGHT:					0.00	5.00	−5.00
P.O. TOTAL					18,925.09	18,913.50	11.59
0008/000	0008	12600	FURNITURE AND ACCESSORIES	Bill Allen Company	45,756.24	45,756.24	0.00
P.O. TOTAL					45,756.24	45,756.24	0.00
0009/000	0009	02480	LANDSCAPING	Easterwood Landscape Service	4,572.00	4,572.00	0.00
P.O. TOTAL					4,572.00	4,572.00	0.00

(continues)

Figure 7-8. (Continued).

Project Financial & Accounting System
CP01-0001 RANDOLPH ST./7TH FL. OFFICE
ABC Organization—Facility and Real Estate Dept.
August 19, 2001

P.O.	VEND ID	UCIC	DESCRIPTION	VENDOR NAME	FUNDS COMMITTED	CHARGES APPROVED AND PAID	COMMITTED BUT NOT PAID
0010/000	0010	01001	CONSTRUCTION	Danny Stanford, Masonry Contractor	1,050.00	1,050.00	0.00
P.O. TOTAL					1,050.00	1,050.00	0.00
0011/000	0011	01001	CONSTRUCTION	City Lumber Company	1,000.00	1,000.00	0.00
P.O. TOTAL					1,000.00	1,000.00	0.00
0012/000	0012	00300	CONSULTING FEES	Roberds Blades & Associates, Elect. Engr	375.00	374.02	0.98
P.O. TOTAL					375.00	374.02	0.98
0013/000	0013	09682	CARPET	Country Fresh	240.00	144.00	96.00
0013/000	0013	09690	CARPET TILE		200.00	200.00	0.00
TAX:					0.00	10.32	−10.32
FREIGHT:					−37.00	48.68	−00.68
P.O. TOTAL					403.00	403.00	0.00
0014/000	0014	16001	ELECTRICAL	DCG Electrical	2,726.11	2,726.11	0.00
P.O. TOTAL					2,726.11	2,726.11	0.00
0015/000	0015	11800	TELECOMMUNICATION EQUIPMENT	AT&T Information Systems	2,040.00	2,040.00	0.00
P.O. TOTAL					2,040.00	2,040.00	0.00
0016/000	0016	12600	FURNITURE AND ACCESSORIES	Truck & Equipment Refurbishing	375.00	375.00	0.00
P.O. TOTAL					375.00	375.00	0.00
0017/000	0017	12600	FURNITURE AND ACCESSORIES	Denny Upholstery & Restoration Shop	72.00	72.00	0.00
P.O. TOTAL					72.00	72.00	0.00
0018/000	0018	11111	CLEANING EQUIPMENT	Action Vacuum Corp.	197.55	197.55	0.00
P.O. TOTAL					197.55	197.55	0.00
0019/000	0002			Jan Lorenc Design, Inc.	0.00	0.00	0.00
P.O. TOTAL					0.00	0.00	0.00
0020/000	0002	00300	CONSULTING FEES	Jan Lorenc Design, Inc.	900.25	900.25	0.00
P.O. TOTAL					900.25	900.25	0.00
0021/000	0020	10001	SIGNAGE	Mark-III Signs, Inc.	757.12	757.12	0.00
P.O. TOTAL					757.12	757.12	0.00

Project Financial & Accounting System
CP01-001 RANDOLPH ST./7TH FL. OFFICE
ABC Organization—Facility and Real Estate Dept.
August 19, 2001

P.O.	VEND ID	UCIC	DESCRIPTION	VENDOR NAME	FUNDS COMMITTED	CHARGES APPROVED AND PAID	COMMITTED BUT NOT PAID
0023/000	0021	11020	SECURITY AND VAULT EQUIPMENT	Vaults of Illinois	2,000.00	1,800.00	200.00
(ADVANCE PAYMENTS:						150.00)	
TAX:					1.00	1.00	0.00
P.O. TOTAL					2,001.00	1,011.00	50.00
(ADVANCE PAYMENTS:						150.00)	
TAX:					1.00	1.00	0.00
P.O. TOTAL					1.00	151.00	−150.00
PROJECT TOTAL					379,675.81	301,148.67	−15,472.01

Last approved budget: $391,620.00   07/27/01

Figure 7-9. Project Financial Status—Summary Report.

Project Financial & Accounting System
FACILITY MANAGEMENT DEPARTMENT
August 11, 2001

Facility Manager: SAM JONES

PROJECT	BUDGET: CURRENT/ ORIGINAL	FUNDS COMMITTED	EST COSTS: CURRENT ORIGINAL	AMOUNT SPENT: THIS YEAR/ PRIOR YEARS	TOTAL SPENT/ OVER-UNDER BUDGET
BRANCH RELATED REGION: CATEGORY:					
CP01-0001	269,850.00	269,838.45	269,850.00	10,500.00	196,838.45
RENOVATIONS TO SUITE					
410	269,850.00		269,850.00	186,338.45	−3,011.55

proven way to manage any size project budget and accounting information. Based on the project accounting management and System process described in this chapter, we recommend that all facility managers ensure that they know and understand key project information at all times, including:

- What funds are included for each line item in the approved budget
- What funds have been committed
- What change orders have been approved and issued
- What funds have been paid to date
- Whether any line items are over budget, and why
- What funds remain to be paid

The development or acquisition and implementation of a project financial and accounting system is an important part of the project financial process. With the information that is contained and maintained within the System database, the facility manager and the organization can easily determine project expenditures in total and for any project at any time. The System can, to the degree to which the input information is accurate, easily and quickly provide management and control information to answer management's project budget, project accounting, expenditure, and related project funding questions.

8

Financial Aspects of Development

Pulse Points

- *The purpose of corporate development is to provide a place and/or the ability for corporate activity to increase or create value for shareholders.*
- *One of the most specific acquisition requirements is how the organization should finance the acquisition of required real estate.*
- *The FM should expect the CFO to recommend particular financial considerations for the acquisition of specific real estate requirements.*
- *Many organizations have made a strategic decision to lease or to purchase the property, buildings, or space that they require.*
- *Lease-versus-purchase analysis provides an excellent example of the value of using a double matrix in a "what-if" analysis.*
- *There are a number of variables that must be compared to reach an "apples to apples" analysis to determine the net present value and effective level rent for each analysis.*
- *The purchase of each piece of property is unique, with specific and special issues that the FM must be prepared to deal with effectively and efficiently.*
- *One of the most common processes for acquiring space, especially office space, is to lease the property and/or facility(ies).*

Keywords

Corporate development, property use, leased property, purchase property, acquisition, disposal, due process, financial and legal review, lease-versus-purchase analysis, lease term, capital funds, rental rate, property taxes, insurance, cost of financing, net present value, effective level rent, site evaluation matrix, cash flow analysis, joint venture development, ground lease, build to suit

Introduction

The purpose of corporate development is to provide a place and/or the ability for corporate activity to increase or create value for stakeholders. The FM needs to focus on the physical location and requirements of the development and on the customer's need for space, furnishings, and equipment. This need should be translated into a space and design program that becomes the basis for the real estate requirement that should answer the following questions:

- Who will occupy the space or property?
- What kind of space or property is needed—leased or owned?
- What type(s) of space or property is (are) needed?
- What space for growth will be required now and at what time in the future?
- When is the space or property needed, and for how long will it be needed?
- How much space or property is needed?
- How long will the FM's customer need the use of the space or property?
- Where should the space or property be located?
- Are there any other pertinent data that will enhance, clarify, or describe the FM's customer's and the FM's corporation's specific requirements?
- What quality of property or space is required?
- What monies (capital or lease) are available?

This chapter will review the financial aspects of development, but not the detailed corporate real estate, legal, or facility management aspects. Other books, publications, and seminars that can provide such information are available.

Financial Considerations in Siting

Once the FM understands the customer's real estate and related space and workplace requirements, it is important that the FM also understand the organization's specific financial, legal, and strategic requirements in the acquisition of this real estate and related space. One of the most specific acquisition requirements is how the organization should finance the acquisition of the required real estate— whether it should be leased or owned, whether it should be new or additional space, and for what length of time it will be needed.

The acquisition and disposition of land and buildings (or the acquisition and disposition of debt, in the case of mortgages or capital leases) can affect the financial stability of the corporation. The organization's board of directors is responsible for providing overall policy development and guidance and is directly accountable to the shareholders. Consequently, the board should have a keen interest in real estate transactions, because these directly affect the balance sheet. The CFO, through the FM, should be required by the board to furnish information on significant real estate transactions—sales, acquisitions, leases, and so on—with a dollar "cutoff" used to determine whether a transaction is included in the board report.

After due process, the aggregate amount of capital dollars that is projected as being available for corporate investment will be allocated among various organizational groups and divisions and their respective departments. The inclusion of specific expenditures for real estate and facilities in the capital plan portion of the annual operating plan will serve as an advance indicator to the FM of potential, near-term acquisition projects. Furthermore, if the FM has had an advisory role in the preparation and review of the annual operating plan, several additional benefits may result.

- The CFO and the FM may be aware of property that has not yet been officially declared surplus but is the subject of a proposed disposition by one of the organization's divisions that may well fit the proposed acquisition program of another division.
- The FM can provide input on the anticipated timing and yield from the sale of projected surplus property.
- The efforts of the FM and of those other service departments that are normally responsible for equipment redeployment should be coordinated.
- The proposed cost of facilities that are scheduled "as required" can be more accurately stated, providing the base for a better understanding of the appropriation request.
- There may be surplus properties and/or space that can be sold if owned or subleased if leased. The resulting income may become available to the organization as cash or as a long-term nonbusiness income stream, reducing the amount of capital the CFO would need to raise to meet the developments approved by the board of directors.

Lease or Purchase Choices

The FM should expect the CFO, whether the organization is private or public, to identify particular financial considerations and recommendations for acquiring real estate to meet specific requirements. These real estate financial considerations could include:

- Lease:
  - *Lease with no capital funds available from the organization for upfit* (expect a higher rental). The organization does not want to invest its cash or go for a capital loan.
  - *Lease to obtain the lowest possible rent* (the organization will provide some or all upfit funds). The organization has capital funds and needs to minimize rent expense.
  - *Lease for a short term (less than two years) for specific business reasons* (expect a higher rent). The organization has strategic reasons to need real estate for a short period only.
  - *Lease for a long term (three to five years).* The organization has a strategic

need for this real estate and plans to use the real estate for specific purposes for an extended period of time.
- *Lease with a purchase option.* The organization does not have the initial capital to purchase the real estate, and so chooses to lease it initially for a minimum lease term with the option to purchase it at some specific later date or dates at a specified price.
- *Ground lease.* The owner of the property does not wish to sell but will provide a long-term lease of the property (ten to twenty-five years or longer). The organization will own any capital improvements to the property, and the ground lease term will usually be a function of the length of the period over which the organization needs to amortize its capital investment.
- *Build to suit.* The organization does not want to make the capital investment to acquire or develop the property and will pay the property owner a rent that will cover the property owner's capital investment and the lease of the property. The build to suit option often results in an agreement for five to fifteen years or longer, depending on the total capital investment, and may include a purchase option by the organization.
- Purchase:
  - *Purchase the real estate.* The organization has a strategic need to keep and control the real estate, site improvements, and related facilities by owning them. This is often due to the need to make a substantial capital investment in equipment or to the fact that this is a strategic business/location. Manufacturing companies, banks, and multiunit restaurant organizations often purchase their real estate, as they will be making a long-term capital investment and need to control the real estate and related property expenses over time.
  - *Purchase the real estate with a development partner.* The organization wants to share the capital investment with a partner, with each owning a percentage of the real estate. The organization will pay the development partner a fee for the developer's time and expenses and make ongoing payments to cover the use of the developer's capital investment.

With each of these options, there are not only financial considerations but also associated legal issues that the FM, the CFO, and organization management must consider. The FM should be aware of these legal issues and work with the CFO and the organization's legal counsel to ensure that the organization's legal rights and associated benefits are being properly protected. These financial and legal issues are subject to negotiation, and the FM should understand these issues and be prepared to participate in and, where appropriate, to lead these negotiations.

At this point, the FM has an important opportunity to lead the development and, working with the CFO and the customer, to provide and manage a realistic capital development budget. As related in an earlier chapter, the FM must also provide the CFO and the customer with the maintenance and operations requirements and related budgets that must be implemented during the start-up and the ongoing management of the completed project.

Lease-versus-Purchase Analysis

Many organizations have made a strategic decision, because of their business services or product requirements, either to lease or to purchase the property, buildings, or space they require. The specific business and the organization's current ability to raise capital funds can be influential factors in the organization's decision to lease or to purchase. The organization may also choose to fund its property and related requirements with a mixture of leases and purchases. The CFO and the FM should provide input into that decision process and should be ready to provide valid financial and business-related information and reasons for recommending one method of acquisition rather than another.

The purchase decision is usually based on the cost of alternative decisions, the FM's organization's relative cash and tax positions and preferred leased/owned property ratio, the anticipated term of use of the facility, asset risk management factors, the desirability of flexibility, and other such factors. Traditionally the acquisition of real estate or space through financing leases is most advantageous when the following conditions exist:

- *Tax shelters.* When the organization (lessee) cannot take advantage of additional tax credits and the property owner/landlord (lessor) can, thereby affecting the terms of the lease.
- *Cash flow.* When the lessee is willing to pay a premium to lease in order to minimize cash outflow or to utilize a fixed cash allocation for other purposes.
- *Cost of capital.* When a highly developed lessor has a lower cost of capital than a lessee who is not highly leveraged.
- *Opportunity cost.* When the yield on the lease provides a good return to the lessor and the lessee has more profitable opportunities than purchasing available for its funds.
- *Asset appreciation.* When the probability of the asset's appreciating in value is low or there is decreasing demand for the specific type of asset.
- *"Priceless asset."* When the lessor is unwilling or unable to sell the asset because of personal desires or legal restrictions.
- *Asset appraisal.* When testing or experience with the use of an asset is required in order to provide data for economic evaluation.

The lease-versus-purchase decision involves both qualitative and quantitative analysis. The quantitative information requirements include the impact of the asset on the balance sheet, the income statement, the ROA (return on assets) base, and the discounted cash flow. The following is a list of comparative advantages of both leasing and purchasing to meet the FM customer's real estate and space needs.

- Advantages of leasing or subleasing
  - Preservation of capital
  - Keeps debt off books
  - Greater selection of space
  - Variety of space configurations
  - Flexibility
  - Limits financial commitment and risk of long-term capital debt
  - Landlord provides services—allows you to keep your attention on running your business
  - Consequences of new tax laws on ownership
- Advantages of purchasing (ownership)
  - Opportunity for property appreciation
  - Right of occupancy—control
  - Predictability of occupancy cost
  - Right of property use
  - Freedom to change or alter

Once the FM has evaluated the subjective factors involved, the lease-versus-purchase analysis can help the FM, the CFO, and the customer make recommendations to the organization's president, chairman, and board of directors concerning which option is financially right for the organization. All calculations should show both straight-line and net present value returns.

As with any financial analysis, there are both known and unknown factors. Factors that are often known include:

- Beginning rental rates
- Beginning operating expenses
- Purchase price
- Capital outlay for purchase
- Mortgage terms
- Current tax rates—income, property, capital gains
- Current depreciation schedules available

While these factors may not be final, they can be closely estimated. What are unknown are the factors that evolve down the road and are influenced by similarly unknown future events. These include:

- Future yields on alternative investments
- Future value of the dollar
- Changes in tax laws
- Operating expense increases
- Tax increases
- Rent increases based on inflation

- Resale or property residual values
- Inflation or recession

Figure 8.1, lease-versus-purchase analysis, can be particularly helpful because it gives the FM the opportunity to observe the result of varying these unknown factors. While no one has come up with a way to protect against wild value swings or catastrophic events, evaluating the results of reasonable high and low estimates enables the FM to better understand the opportunity and/or risk involved. This analysis may also help the FM determine what purchase price should be considered in order to make this a realistic investment opportunity.

The lease-versus-purchase analysis provides an excellent example of the value of using a double matrix in a "what-if" analysis. The first step is to input known factors, which in this case are:

- Total purchase costs of the new building
- Cost of financing
- Depreciation schedule
- Current property tax

The next step is to vary two of the other factors, which in this case are:

- Starting rent
- Future value of the building

The FM can then determine what a reasonable rent might be based on the FM's estimate of what the building's future value might be (e.g., breakeven starting rent for a future value of $15,000,000 would be between $19.00 and $20.00 per rentable square foot). Conversely, you could analyze what the future value must be to offset the starting rent you are considering. Any other two factors can be varied to broaden the analysis.

After the FM and the customer have developed the specific requirements for a real estate need, a request for proposal can be written and sent out to a number of prequalified building owners and/or landlords. The FM's real estate broker can receive the responses to the RFP and deliver them to the FM. Some of the responses may not follow the requested response format or provide the requested information. The FM's customer will expect to receive an "apples to apples" comparative financial analysis of the responses to help in reviewing and identifying the responses that meet its requirements. Depending on the size of the requirement and the complexity of the RFP, the apples to apples financial analysis may be very straightforward or very complex. Unless the FM has the time and resources to perform the more complex financial evaluations, he should expect his broker to provide this capability and service.

The financial analysis should be provided in a format that both the FM and the customer can recognize and understand. All responses should be listed using the same format, with each item quantified. As shown in Figure 8-1, the FM may find that each response quotes a different amount of rentable square feet (R.S.F.),

Figure 8-1. Lease-Versus-Purchase Analysis.

15-Year Analysis	Lease Side			Ownership Side				Results	
Year	Rent	Improvements	Amortization	Equity	Depreciation	Income	Expenses	NCFAT	NPV
0	0	0	0	3,408,000	0	0	0	(3,408,000)	
1	1,800,000	0	0	344,803	419,048	0	1,820,499	(210,445)	
2	1,868,000	0	0	380,467	419,048	0	1,819,435	(201,714)	
3	1,938,740	0	0	420,306	419,048	0	1,816,345	(193,668)	
4	2,012,337	0	0	464,318	419,048	0	1,810,921	(186,426)	
5	2,088,914	0	0	512,938	419,048	0	1,802,818	(180,123)	
6	2,168,599	0	0	566,659	419,048	0	1,791,649	(174,907)	
7	2,251,524	0	0	625,985	419,048	0	1,776,984	(170,944)	
8	2,337,832	0	0	691,534	419,048	0	1,758,338	(168,421)	
9	2,427,666	0	0	763,946	419,048	0	1,735,174	(167,543)	
10	2,521,180	0	0	843,942	419,048	0	1,706,890	(168,540)	
11	2,618,534	0	0	932,313	419,048	0	1,672,815	(155,866)	
12	2,719,895	0	0	1,029,939	419,048	0	1,632,200	(152,868)	
13	2,825,436	0	0	1,137,787	419,048	0	1,584,214	103,435	
14	2,935,341	0	0	1,256,928	419,048	0	1,527,928	150,485	
15	3,049,801	0	0	1,388,545	419,048	0	1,462,309	199,947	
END	0	0	0	(13,950,000)		0	0	11,672,651	
TOTALS	35,563,800	0	0	818,000	6,285,714	0	25,718,520	6,586,054	(1,230,424)

Lease Factors

Start rent	$18.00
Operating expense	$7.00
Rent escalation %	3.00%
Operating expense escalation	5.00%
Square feet	100,000

NPV	8.00%

Results:

Favors lease by $1,220,424

Ownership Factors

Land cost	1,000,000	Term—yrs	15
Improvements	13,200,000	Interest	10.00%
Purchase price	14,200,000	Principal	11,360,000
		Closing costs	658,000
Future value	1,500,000	Down payment	2,840,000

Building/interiors	12,000,000	Start tax	$250,000
Parking & landscaping	$1,200,000	Start operating expense	$450,000
		Tax escalation %	5.00%
		Operating expense escalation %	5.00%

Selling cost	$1,050,000	Tax on capital gains	32.10%
		Tax on income	35.10%
		Depreciation period, yrs	31.5

although the number of usable square feet (U.S.F.), which is a function of the efficiency (Eff.) of the floor and building design, is quoted as requested:

Location	U.S.F.	Eff.	Rent/ R.S.F.	R.S.F.	Rent/Yr.	Rent for 5 Yrs.
Building A	13,500	10.0%	15,000 × $15.00 =	$225,000 =		**$1,125,000**
Building B	13,500	12.5%	15,429 × $15.00 =	$231,435 =		**$1,157,175**
Building C	13,500	15.0%	15,882 × $15.00 =	$238,230 =		**$1,191,150**

This easily shows that based on rentable square feet alone and assuming that all landlords quoted a $15.00/R.S.F. rental rate, the customer would be paying over $6,000 more per year at Building B than at Building A and over $13,000 more per year at Building C than at Building A. The total rent for the five-year term, assuming a constant $15.00 per R.S.F., would amount to a savings of more than $30,000 at Building A over Building B and a savings of more than $66,000 at Building A over Building C.

However, the evaluation and analysis must also look at many other items, such as the upfit allowance and what it includes in real dollars based on new or existing space; comparing and equating floor-to-ceiling heights; whether mechanical, electrical, ceiling, sprinkler, and other such systems are in place or have to be installed; the rental rate; escalations; free rent; parking costs; operating expenses; and other such factors (see Figure 8-2). As the FM should see, there can be a number of variables that must be compared in order to perform an apples to apples analysis to determine the effective level rent for each analysis (see Figure 8-3; also Figure 8-9 for effective level rent). Effective level rent translates the net present value of periodic lease payments into an annualized dollar amount per square foot. A net present value calculation is one of the few ways in which all the dollar values of the concession package can be taken into account while allowing for the alternative cost of money leasehold. The advantage of using a constant payment as the net effective rent is that it is easier to compare in different transactions and is close to the actual rent that would be paid on an annualized basis.

Figure 8-2 is a site evaluation matrix showing three sites that have been evaluated. This spreadsheet format provides an objective ranking of site evaluation criteria that have been weighted. Each criterion is then scored by the customer and other members of the site identification team, and the ratings and scores for each property on each criterion are shown. The analysis provides a total score for each site, and weighting, site upfit, and general site selection notes and information to assist in the decision-making process are provided at the bottom of the page. In any event, your line operating executives should concentrate on "making their plan" by manufacturing and marketing products—not by real estate sales.

Figure 8-3 is an analysis of twenty-four-month proposals that provides a comparative analysis of five different buildings and the lease and capital costs for each location. The notes section at the bottom of the page gives subjective infor-

Figure 8-2. Site Evaluation Matrix.

ABC Company Relocation—Northern Chicago

Evaluation Date: JUNE 18, 2002
Evaluation By: BILL ROBERTS, SUSAN ADAMS, AND WALTER LITTLE.

Office Location/Landlord Evaluation Criteria	Weight	Summerfield/Glenv'. Mayfield Invest.		Richland/Niles Fairfield Develop.		Westlake/Skokie Westlake & Assoc	
		Rating	Score	Rating	Score	Rating	Score
Total Cost/Value	9.0	9.5	85.5	9.0	81.0	9.0	81.0
Land Cost/Value	7.0	9.0	63.0	8.5	59.5	5.0	35.0
Upfit Cost/Value	8.0	9.5	76.0	8.5	68.0	9.5	76.0
Location	8.0	10.0	80.0	9.0	72.0	8.5	68.0
Building Configuration	6.0	10.0	60.0	8.5	51.0	8.5	51.0
Amenities (Food Service, etc.)	10.0	9.5	95.0	8.5	85.0	8.5	85.0
Free Parking	9.0	9.5	85.5	9.5	85.5	7.0	63.0
Building Services & Security	8.0	9.5	76.0	9.0	72.0	6.0	48.0
Collocation with XYZ Corp.	6.0	6.0	36.0	9.5	57.0	6.0	36.0
Bus Route to & from Site	8.0	9.0	72.0	8.0	64.0	8.0	64.0
Courier Service Available	10.0	9.0	90.0	8.5	85.0	8.5	85.0
Real Property, etc., Taxes	6.0	8.0	48.0	8.0	48.0	8.5	51.0
Housing/Local Labor Market	6.0	8.5	51.0	8.0	48.0	8.0	48.0
Operational Cost Savings	7.0	9.0	63.0	8.0	56.0	8.0	56.0
Human Resources Issues	7.0	8.0	56.0	8.0	56.0	8.0	56.0
Ability to Meet Schedule	10.0	9.5	95.0	9.0	90.0	10.0	100.0
Landlord Resources Avail.	9.0	9.5	85.5	9.5	85.5	10.0	90.0
Overall Landlord Exper.	9.0	9.5	85.5	9.0	81.0	9.0	81.0
Overall Evaluation	8.0	9.5	76.0	9.0	72.0	8.5	68.0
Total Score:			1379.0		1316.5		1242.0

(continues)

Figure 8-2. (Continued).

Evaluation Notes:
1. Weights are between 0 and 10 (10 being best)
2. Ratings are between 0 and 10 (10 being best)
3. Ratings × weights = score

Upfit Notes:
1. Full turnkey construction.   Full turnkey construction.

                 $38.00 per sq. ft. for office & $95.00 for computer room.

Information Notes:

1. TAXES:	Niles (City & County)	Glenview (City) and Skokie (City)
Real Estate	$1.38/$100 + fire & rescue levy	$0.88/$100
Personal Property	$3.75/$100	$4.20/$100
	No merchants capital tax	No merchants capital tax
	Gross receipts tax in effect	Gross receipts tax in effect

2. Housing Costs		
2 Bedroom (Median—1989)	$99,500	$136,000
3 Bedroom (Median—1989)	$107,000	$193,000
2 Bedroom—Rental	$570 per month	$690 per month

Figure 8-3. Analysis of Twenty-Four-Month Proposals for the Relocation of ABC Company.

June 18, 2002

Proposed Location/Term	Rate/ R.S.F.	Esc./ Year	Total R.S.F.	Total U.S.F.	First Year's Rent	Estimated Upfit Allow./ U.S.F.	Total Allow.	Total Improve. Cost	Total Rent	Total Commitment = Total Rent + Total Improve. Cost	Estimated Balance of Improve. Cost Paid by ABC CO.	Remarks
1. *1245 Wacker Avenue, 3rd & 4th Floor*												
24 Months	$17.75	4%	50,000	44,000	$875,500	$5.00	$250,000	$480,000	$1,798,500	$2,278,000	**$230,000**	Note 1
2. *769 Michigan Drive, 4th Floor & partial 2nd, 5th & 8th Fls.*												
24 Months	$19.50	3%+	45,000	40,284	$877,500	$8.00	$322,272	$445,000	$1,782,000	$2,227,000	**$122,800**	Note 2
30 Months	$19.50	3%+	45,000	40,284	$877,500	$10.00	$402,840					Note 2
36 Months	$19.50	3%+	45,000	40,384	$877,500	$12.00	$484,608					Note 2
3. *849 Wacker Avenue, 5th & 6th Floors*												
18 Months	$12.00	Fixed	47,743	45,481	$572,916	$1.00+	$ 45,481					Note 3
24 Months	$12.15	Fixed	47,743	45,481	$580,078	$1.00+	$ 45,481	$446,600	$1,160,200	$1,606,800	**$204,700**	Note 3

(continues)

Figure 8-3. (Continued).

4. *982 Michigan Drive, 14th & 15th Floors, with Basement/Computer Room*

18 Months	$15.00	Fixed	49,439	44,754	$741,585	$4.47	$200,000	$300,000	$380,400	$1,483,200		Note 4
24 Months	$15.00	Fixed	49,439	44,754	$741,585	$6.70		$300,000	$380,400	$1,863,600	**$ 80,400**	Note 4

5. *1200 Richards Street, 8th & 9th Floors*

18 Months	$14.66	Net Market	47,000	43,519	$806,500	$8.00	$348,152			$1,397,100		Note 5
24 Months	$12.00	Net Market	47,000	43,519	$681,500	$8.00	$348,152	$522,300		$1,919,400	**$174,200**	Note 5

Notes:

1. 1245 Wacker Avenue did not make an 18-month proposal, but it stated that this would not be a deal-breaker. Proposal provided an option for an additional 18 months and included the landlord providing preliminary and working drawings.

2. 769 Michigan Drive did not make an 18-month proposal and, again, expressed a serious interest in ABC Co. If 18 months is required, the upfit allowance would be $0.00 (i.e., that cost would be totally ABC Co.'s). Rent would be $20.10 for year 2 and $20.70 for year 3.

3. 849 Wacker Avenue proposal provides for recarpeting and repainting and an additional upfit allowance of $1.00 per U.S.F. The lease term may be extended to a total of 60 months at a rental rate of $13.00/R.S.F. at the end of the initial lease term.

4. 982 Michigan Drive proposal recognized the possible need to alter 60% of the space and has provided for a renewal term of 36 or 42 months at $16.00/R.S.F. This is the only proposal to include a computer room that meets ABC Co.'s needs without having to build one from scratch. This proposal includes our subleasing and using the current major tenant's facilities, including food service, catering, vending, parking, security, and card access, and includes space planning, construction drawings, building permits, and certificate of occupancy. The above yearly rental includes an existing computer room of 3,878 R.S.F., and not all of this space has to be leased.

5. 1200 Richards Street proposal is *net* of janitorial and utilities, which are estimated to be $2.00 to $2.50/R.S.F. Existing space will be vacated by Jan. 15, 2003 by the current tenant, and because of the age of the building and wear on the space, the entire inside of the existing office/warehouse will require *gutting* and is included in the $8.00/R.S.F. Proposal includes one preliminary drawing and one completed set of construction documents.

mation that was provided by the various landlords as part of the proposals or was determined from research on each location. This analysis provides objective bottom-line comparisons that become part of the information to be used in making a selection.

Figure 8.4 provides a relocation analysis that compares three sites; it includes rents per year, purchase option price, lot size, operating expense, escalations, free rent and total rent, and expenses by year and over the term.

In the analysis of the proposed lease alternatives, the FM may choose to have her real estate broker assist her in determining the real estate requirement. The lease analysis must look at many items, including:

- The upfit allowance
- What the upfit allowance includes in real dollars based on new or existing space
- Comparing and equating floor-to-ceiling or floor-to-bottom-of-structure costs versus the landlord's improvement allowance or work letter
- Whether mechanical, electrical, ceiling, sprinkler, and other such systems are in place or to be installed
- The rental rate
- Escalations
- Free rent
- Parking costs
- ADA compliance and associated operating expenses
- Rentable square feet
- Usable square feet
- Common area factor
- Lease term (years)
- Commencement month
- Move-in month
- First year's rent (per square foot)
- Percentage of rent escalated
- Amount escalated (per square foot)
- Escalation percentage
- Stepped rent structure (per square foot)
  - Year 1 rent structure
  - Year 2 rent structure
  - Year 3 rent structure
  - Later years rent structure
- Lease obligation
- Lease buyout
- Number of employees in facility
- Build-out allowance
- Build-out cost
- Parking spaces required
- Parking cost (per space, per month)
- Total annual cost (aggregate $)

Figure 8-4. Relocation Analysis for Northern Chicago.

ABCCOIN1.WK1
PAGE 1

Prepared By: BILL ROBERTS
Date: JUNE 18, 2002

Development Name:	SUMMERFIELD	RICHLAND OFFICE PARK	WESTLAKE TERRACES
Address:	3298 Summers Ct.	9100 Bakers Avenue	West Terrace Drive
	Suite 100	Suite 120	Building 200, Suite 105
City, St. & Zip:	GLENVIEW, IL	NILES, IL	SKOKIE, IL
Lease Starts:	DECEMBER 1, 2002	DECEMBER 1, 2002	DECEMBER 1, 2002
Lease Ends:	NOVEMBER 30, 2007	NOVEMBER 30, 2007	NOVEMBER 30, 2007
Total Leased Area:	32,000 Square Feet	32,000 Square Feet	32,500 Square Feet
Yr 1 Lease Rate:	$7.00 /S.F.;	$7.20 /S.F.;	$6.10 /S.F.;
Yr 2 Lease Rate:	$8.28 /S.F.;	$7.42 /S.F.;	$6.10 /S.F.;
Yr 3 Lease Rate:	$8.75 /S.F.;	$7.64 /S.F.;	$6.10 /S.F.;
Yr 4 Lease Rate:	$8.88 /S.F.;	$7.87 /S.F.;	$6.10 /S.F.;
Yr 5 Lease Rate:	$9.34 /S.F.	$8.10 /S.F.	$6.10 /S.F.
Bldg. Rent Inc.:	100.00% Per Year	100.00% Per Year	100.00% Per Year
Tot. Parking Area:	50,000 Square Feet	48,875 Square Feet	0 Square Feet
Yr 1 Park. Rate:	$0.00 /S.F.;	$1.21 /S.F.;	$0.00 /S.F.;
Yr 2 Park. Rate:	$0.00 /S.F.;	$1.25 /S.F.;	$0.00 /S.F.;
Yr 3 Park. Rate:	$0.00 /S.F.;	$1.28 /S.F.;	$0.00 /S.F.;
Yr 4 Park. Rate:	$0.00 /S.F.;	$1.32 /S.F.;	$0.00 /S.F.;
Yr 5 Park. Rate:	$0.00 /S.F.;	$1.36 /S.F.;	$0.00 /S.F.;
Park. Rent Inc.:	100.00% Per Year	100.00% Per Year	100.00% Per Year
Yr 1 Total Rate:	$7.00 /S.F.;	$8.41 /S.F.;	$6.10 /S.F.;
Yr 2 Total Rate:	$8.28 /S.F.;	$8.67 /S.F.;	$6.10 /S.F.;
Yr 3 Total Rate:	$8.75 /S.F.;	$8.92 /S.F.;	$6.10 /S.F.;
Yr 4 Total Rate:	$8.88 /S.F.;	$9.19 /S.F.;	$6.10 /S.F.;
Yr 5 Total Rate:	$9.34 /S.F.;	$9.46 /S.F.;	$6.10 /S.F.;
Total Rent Inc.:	106.69% Per Year	102.89% Per Year	100.00% Per Year
Purchase Option:	$3,395,000 @ YEAR 5	First Right of Refusal	NONE
Lot Size:	5.21 Acres	3.75 Acres	NONE
Operating Expense	$6.50 /RSF	$6.55 /RSF	$6.35 /RSF
Oper. Ex. Inc.:	104.50% Per Year	105.50% Per Year	104.75% Per Year

	YEAR 0	2002 (1 Mo.)	2003 (12 Mos.)	2004 (12 Mos.)	2005 (12 Mos.)	2006 (12 Mos.)	2007 (11 Mos.)	Total (60 Mos.)	LESS 1 YR. FREE RENT
SUMMERFIELD EXPENSES:									
Building Rent Expense	N/A	$18,667	$227,413	$266,213	$280,347	$285,387	$273,973	$1,352,000	($ 224,004)
Parking Expense	N/A	$0	$0	$0	$0	$0	$0	$0	
Operating Expense	N/A	$4,000	$48,180	$50,348	$52,614	$54,981	$52,471	$262,594	
TOTAL EXPENSES	N/A	$22,667	$275,593	$316,561	$332,960	$340,368	$326,444	$1,614,594	**$1,390,590**
	YEAR 0	2002 (1 Mo.)	2003 (12 Mos.)	2004 (12 Mos.)	2005 (12 Mos.)	2006 (12 Mos.)	2007 (11 Mos.)	Total (60 Mos.)	LESS 1 YR. FREE RENT
RICHLAND EXPENSES:									
Building Rent Expense	N/A	$19,200	$230,987	$238,027	$245,093	$252,453	$237,600	$1,223,360	($ 230,400)
Parking Expense	N/A	$4,928	$59,302	$61,216	$62,723	$64,678	$60,931	$313,778	
Operating Expense	N/A	$4,000	$48,180	$50,348	$52,614	$54,981	$52,471	$262,594	
TOTAL EXPENSES	N/A	$28,128	$338,468	$349,591	$360,430	$372,113	$351,002	$1,799,732	**$1,569,332**
	YEAR 0	2002 (1 Mo.)	2003 (12 Mos.)	2004 (12 Mos.)	2005 (12 Mos.)	2006 (12 Mos.)	2007 (11 Mos.)	Total (60 Mos.)	LESS 1 YR. FREE RENT
WESTLAKE TERRACES EXPENSES:									
Building Rent Expense	N/A	$16,521	$198,250	$198,250	$198,250	$198,250	$181,729	$991,250	($ 198,252)
Parking Expense	N/A	$0	$0	$0	$0	$0	$0	$0	
Operating Expense	N/A	$3,656	$44,040	$46,021	$48,092	$50,256	$47,962	$240,027	
TOTAL EXPENSES	N/A	$20,177	$242,290	$244,271	$246,342	$248,506	$229,691	$1,231,277	**$1,033,025**

- Free parking (aggregate $)
- Operating expense increase (annually)
- Operating expense stop (per square foot)
- Discount rate
- Tenant improvement amortization rate (percentage)
- Moving allowance (aggregate)
- Moving expense (aggregate)
- Breakout of operating expense line items, including:
  - Common area maintenance (per square foot)
  - Taxes (per square foot)
  - Utilities (per square foot)
  - Insurance (per square foot)
  - Janitorial (per square foot)
  - Management fee (per square foot)
  - Projected total operating expense (per square foot)

The cash flows section compares and calculates the following:

- Operating expense increases over expense stop (per calendar year, per square foot)
- Total cumulative operating expense projection and incremental increase (per annum, per square foot)
- Base rent increases (per annum, per square foot)
- Total rent per year and its relationship to cash flows regarding:
  - Operating expense increases passed through per year
  - Total rent—cumulative total of base rent, expense stop, and passed-through increases
  - Breakout of any existing lease obligations (per annum)
  - Excess tenant improvement costs (per annum)
  - Parking costs (per annum)
  - Moving expenses
  - Total cost before incentives—total rent plus lease obligations, excess tenant improvement costs, parking costs, and moving expenses (per annum)
- Incentives:
  - Free rent (per annum)
  - Lease buyout (per annum)
  - Tenant improvement allowance (total dollars)
  - Free parking value (per annum)
  - Moving allowance
  - Total incentives
- Total effective cost per annum
- Average monthly cost (per annum)
- Effective rate (per square foot, per annum)
- Any credits to carry forward (per annum)
- Total aggregate cost of occupancy
- Total NPV of aggregate cost of occupancy

- Equivalent rentable rate (aggregate, per square foot, per annum)
- Equivalent usable rate (aggregate, per square foot, per annum)
- Aggregate cost (per annum)
- NPV cost per annum
- NPV cost rentable rate (per square foot, per annum)
- NPV cost usable rate (per square foot, per annum)
- After 38 percent tax aggregate cost per annum
- After 38 percent tax NPV cost per annum
- After 38 percent tax rentable rate (per square foot, per annum)
- After 38 percent tax usable rate (per square foot, per annum)
- Per employee desk cost after 38 percent tax, aggregate
- Per employee desk cost after 38 percent tax, NPV

There can be a number of variables that have to be compared in order to perform an apples to apples analysis to determine the net present value and effective level rent for each analysis. Based upon the FM's NPV and effective level rent analysis, the landlords' reputations, and the landlords' responses to the RFP, the FM will be in a position to make a site recommendation. The FM's brokerage company may need to obtain clarification of any elements stated in the RFP that were unsatisfactorily specified. Depending on the FM's organization's needs, graphics depicting any of the analyzed factors could be included. The value rating analysis discussed in the market analysis section of this proposal evaluates:

- Building systems
- Geographic locations
- Floor plate size
- Life safety systems
- Many other features, as requested in your RFP

Based upon the results and the analysis of the responses to the RFPs, the FM is responsible for making an informed and accurate recommendation to the CFO and the customer as to which property/facility the organization should select. Knowledge of the total financial and legal consequences is generally the key basis for a final selection. However, there are times when the final selection may prove to be a political or personal choice. It is important that the FM understand the process by which the organization's decisions are made and, where possible, influence the use of a business approach to the selection process.

Development Case Studies

As discussed earlier, there are many ways for the FM to acquire purchased or leased property for the organization. The following cases are provided for consideration and review.

Build by Owner

When the FM's organization chooses to buy the property, develop the property, and build facilities that it will own, the property is usually developed to meet the organization's unique requirements; this is known as build by owner. In the past, many organizations did not consider the ultimate disposal of the property or facility during development and found, when the property or facility was no longer useful to their business, that it was so unusual that there was no viable market for it. The FM today must advise the CFO and the customer to take the disposal or sale of the property or facility at some time in the future into consideration when developing the property or facility.

For a build by owner project, the FM must develop a very detailed property acquisition, property or facility development, and property or facility management operations and maintenance budget that will include most or all of the following cost items:

- Property acquisition budget items:
  - Travel (as required)
  - Property or facility value appraisal
  - Property or facility survey
  - Environmental survey(s) for wetlands, soil and/or facility contamination, and other such problems
  - Property review (soil borings)
  - Total property purchase price
  - Project management fees
  - Purchase price for additional property option(s)
  - Brokerage fees (if any)
  - Purchase contingencies
  - Clear title and title insurance for the property
  - Legal fees for development of the purchase agreement
  - Property closing fees
  - Engineering/architectural study fees
  - Change of zoning fees (if required)
  - Property taxes
  - Municipality/state development incentives
  - Property infrastructure costs (waste and sewer, electrical, natural gas, water, etc.)
  - Insurance
- Property or facility development budget items:
  - Internal mortgage expenses (understand how funds will be obtained to finance or repay the development costs) and/or payments for construction and/or permanent loan expenses
  - Construction permits
  - Construction cost
  - Construction contingencies

- New information and telephone technology requirements (equipment, software, and installation)
- Relocation of existing information and telephone technology
- Landscaping and site improvements
- New furniture, fixtures, and equipment (F.F.&E.)
- Other owner-furnished F.F.&E. (purchase and installation)
- Relocation of existing F.F.&E., including files and personnel boxes
- Cleanup of old and new property or facilities
- Personnel relocation (if any)
- Relocation security
- Occupancy permit(s)
- Utility connection fees
- Property, construction, and content insurance
- Start-up costs
- Project contingencies (unexpected rock, poor bearing soil, etc.)
- Property or facility management operations and maintenance budget
  - The FM should develop a detailed operations and maintenance budget based upon the property and facility staffing and operations requirements.

The purchase of each property is unique, with specific and special issues that the FM must be prepared to deal with effectively and efficiently. The FM, as the representative of the owner, must ensure that the funds that are budgeted and spent for each property development are managed in keeping with good business and project management practices as required by the FM's organization.

Figure 8-5 provides a sample letter of intent to purchase and sell property. This type of document is usually developed after a property has been selected and the FM's organization is ready to make a deal.

Joint Venture

A joint venture is normally created between a developer and a corporate land-owner. In this type of joint venture, the developer will offer the corporate land-owner one of two postures: Either the developer will have the in-house capability to furnish all of the necessary development services, or the developer will offer its skills as a development project organizer (a "bringer together" of the ingredients for a successful project). The corporate landowner, represented by the FM, will offer its land, to be sure, and usually also a parcel or tract of land that is largely or entirely unencumbered, so that the equity in it can be used as leverage for development purposes. Whatever the posture of the developer, it will be seeking a percentage split of the profits as well as compensation for its development skills, while the landowner will be seeking a fair purchase price for its land and a split of the profit, the sum total of which would exceed the profit from an outright sale.

This type of joint venture will require a meeting of the minds on many essential points. Probably the most critical element from the FM's point of view will be the method by which the organization will be paid for its corporate land. This

method must permit the developer leverage latitude, or the essential reason for the joint venture will not exist. In any event, the basics of the agreement between the two parties will usually be spelled out in a letter of agreement or intent and then elaborated upon by attorneys representing the two sides in a formal written agreement. Figure 8-6 shows the wording of a sample letter of intent that illustrates one method for expressing the relationship between the parties—in this case, a full-service development company and a landowner with unencumbered land.

Please note from the wording of this agreement that it attempts to address the underlying principle of participation, that is, equity among the parties. Although limitless variations are possible, this example does serve to illustrate the types of legal relationships that participants in joint ventures will enter into *for the lure of higher yield*. The key, then, is to adequately assess the realities of an equation that begins with your operating structure and profit philosophy and ends with an estimate of risk and offsetting potential gain, as shown in Figure 8-7.

Ground Lease Property and Build to Suit

There may be times when the FM cannot locate a property that is for sale but may find a site with an owner who is willing to ground lease it to the FM's organization. The ground lease is usually for a term of from ten to thirty or more years. The term of the ground lease is a function of the amortization requirements of the site or facility improvements made by the FM's organization.

Many of the requirements for the ground lease are similar to those for the purchase of property. The FM will need to develop budgets and may need to see that the property is rezoned, provide an environmental study, and carry out other such tasks before the ground lease agreement is signed by the FM's organization.

Purchasing a Building Built to Specifications

The FM may find that a property developer has both the property and the unique expertise to build a facility to the organization's unique and specific requirements. Such a property developer usually has the staff, track record, and reputation to build a quality building in a timely manner for a reasonable price.

The FM may choose to hire an architect/engineer/interior designer to assist in the development of requirements, specifications, and design/construction plans in coordination with the developer or may choose to use the developer's architect/engineer/designer. The FM, as the organization's representative and manager, must work with the customer to develop the specific building requirements and specifications, work with the developer to establish the final sale price, and, working with the CFO, put together a financing program that will receive board approval.

When this process for acquiring a building is selected, the FM will need to develop budgets and schedules similar to those for purchasing property. The main difference will be the cash flow requirements, as the developer will either self-fund the construction cost or obtain a construction loan.

Figure 8-5. Sample Letter of Intent to Purchase and Sell Property.

This Letter of Intent is made and entered into this *21* day of *September 2002* by and between *ABC Company* ("Purchaser") and *Warehouse Developers, Inc.* ("Seller").

In consideration of the agreements hereinafter set forth, the parties hereto mutually agree as follows:

1. Seller agrees to sell and Purchaser agrees to purchase the property *located at 2548 West Wacker Drive, Chicago, IL 60638,* in the County of *Cook*, State of *Illinois*, as more specifically described in Exhibit A, which is attached hereto and incorporated herein by this reference, together with all rights and appurtenances thereto and all rights, title and interest of Seller in and to any and all roads and streets bounding such property. A more definitive description shall be provided by the Seller to the Purchaser from an accurate boundary and topographic survey acceptable to the Seller and Purchaser, at Seller's cost to be reimbursed by Purchaser at closing.

2. The purchase price shall be as agreed to by the Seller and Purchaser based upon an appraisal of the property not later than 90 days from the date of this Letter of Intent by a minimum of three (3) appraisers retained by the Purchaser and approved by the Seller. Seller and Purchaser agree that the purchase price shall not exceed *$6.60* nor be less than *$5.15* per square foot of the appraised and surveyed property. Failure to agree on a reasonable purchase price shall render this Letter of Intent null and void.

3. Conveyance of the property shall be by general warranty deed and shall be covered by a fully paid title insurance policy.

4. Purchaser proposes to use the property for the construction and operation of a free-standing warehouse distribution center with outside storage. In the event that the property is restricted in any way which prohibits, limits, or restricts the use of the property for such purpose, Seller shall obtain appropriate authorization so that the property may be used for the purposes described above. In the event Seller is unable to secure the authorization necessary for utilizing the property within 180 days from the date of this Letter of Intent, Purchaser may so notify Seller in writing, whereupon this Letter of Intent shall become null and void.

5. Further, Purchaser's obligation to purchase is also subject to the following within 180 days from the above date:
   a. Purchaser's obtaining approval and funding of the purchase of the property and construction of the warehouse distribution center from their parent company, *XYZ Corporation;*
   b. Seller's acquisition of clear title to an entrance way to the property from the adjacent property owner (whereby the adjacent property owner will exchange a portion of the adjacent property to create an entrance way to the subject property in exchange for a portion of the subject property which borders *West Wacker Drive* and *4th Avenue* and the adjacent property);

(continues)

Figure 8-5. (Continued).

---

    c. Seller grants Purchaser access to the site, and the right to physically investigate the site. Purchaser, as part of the due diligence and contingency phase of the agreement, shall be completely satisfied before closing shall take place that the site and/or building are free and clear of any and all current airborne, surface, and subsurface environmental contaminates and/or wetland restrictions which affect the current and possible future use of the site and/or building. Purchaser shall employ an environmental audit process to make this determination, which includes but is not limited to retaining a qualified consulting organization to investigate and research the site and adjacent sites, obtain and analyze samples of site materials and soil via borings, investigate wetland issues and restrictions to the site, and provide a written report satisfactory to the Purchaser that the site and/or building is free and clear of contaminates and the site and/or building use(s) are not limited by wetland restrictions. If the environmental audit process through the above report or other Purchaser investigation does not provide the Purchaser with a "clean" and "usable" site, the Purchaser may at the Purchaser's option cancel the Sale and Purchase Agreement without penalty;

    d. Seller shall provide the Purchaser with a written statement that the site and/or building meets the requirements of the federal "Americans with Disabilities Act of 1990" (ADA) and all other federal, state and local rules and regulations. The Purchaser shall have the option to investigate the site and/or building to verify the Seller's claim;

    e. Purchaser's obtaining the necessary licenses, permits, and other authorizations, including curb cuts for reasonable traffic access;

    f. Seller's obtaining letters of service and supply from the appropriate agencies for water, gas, electricity, sanitary sewer, storm sewers, and any other necessary public utilities stating that the services and supply are immediately on or contiguous to the subject property and are available to the Purchaser for a connection fee for all such utilities at the time of occupancy; and

    g. Purchaser's obtaining title insurance binder, title insurance, and a general warranty deed.

6. Real estate taxes for the current year shall be prorated as of the date of closing.

7. The closing of the herein described purchase and sale shall be subject to the conditions set forth in this Letter of Intent and shall be scheduled at a mutually agreeable time and date on or after 180 days following the date of this Letter of Intent.

In WITNESS WHEREOF, the Seller has caused this Letter of Intent to be executed on the date noted above.

Witness:

SELLER:
WAREHOUSE DEVELOPERS, INC.

_____

By: _____
      Walter H. Simpson

Its: Chairman _____

In WITNESS WHEREOF, the Purchaser has caused this Letter of Intent to be executed on the date noted above.

Witness:

PURCHASER:
ABC COMPANY

_____

By: _____
      Robert C. Wilson

Its: President _____

Lease Space

One of the most common methods for acquiring space, especially office space, is to lease the property and/or facility(ies). As was discussed earlier in this chapter, the decision to lease space is generally the result of a business/financial strategy set by the board for meeting short- and long-term property/space requirements.

The FM, with the CFO's and the customer's support, may choose to bring a knowledgeable real estate broker onto the team to assist in the search and acquisition process. Before bringing a real estate broker onto the team, however, it is important for the FM to understand how the broker will be compensated—whether by the FM's organization or by the landlord or owner of the space leased. All parties to the lease process should understand what the brokerage fee will be, the broker's responsibilities, and who will pay the fee.

If the FM's broker is being paid by the FM's organization, the FM or the broker should develop a service agreement containing a formal detailed listing of the services to be provided. This agreement will document the specific services that the broker will provide and the compensation to be paid and when. The FM may require the broker to write the RFP, which provides specific property/space information that the FM may choose to include in the RFP, with the broker's assistance. Some FMs require that the broker identify the landlords/owners to receive the RFP and specify that the broker will receive the responses to the RFP. Many of the financial and legal items in the RFP will become important during the

Figure 8-6. Joint Venture Letter of Intent.

1. The basic vehicle for property ownership, development, and management will be a limited partnership, with the Owner or its designees owning a _____ percent (____%) interest therein, and XYZ Development, or its designees, owning the remaining _____ percent (____%) interest therein. The Owner shall hold its interest as a limited partner, and XYZ Development shall hold its interest as a limited partner and/or a general partner, with one or more of its principals acting as additional general partners.

2. Agreement as to the master development plan and all basic decisions in connection with the development of the proposed project prior to the execution of the partnership agreement shall be made by a designee of the Owner and a designee of XYZ Development. Following the execution of the partnership agreement, the general partners shall be responsible for obtaining and supervising the planning, design, financing, construction, and marketing of the proposed dwelling units, facilities, and appurtenances in the development.

3. Upon the execution of the limited partnership agreement, the Owner shall convey to the limited partnership title to that property, agreed upon in accordance with paragraph 2 above, to be developed as Phase I of the project. Additional properties in phase development shall be deeded into the partnership when the general partners deem it an appropriate time to start the development of the additional phases. The agreed-upon value of all the properties deeded into the partnership for any phase shall be _____ dollars ($_____) per acre, which amount shall be evidenced by a partnership note secured by a mortgage subordinated to the lien of any institutional lender or lenders furnishing funds for the development of the property. Said note shall provide for interest at the rate of _____ percent (____%) per annum, commencing on the date of conveyance, but payments being deferred until proceeds from sales of dwelling units (cash flow) allow such payments. Interest payments shall be junior only to partnership debts owed to third-party creditors.

4. Upon execution of the partnership agreement, the costs theretofore incurred by the Owner and/or XYZ Development in obtaining the services of _____ for the investigation of the development potential of the subject property shall become an obligation of the partnership.

5. XYZ Development agrees to accept a partnership note in payment of its services rendered to the partnership, which note shall bear interest and be repaid in like manner as the Owner is repaid for his land (i.e., in proportion on a _____-_____ basis), so that XYZ Development shall be paid its compensation no later than the Owner is paid for his land.

The above notes shall be subordinated, if requested by the partnership, to all other debts of the partnership, and shall be repaid in full before there is any distribution of profits to the partners from the development. XYZ Development's estimated cost of developing each phase is _____ percent of the total development cost (exclusive of land). In the event that the compensation due XYZ Development exceeds this estimate, said excess shall be paid by the partnership, as are the other expenses of the partnership. In the event that said compensation is less than the estimated amount of said note, said savings shall accrue to the benefit of the partnership and shall be reflected in profits. XYZ Development shall give the partnership credit against its development compensation for Phase I in an amount equal to that paid by the partnership in fees for the market and feasibility study and the cost of acquiring utilities and proper zoning (said fees presently estimated to be a maximum of $_____). It is understood that the above-mentioned deferred compensation arrangement with XYZ Development does not include the services, if any, rendered to the partnership by Professional Brokerage Corporation or any of its subsidiaries, which services shall be contracted for and paid for, as are obligations to all other third parties to the partnership.

---

analysis of the landlords' responses, and eventually these items will become important items in the lease abstract as described in Chapter 9.

Figure 8-8 is an example of a landlord's response to an RFP. The FM will often receive a number of responses to the RFP; after evaluating these responses, the FM and the customer can then, with senior leadership and legal support, begin the process of developing the lease document, with corporate legal support for the legal issues/items involved in the lease.

Figure 8-9 provides a listing of seven properties that are available for lease. This analysis looks at a number of issues that the FM should review with the customer and the CFO in the process of making a selection recommendation. While the customer may focus on the rent costs, the building/space efficiency, the effective rent, the factors that make up the effective rent, rent escalation, operating expenses, and other such factors, all factors need to be considered in order to ensure that the FM can provide an apples to apples comparison.

This type of analysis is an important requirement when leasing space, and the FM must be prepared to look at nonfinancial issues that could make the deal that is best from a financial/legal perspective unsatisfactory. The financially best deal could include unacceptable location, transportation, parking, zoning issues, amenities, or landlord/owner reputation issues that the FM must understand in making a recommendation to the customer and the CFO.

Conclusion

The FM should consider the information in this chapter as a starting point in the financial aspects of development. The material provided in the text and exhibits should be used by the FM in conjunction with the actual experience in property development that the FM will face or has faced in serving the customer and the organization.

Figure 8-7. Estimated Yield from a Joint Venture.

A Joint Venture Between
ABC COMPANY & XYZ DEVELOPMENT

DISTRIBUTION CENTER
Perimeter Business Park
7645 Warehouse Drive
Chicago, IL

Building Area:	32,000 RENTABLE SQUARE FEET
	33,546 GROSS SQUARE FEET

	Office—	1,500 Square Feet
	Warehouse—	30,500 Square Feet

Ext. Storage Area: 85,378 SQUARE FEET (Fenced)

Property Area: 5.1783 ACRES

Lease:	LEASE COMMENCEMENT—	December 1, 2003
	LEASE EXPIRATION—	November 30, 2023
	BASIC RENT AMOUNTS—	

Lease Year	Rate Per Sq. Ft.	Rents
Year One	$ 7.00	$ 224,000.00
Year Two	$ 8.28	$ 264,960.00
Year Three	$ 8.75	$ 280,000.00
Year Four	$ 8.88	$ 284,160.00
Year Five	$ 9.34	$ 298,880.00
Year Six	$ 9.81	$ 313,920.00
Years Seven through Ten	$10.09	$ 322,880.00
Years Eleven through Fifteen	$11.79	$ 377,280.00
Years Sixteen through Twenty	$14.14	$ 452,480.00
Total Rental Commitment		**$7,106,240.00**

Option to Purchase:	End of Year Five—	$3,395,000.00
	End of Year Eight—	$3,500,800.00

Expansion Option: Lease an additional 2 acres within one year of Certificate of Occupancy (December 1, 2003).

Figure 8-8. Lease Proposal Letter.

WEST WACKER TOWERS, L.P.
4425 West Wacker Drive
Suite 2100
Chicago, IL 60630
(312) 555-3400

June 30, 2002

Ms. Sandra K. Broker
Vice President—Brokerage
Professional Brokerage Company
304 E. Wacker Drive
Suite 2210
Chicago, IL 60630

Re: West Wacker Towers
     Second Floor Lease Proposal
     4425 W. Wacker Drive
     Chicago, IL 60630

Dear Ms. Broker:

In response to your Request for Proposal dated June 18, 2002, I have been authorized by Westland Development Company, Inc. (Landlord) to submit the following proposal to your client, ABC Company (Tenant), for the leasing of new office space at the referenced location:

PREMISES:	Approximately 16,535 rentable square feet (15,683 usable square feet) on the second (2nd) floor known as Suite 200 and as shown in the enclosed Exhibit A.
COMMENCEMENT:	October 1, 2002.
LEASE TERM:	Five (5) years—October 1, 2002 to September 30, 2007.
RENEWAL OPTIONS:	Two (2) options for five (5) years for each option. Landlord must be notified in writing one hundred eighty (180) days in advance of the end of the current lease term if Tenant elects to remain in the lease space.
RENTAL RATE:	$21.00 per rentable square foot, which includes a Base Rental component of $13.41 per rentable square foot and an Operating Expense component (expense stop) of $7.59 per rentable square foot.

(continues)

Figure 8-8. (Continued).

ESCALATION:	On the first day of each lease year, commencing October 1, 2002, the Base Rental component shall be increased by four and one-half percent (4.5%). Option period Base Rent and Operating Expense component shall be market.
IMPROVEMENTS:	Landlord shall provide to the Tenant an allowance of $17.00 per rentable square foot toward the Tenant's improvement of the space. Should Tenant elect to take the option to extend the lease term, Landlord shall provide Tenant an allowance of $8.00 per rentable square foot at the beginning of each option period for painting, carpeting, and minor alterations.
RENT ABATEMENT:	Tenant shall receive twelve (12) free months of Base Rent abatement starting on October 1, 2002 and will begin Base Rental payments effective October 1, 2003. Operating Expenses shall be paid for the term of the lease.
PARKING:	Landlord shall provide to the Tenant three (3) parking spaces per thousand rentable square feet at $10 per month per space through September 30, 2007. Landlord shall provide Tenant five (5) reserved and free spaces for the initial term of the lease on the 1st parking level.
CONF. FACILITIES:	Landlord's 600 square foot conference facilities on the first floor shall be available for reservation by the Tenant at no additional cost.
HEALTH FAC.:	Landlord shall provide five (5) Executive memberships in the West Wacker Towers Health Club at no cost to the Tenant through the end of the initial term of the lease. Landlord shall provide up to seventy-five (75) Standard memberships for Tenant employees in the Health Club at $40 per month per member through September 30, 2007 when these memberships are paid by the Tenant.
SECURITY DEPOSIT:	One (1) month's rent to be held for the term of the lease.
ASBESTOS:	Landlord warrants to the Tenant that the space, building systems, and the building contain no friable asbestos.

If the terms and conditions set forth in this proposal are acceptable, please have the proposal executed by your client where indicated below and return one executed copy to my attention not later than 5:00 P.M. (CT), July 6, 2002. Should you have any questions, please do not hesitate to contact me.

Sincerely,

Robert A. Thompson
Vice President
Property Management

enclosures
cc: Linda B. Stone (w/enclosures)
       W. Wacker/ABC Co. file (w/enclosures)

AGREED AND ACCEPTED:
ABC Company
By: _____   Date: _____

Title: _____

Figure 8-9. Preliminary Evaluation of Lease Proposal Responses—Lease Financial Analysis.

Lease Year	Building A Rent	Building B Rent	Building C Rent	Building D Rent	Building E Rent	Building F Rent	Building G Rent
0	(279,275)	0	(236,254)	(35,000)	0	(300,000)	36,094
1	166,250	0	0	0	145,882	341,253	0
2	253,750	0	210,004	313,547	245,882	341,253	331,439
3	280,000	420,000	420,007	376,257	345,882	411,253	453,108
4	315,000	420,000	455,008	376,257	345,882	411,253	463,551
5	341,250	420,000	455,008	376,257	345,882	411,252	474,308
End	0	0	0	0	0	0	(36,094)
TOTAL	**1,076,975**	**1,260,000**	**1,303,773**	**1,407,317**	**1,429,410**	**1,616,265**	**1,722,405**

Loss Factor—Building Efficiency

	Building A	Building B	Building C	Building D	Building E	Building F	Building G
Usable sq. ft.	15,625	15,625	15,487	15,847	20,346	15,351	15,419
% Loss Factor	12.0	12.0	13.0	13.0	0.0	14.0	13.5
Rentable sq. ft.	17,500	17,500	17,500	17,500	20,346	17,500	17,500

Effective Rent—Annual Average Rent

/Rentable sq. ft.	15.50	14.40	17.60	16.48	14.05	21.90	19.68
/Usable sq. ft.	17.36	16.13	19.89	18.63	14.05	24.97	22.34
Annual cost	215,395	252,000	260,755	281,463	285,882	323,253	344,481
After-tax cost	148,012	166,320	177,048	186,499	188,682	219,633	226,601

Factors that Compose Effective Rent

Gross/net lease	Gross	Gross	Gross	Gross	Gross	Gross	Gross
Starting rent*	9.50	24.00	24.00	21.50	17.00	19.50	24.75
Operating Expense†	6.75	6.81	0.00	0.00	0.00	6.30	6.00
Months free rent	0.0	24.00	18.00	14.00	0.00	0.00	15.00
Ave. yr. inc.†	2.50	0.00	0.50	0.00	0.00	1.00	0.59
Operating expense escalation %	(None used for this comparison)						
Last year rent	19.50	24.00	26.00	21.50	17.00	23.50	27.10

*Operating expense estimate added to net lease rent (to compare properly to gross lease).
†Part of rent.
~ Average annual effective/rentable sq. ft.—for increases.

Final Comparison—Annual Cost Differerence

Low to high	$0.00	$36,605	$45,360	$66,068	$70,487	$107,858	$129,086

Additional Fitup Cost per Rentable sq. ft. Over Best Allowance

$'s rent sq. ft.	—	7.00	6.00	—	4.00	—	—

9

Leasing and Letting

Pulse Points

- *The FM, representing the lessee (customer), has the opportunity and the requirement to protect the legal, financial, and physical aspects of the leased property that is being managed for the customer and the organization.*
- *The lease should provide a listing of business/financial elements that the FM can use to ensure that monthly lease and service payments to the landlord are accurately made.*
- *The lease should provide your customer and your organization with advantageous lease renewal terms, advantageous rates, upfit allowances, free rent, and so on.*
- *The FM should make a careful review of all lease escalation clauses, including a review of lease escalation invoices from the landlord.*
- *Property that is deemed unnecessary to the pursuit of the organization's objectives should be identified as surplus and divested.*
- *The specter of environmental liability under federal or state legislation over the last two decades has posed serious realty divestment problems for certain organizations.*
- *The breakeven amount can provide a beginning point, even though your initial buyout offer may be higher or lower than the breakeven amount.*
- *Each year, millions of dollars are lost by organizations and made by landlords because the tenant does not review the lease and does not have an audit program to ensure that lease and related expenses are accurate and correct.*

Keywords

Financial management, real estate terms, certificate of occupancy, landlord, options, rent, operating expenses, lease document, lease escalation clauses, capital costs, management expenses, taxes and insurance, disposing of assets, subleasing, donate property, environmental issues, breakeven point, total buyout obligation, net present value, sublease analysis, lease deposit

Introduction

Leasing and letting are two related aspects of property use. Leasing is the aspect in which an organization (lessee or tenant) chooses to occupy, for a fee (*rent*), a property or site that another entity owns or legally controls. Letting is the aspect in which a legal entity (lessor or *landlord*) owns or legally controls a property or site that is intended to produces income through the operation or occupancy of the property by a lessee.

The FM, representing the lessee (customer), has the opportunity and the requirement to protect the legal, financial, and physical elements of the leased property managed for the customer and the organization. This requires that the FM fully understand leasing from the landlord's perspective, the customer's lease requirements, and the business requirements of that lease, in order to support the FM's customer, who is occupying the leased space. In addition, the FM as the lessee must have a working relationship with the landlord, the lessor, that must be successfully managed. Conversely, the landlord should be providing the specific services required by the lease, providing a safe and secure building (inside and outside the building), and protecting the company's right to occupy the space.

This chapter will review many of the financial issues that the FM faces in the *financial management* of leased property. In many ways these are similar to the issues and requirements the landlord faces. But the landlord is expected to make a profit from the management of leased property while providing required services to tenants. The FM must manage lease and related costs and reduce expenses for the customer wherever possible.

Financial Management

You as the FM have a very important role in the financial management of the properties your customer or organization has obtained. Once the property or space has been occupied, the FM and the FM staff must manage the lease, understand the details of the business issues included in the lease, be familiar with the legal issues involved in the lease, and ensure that the landlord provides all the services required by the lease.

Note that the FM must clearly understand *real estate terms* and issues, and must seek assistance from a peer or consultant and sometimes from corporate legal counsel when lease issues arise with which the FM has no experience or in which she or he is uncertain of what should be done. For the most part, financial management of the lease should be straightforward if the FM is working with a good **lease document**. The lease should provide a listing of business/financial elements that the FM can use to ensure that monthly lease and service payments to the landlord are accurately made.

Certificate of Occupancy and Utilities

Your customer has moved into the leased facility, the punch list items and project close-out have been completed, and you or your landlord has received a certificate of occupancy from the local permitting authority. The *certificate of occupancy* is a key document, and the lease commencement date, or the start date of the lease, should be tied to the date on which it is obtained, as being the date on which your customer can operate the business from this new address. You may also wish to tie the lease commencement date to the acquisition of all or certain utilities, including the payment of utility deposits, that your customer must have in order to meet business requirements. If, for example, your customer requires two feeders of main electric power to the facility and only one has been installed, your lease may state that the lease start date will not occur and lease payments will not start until the second feeder has been installed.

Your landlord may have difficulty in providing the parking space your customer's staff requires. The space may be ready, but the site may not be completed. You should monitor the support services provided by the landlord, ensure that the free rent period is taken, and ensure that all the terms and conditions of the lease are being met. This may also include follow-up on customer and building budgets, signage, parking, keys, and janitorial and maintenance services; and ensuring that information on the correct monthly rent payment, rent and/or *operating expense* escalations, and the rent payment address is transmitted to the accounts payable department.

Options

When you review the lease document, it is not unusual for you to find that during the lease negotiation, one or more lease *option* periods were included. There may be a number of option periods with years for each and the dates that the options would begin and end, including the number of days notice that you are taking the option that must be given to the landlord. These options are there because either you or your customer believed that the customer would like to have a specific option to stay in the space. There could also be an option for other space within the property, in which case the amount of space being optioned; the amount of rent for the option period(s) and whether it is fixed, increases with the consumer price index (CPI), increases by a certain percentage per year, or is set at market; specific option information that may be unique to your location; the right of first refusal on specific floors or space; and other such information should be included in the lease.

The lease could also include options to purchase the space, building, site, or other item(s) (equipment, furnishings, license, etc.), in which case it should include the number of options to purchase that are available, the date on which each option is due, and the purchase cost for each option. Options to purchase can prove to be very beneficial, as your customer may need to control the building or site and this option could assist it in obtaining the building or site for a reasonable cost that was set a number of years ago.

The lease options should provide your customer and your organization with advantageous lease renewal terms, advantageous rates, upfit allowances, free rent, and so on. The lease should require that the tenant (your customer) notify the landlord in writing (see Figure 9-1) in a specific way by a specific time before the expiration of the current lease should the tenant wish to exercise the option to renew the lease in accordance with the option provisions of the lease.

Unfortunately, tenants sometimes forget to notify the landlord in writing of their desire to take the option. We know of at least one FM who lost his job because he failed to notify his landlord in writing concerning the option for a strategic facility, and this cost his organization more than $1 million in additional rent when a new lease had to be negotiated. Unless the notice is given in writing, the tenant, your customer, is in the unfortunate position of having to negotiate a new lease, or to relocate quickly if the landlord demands that the tenant move. Figure 9-1 provides an example of one method of notifying the landlord in writing of your customer's intent to exercise its option to renew the lease. The lease could also include an option to purchase the space/building/site, and the legal requirements in the lease must be carefully followed in order for your customer or organization to take advantage of the purchase option/opportunity.

Rent, Operating Expense Payments, and Other Such Payments

Almost all leases have an annual rent increase, which usually take effect after a year of the start of the lease, and an operating expense adjustment, which is often based on a calendar year (see Figure 9-2). The landlord's annual rent and operating expense escalation statements, and the statements should include all required backup information, should be reviewed in detail. You should review the backup information for justification of the amount of change in the Consumer Price Index (CPI) (if applicable) and operating expenses for the previous year, and you should check all mathematical calculations, including increases in the operating expenses. When you and your customer are satisfied that the increase(s) are in accordance with the terms and conditions of the lease, accounts payable should be advised accordingly and given the new rent payment amount.

A careful review should be made of all *lease escalation clauses*, and you should review the lease escalation invoices from your landlord to ensure that your company is making increased payments for only those items and expenses that are subject to escalation. With many tenants and leases to monitor and manage, the landlord's property management agent or company may inadvertently or as a matter of policy send out invoices without specifically reviewing each of the lease escalation clauses. It is important that you understand the invoice and challenge any item or amount that your customer is not obligated to pay.

A typical issue arises when you or your customer finds that your organization is paying or has paid too much in either rent or operating expenses. One of the authors has had experience reviewing many hundreds of rent and operating expense statements provided by landlords, and when these statements were reviewed in detail against the actual lease document and past historical costs, there have been a number of errors, some of them very large. The landlord should then be contacted for a possible refund. Also, you should be sure that operating expenses are based on actual expenses with actual receipts, especially for property

Figure 9-1. Option Notification Letter.

ABC COMPANY
4425 W. Wacker Drive
Suite 200
Chicago, IL 60630
(312) 555-7890

March 2, 2003   **CERTIFIED MAIL**
                                                    RETURN RECEIPT REQUESTED

Mr. Robert A. Thompson
Vice President—Property Management
West Wacker Towers, L.P.
4425 West Wacker Drive
Suite 2100
Chicago, IL 60630

      Re: West Wacker Towers
          4425 W. Wacker Drive
          Suite 200
          Chicago, IL 60630

Dear Mr. Thompson:

An option was included in a lease dated November 14, 1998, by and between West Wacker Towers, L.P., an Illinois Limited Partnership, with a place of business in Chicago, IL (the "Landlord), and ABC Company, a Delaware Organization with a place of business in Chicago, IL (the "Tenant").

As Tenant, ABC Company does hereby exercise its Option to renew the above lease for an additional term of five (5) years commencing (May 1, 2003) at the expiration of the initial five (5) year term of this lease (April 30, 2003) as stated in Article V of the lease.

The terms for the additional five (5) year period are as describe in the original lease that was referenced in the first paragraph including an additional renovation allowance of $5.00 per rentable square feet provided by the Landlord to the Tenant to paint and re-carpet Suite 200.

In Witness Whereof, the parties have executed this Option of a lease renewal on the following dates:

WITNESS   **ABC COMPANY**

_____   By: _____ Date _____ _____, 2003
                                 Raymond A. Samulson

                                 Its: <u>Vice President</u>

West Wacker Towers
4425 W. Wacker Drive
Suite 200
Chicago, IL 60630
Option Letter
March 2, 2003
Page 2

State of Illinois
County of Cook

The foregoing instrument was acknowledged before me this _____ day
of _____, 2003, by Raymond A. Samulson, Vice President,
ABC Company, a Delaware Organization on behalf of the Organization.

_____
(Notary Public)

My Commission Expires:

WITNESS   **WEST WACKER TOWERS, L.P.**

_____   BY: _____ DATE _____ _____, 2003
                                  Vincent C. Comer

                           ITS: General Partner

State of Illinois
County of Cook

The foregoing instrument was acknowledged before me this _____ day
of _____, 2003, by Vincent C. Comer, ———West
Wacker Towers, L.P., an Illinois Limited Partnership on behalf of the Limited Partnership.

_____
(Notary Public)

My Commission Expires:

Please sign, have both copies notarized and return one copy to me.

Sincerely,

William S. Roberts
Director of Facility Services

cc: Raymond A. Samulson
      West Wacker Towers/ABC Co. Suite 200 Lease File

Figure 9-2. Lease Operating Expense Escalation Letter.

WEST WACKER TOWERS, L.P.
4425 West Wacker Drive
Suite 2100
Chicago, IL 60630
(312) 555-3400

September 3, 2003

Mr. Bill Roberts
Facility Manager
ABC Company
4425 W. Wacker Drive
Suite 200
Chicago, IL 60630

      Re: 2003 Operating Expense Escalations for
          West Wacker Towers
          4425 W. Wacker Drive
          Suite 200
          Chicago, IL 60630

Dear Mr. Roberts:

Enclosed are the calculations and invoice that represent your proportionate share of the 2002/2003 expenses for the above referenced address.

Please feel free to call me if you have any questions concerning this matter.

Sincerely,

Robert A. Thompson
Vice President
Property Management

enclosures

cc: Linda B. Stone (w/enclosures)
     W. Wacker/ABC Co. file (w/enclosures)

WEST WACKER TOWERS, L.P.
4425 West Wacker Drive
Chicago, IL 60630

2002/2003—Building Operating Expenses:

Bldg. Sq. Ft.: 122,432

Run date: 9/01/2003

I. **OPERATING EXPENSES:**

Gas	$ 24,860
Electricity	141,921
Water & sewer	11,590
Repairs & maintenance	190,888
Electrical	15,663
Housekeeping/janitorial	112,614
Landscaping	16,160
Snow removal	5,800
Fire protection	9,224
Security	10,644
C/A improvements	9,352

    Total Operating Expenses   **$548,316**

II. **TAXES:**

County	$135,671
City	30,172
School	32,657

    Total Taxes   **$198,500**

III. **INSURANCE**   **$ 22,700**

IV. **TAX CONSULTANT'S FEE**   **$ 900**

V. **PROPERTY MANAGEMENT FEE**   **$ 80,000**

    TOTAL EXPENSES   **$850,816**

(continues)

Figure 9-2. (Continued).

WEST WACKER TOWERS, L.P.
4425 West Wacker Drive
Chicago, IL 60630

2002/2003—Suite 200 Operating Expenses:

Run date: 9/01/2003

ABC Company
Suite 200
Suite Sq. Ft   16,535 Rentable

ABC Company Pro Rata Share: 16,535 Sq. Ft. ÷ 122,432 Sq. Ft. = 0.13505

I. **OPERATING EXPENSES**	**$74,050**	
II. **TAXES:**	**$26,807**	
III. **INSURANCE**	**$3,066**	
IV. **TAX CONSULTANT'S FEE**	**$ 122**	
V. **PROPERTY MANAGEMENT FEE**	**$10,804**	
TOTAL EXPENSES		**$114,849**
TOTAL EXP. PAID BY ABC CO. IN 2003		**$112,531**
TOTAL DUE		**$ 2,318**

New Monthly 2003 Operating Expense Payment: $114,849 × 7% Increase =
$122,888 ÷ 12 Months = **$10,241 Per Month,** Due October 1, 2003, through
September 31, 2004.

taxes and utility bills for the property your customer occupies. There are also
consulting companies that will review all of the client's rent and operating expense statements; they generally charge a percentage of the amount of refunds
paid by landlords as their fee. Some of these firms appear to be very successful
for their clients.

The following are items that you should consider in your review of the lease
escalation clauses and associated invoices from your landlord:

- *Operating Expenses*
  - Maintenance costs
    —Maintenance contracts
    - Elevator
    - Filter service
    - Electrical
    - Mechanical
    - Snow removal
    - Controls service
    - Emergency power
    - Building automation
    - Trash removal
    —Salaries for employees
    - Fringe benefits
    - Uniforms
  - Repairs and replacements
    —Normal repairs
    - Electrical
    - Mechanical
    - Painting
    - Carpeting
    - Sun control (drapes, blinds, etc.)
    - Relamping
    - Filters
    —Landscaping (exterior and building common area)
    - Leasing and/or purchase costs
    - Plants
    - Plant replacement
    - Containers
    - Regular maintenance

- *Management Expenses*
  —Fees
  —Salary; fringes
  —Mark-up/accounting/finance
  —Telephone
  —Stationery and postage
  —Rent or cost of space
  —Security contract
  —Equipment
  —Vehicle
  - Utilities
  —Vehicle
  —Natural gas
  —Fuel oil
  —Water
  —Sewer
  —Electricity
  —Propane
  - Janitorial/housekeeping contract
  —Janitorial salaries
  —Fringe benefits
  —Uniforms
- *Capital Costs*
  - Amortized capital expenditures
  - Term of amortization
  - Interest
  - Financing costs
- *Miscellaneous Expenses*
  - Entertainment
  - Tax consultant
  - Bad debts
  - Taxes
  - Dues to related organizations
  - Meetings
  - Travel

If you have acquired property, then depending on how your organization is organized, your real estate work will include managing the property after your customer has moved in and project closeout has been completed. You may be required to work with the local fire department, develop building budgets, and provide facility and maintenance services. Your responsibilities may also include reviewing and monitoring operating expenses, monitoring facility and maintenance services and costs provided by others, ensuring that an appropriate insurance policy is in place, reviewing property tax invoices, and being aware of zoning and development issues and property values in the local area. Conversely, when you lease property, your landlord will develop an income and operating budget (see Figure 9-3) and provide maintenance services. The landlord will review and monitor operating expenses, maintenance and tenant services, building and site insurance, and billing of tenants for rent and operating expenses. If at some time in the future you are asked to take an owned customer property and develop it as an income-producing leased property, you would then become a landlord, and you would need to develop an income and operating budget similar to that in Figure 9-3.

Taxes and Insurance

Your lease may require you to pay property *taxes* directly to the local government authorities, or you may be required to pay a pro rata share based on the ratio of the rentable square footage that you are leasing to the total rentable square footage in the building in which your customer is leasing space. The amount of property taxes can be substantial or minor, depending upon your location and the type of facility. With today's increasing property taxes, many organizations will hire consultants to research current tax rates being paid by similar businesses in order to ensure that the organization is not paying more than it should be paying. These consultants can also assist the organization in reviewing bills, payments, and petitions for review of the current appraised values.

Insurance is a very important requirement for leased and purchased property. The landlord may require a certificate of insurance before allowing a tenant to move in. Your risk management manager should be kept informed of the projects that are being started, when they will be completed, and when they will be occupied. The risk management manager should also review the insurance requirements in a lease before the lease is signed to ensure that it includes no unfavorable insurance requirements. Also, the risk management manager will often request a replacement cost estimate for owned facilities from you to ensure that the organization's assets are fully protected (see Figure 9-4). Taxes and insurance can be very expensive and should be reviewed before the project is approved by the parent company and your customer.

Disposing of Assets

Organizations change management, change direction, grow, or decline. As your organization goes through these cycles, you may find that leased space has been vacated or owned property is now surplus, and that the space or property is not required to meet the organization's immediate business plans.

Your organization or customer may wish to keep the vacant leased space or surplus owned property and be willing to carry the ongoing costs if there will be a business need for it in the near future. However, property that is deemed unnecessary to the pursuit of the organization's objectives should be identified as surplus and the organization's interest therein divested. This is a rule that should

Figure 9-3. ABC Building Income and Operating Budget—2003.

ABC BUILDING (ACCOUNT NO. 1456)
INCOME AND OPERATING PLAN
2003

JANUARY 5, 2003
PREPARED BY: STEVEN ADAMS

CODE	ACCOUNT	JAN	FEB	MAR	APR	MAY	JUN	JUL	AUG	SEP	OCT	NOV	DEC	TOTAL
42260	RENTAL INCOME	163,014.00	163,269.00	171,112.00	169,972.00	170,026.00	170,472.00	171,220.00	172,248.00	172,362.00	172,362.00	173,480.00	173,608.00	2,043,145.00
	EXPENSES													
42264	Utilities													
	Electric	9,559.00	8,869.00	9,089.00	10,078.00	10,622.00	15,359.00	14,323.00	15,215.00	15,878.00	14,744.00	10,207.00	7,978.00	141,921.00
	Gas/Fuel Oil	4,042.00	4,417.00	4,716.00	2,795.00	1,152.00	679.00	35.00	35.00	35.00	150.00	2,079.00	4,725.00	24,860.00
	Water	0.00	0.00	2,576.00	0.00	2,767.00	0.00	0.00	0.00	3,360.00	0.00	2,887.00	0.00	11,590.00
	Total Utilities	13,601.00	13,286.00	16,381.00	12,873.00	14,541.00	16,038.00	14,358.00	15,250.00	19,273.00	14,894.00	15,173.00	12,703.00	178,371.00
42269	Mechanical	13,421.00	30,971.00	18,821.00	14,621.00	15,571.00	13,421.00	13,421.00	14,971.00	15,030.00	13,430.00	13,780.00	13,430.00	190,888.00
42270	Electrical	2,676.00	2,325.00	450.00	450.00	825.00	3,887.00	450.00	2,425.00	450.00	450.00	825.00	450.00	15,663.00
42274	Fire Protection	3,126.00	573.00	62.00	244.00	231.00	62.00	244.00	4,063.00	62.00	254.00	241.00	62.00	9,224.00
42267	Cleaning	9,154.00	9,154.00	9,154.00	9,154.00	11,920.00	9,154.00	9,154.00	9,154.00	9,154.00	9,154.00	9,154.00	9,154.00	112,614.00
42268	Landscaping	955.00	955.00	985.00	985.00	4,185.00	985.00	985.00	985.00	985.00	2,185.00	985.00	985.00	16,160.00
42273	Security	808.00	808.00	808.00	808.00	808.00	1,372.00	872.00	872.00	872.00	872.00	872.00	872.00	10,644.00
42271	Elevators	872.00	872.00	872.00	898.00	898.00	898.00	898.00	898.00	898.00	898.00	898.00	898.00	10,698.00
42269	Snow Removal	1,400.00	1,200.00	0.00	0.00	0.00	0.00	0.00	0.00	0.00	0.00	750.00	500.00	3,850.00
42269	Miscellaneous	485.00	799.00	785.00	1,335.00	1,045.00	1,206.00	1,292.00	806.00	542.00	492.00	806.00	492.00	10,085.00
42924	Management Fee	6,655.00	6,655.00	6,655.00	6,655.00	6,655.00	6,655.00	6,655.00	6,655.00	6,655.00	6,655.00	6,655.00	6,655.00	79,860.00
42280	Taxes/Insurance	0.00	0.00	0.00	0.00	0.00	0.00	0.00	0.00	198,535.00	0.00	0.00	0.00	198,535.00
42265	EWO Work	0.00	0.00	0.00	0.00	0.00	0.00	0.00	0.00	0.00	0.00	0.00	0.00	0.00
10504	Leasehold Improv	0.00	0.00	0.00	0.00	5,000.00	0.00	0.00	0.00	0.00	0.00	0.00	0.00	5,000.00
	Total Expenses	53,153.00	67,598.00	54,973.00	48,023.00	61,679.00	53,678.00	48,329.00	56,079.00	252,456.00	49,284.00	50,139.00	46,201.00	841,592.00
	OPERATING INCOME	109,861.00	95,671.00	116,139.00	121,949.00	108,347.00	116,794.00	122,891.00	116,169.00	(80,094.00)	123,078.00	123,341.00	127,407.00	1,201,553.00
42265	SWITCH EXPENSES													
	Maintenance	0.00	6,678.00	0.00	0.00	6,678.00	0.00	0.00	6,678.00	0.00	0.00	6,678.00	0.00	26,712.00
	XYZ CORP. Payments	(4,913.00)	(4,913.00)	(4,913.00)	(4,913.00)	(4,913.00)	(4,913.00)	(4,913.00)	(4,913.00)	(4,913.00)	(4,913.00)	(4,913.00)	(4,913.00)	(58,956.00)
	Total Switch	(4,913.00)	1,765.00	(4,913.00)	(4,913.00)	1,765.00	(4,913.00)	(4,913.00)	1,765.00	(4,913.00)	(4,913.00)	1,765.00	(4,913.00)	(32,244.00)
	NET OPERATING INCOME	114,774.00	93,906.00	121,052.00	126,862.00	106,582.00	121,707.00	127,804.00	114,404.00	(75,181.00)	127,991.00	121,576.00	132,320.00	1,233,797.00
	CHECKBOOK BALANCE													
	Account Minimum	5,000.00	5,000.00	5,000.00	5,000.00	5,000.00	5,000.00	5,000.00	5,000.00	5,000.00	5,000.00	5,000.00	5,000.00	
	Net Oper Income	114,774.00	93,906.00	121,052.00	126,862.00	106,582.00	121,707.00	127,804.00	114,404.00	(75,181.00)	127,991.00	121,576.00	132,320.00	
	ABC COMPANY A/C	0.00	0.00	0.00	0.00	0.00	0.00	0.00	0.00	0.00	0.00	0.00	0.00	
	Transfer to ABC CO.	(114,774.00)	(93,906.00)	(121,052.00)	(126,862.00)	(106,582.00)	(121,707.00)	(127,804.00)	(114,404.00)	75,181.00	(127,991.00)	(121,576.00)	(132,320.00)	
	Balance Sheet Items	20,027.21	20,027.21	20,027.21	20,027.21	20,027.21	20,027.21	20,027.21	20,027.21	20,027.21	20,027.21	20,027.21	20,027.21	
	MONTH END BALANCE	25,027.21	25,027.21	25,027.21	25,027.21	25,027.21	25,027.21	25,027.21	25,027.21	25,027.21	25,027.21	25,027.21	25,027.21	

Figure 9-4. Replacement Cost.

MEMO

FROM: Bill Roberts   **DATE:**   June 18, 2003

TO: Risk Management   **SUBJECT:** Replacement Cost
                                                                              ABC Building
                                                                              3215 North Michigan Ave.
                                                                              Chicago, IL

The XYZ Building is approximately 97% occupied, and per your request, the following is our estimated replacement cost for this building:

Construction Cost Method	*Lost Income Method*
• Building = 130,000 Gross S.F.	• 2003 Lease Income = $ 2,035,000
• Land = 5.57 Acres	
• Land & Bldg. Cost = $150/G.S.F.	• Income Value = $156.50/G.S.F.
• Land & Bldg. Cost = $19,500,000	• 10 Year Value = $20,350,000
• Less Land Cost = $ 1,100,000	• Less Land Cost = $ 1,100,000
• Construction Cost = **$18,400,000**	• Lost Income = **$19,250,000**

We feel that for insurance purposes, the minimum replacement cost in 2003 would be $18,400,000.
cc: ABC Building file

have no exceptions. For example, if a new property will better serve the organization, the old property should not be ignored, but should be considered surplus and sold. On the other hand, if the organization does not need a property for current operations, yet determines that it should be held for future use, the property is not surplus.

If, with the objective of enhancing corporate profitability, an organization determines that it should lease or sublease idle space for which it has identified no current or future use, that space is *not* surplus. It is a key asset in the organization's (presumably) new business mission, effectively or in fact. However, in this situation, the organization either has made or should make a clear statement of its intention to be active in the business of real estate investment (at least with respect to this property), since it is now competing in a new marketplace for profitability, rather than for income that might offset the cost of carrying idle property held for a separate purpose.

The determination that a property is surplus should be made as quickly as possible, for the cost of carrying idle assets can be very substantial. Moreover, in the case of owned surplus property, the proceeds from the disposition of the property can also be substantial, and of considerable aid to the organization's cash position. Therefore, in addition to the "out-of-pocket" carrying costs, the actual carrying cost of surplus real estate also includes the cost of the capital that has not been realized by virtue of the continued holding of and investment in unproductive property. Finally, once the determination that the property is surplus has been made, the organization should act quickly to dispose of the property in the most profitable manner.

If there are no business plans to use the vacant leased space or surplus owned property, the large monthly carrying expenses and the accompanying legal issues will usually dictate timely disposal of the space or property. You and your customer should review the financial, legal, and market issues with your legal counsel and real estate broker and then adopt a disposal marketing strategy, which could include one of the following:

- Locate another in-house division or department that can use the space and/ or property and is willing to take over all or part of the remaining obligation.
- Sublease all or part of the space or property, if leased.
- Negotiate a buyout of the remaining lease obligation.
- Sell, if owned.
- Lease all or part of the space or property, if owned.
- *Donate*, if owned, to a government agency, a nonprofit organization, or a university or college when a tax credit could benefit your organization and your customer.

There will always be some costs involved in the disposal of property (e.g., commissions, carrying costs, perhaps some deferred maintenance, and so on). Therefore, in order to determine the net benefit, some form of cost-benefit analysis should be implemented, using present value methods, if necessary. Attempting to convey an interest in real estate for some reasonable amount of consideration (i.e., money or other items of value) may also require marketing savvy. Disposing of property involves much more than just putting up a "For Sale" sign. Even the most straightforward disposal can be a complicated matter. Considerations such as broker selection and even splitting the fee with cooperating brokers are currently receiving much examination in the literature.

While the prompt (though not hasty) disposition of surplus property is always in order, there may be, from time to time, certain constraints on disposing of property of which you and your customer should be aware. The most obvious is the simple lack of a strong enough market, with the result that buyers are few or marketing time is long. Sometimes, because of the nature of the property, its location, or the improvements that have been made to it, there are no ready buyers, even in an otherwise strong general commercial market. For example, a massive mid-rise brick and concrete slaughterhouse in a suburb of a major metropolitan area stood idle for many years following the termination of its operations. While hundreds of thousands of square feet were available, the cost of converting it to another use was prohibitively high. In addition, while the site would have been a valuable location for an industrial park, the cost to raze the mid-rise structure, which had been built very sturdily to accommodate the production process, was more than the land value. The only buyer ended up being the local development authority, which acquired the property at a questionable price and incurred the cost of razing the structure simply to stimulate development in an area that was deteriorating as a result of this property's having been idle for so long.

Environmental issues, especially the specter of environmental liability under federal or state legislation enacted over the last two decades, have also posed serious real estate divestment problems for certain organizations. In years past, disposing of toxic waste by putting it in the ground at or near the site where it was produced was a not uncommon practice, even for the federal government. In most instances, the waste can no longer be recovered or treated, except at extraordinary expense. Nobody wants to buy trouble. Therefore, even if the property is no longer of use to its owner, it is unlikely that it will ever be sold. Asbestos in buildings poses a similar problem. Many investors will not acquire properties that contain asbestos. Even willing buyers typically approach the matter prudently by requiring that the seller remove the asbestos at its own cost as part of a buy/sell agreement. If the cost to cure the asbestos problem exceeds the property's value, which can happen, selling the property may not be cost-effective.

Finally, even when a property is both marketable and in demand, there may be legal hurdles or prohibitions that prevent disposition. Perhaps the most common such hurdle is a prohibition on subletting or assigning leased space. Reasonably constructed lease clauses that restrict the corporate lessee from *subleasing* or assigning a lease to a third party by requiring the lessor's consent are often upheld if they are challenged in court or ignored. The court's rationale respects the lessor's interest in protecting the value and income stream from the property, which might be put in jeopardy by an unwelcome tenant. While corporate property owned in fee simple may generally be sold in spite of "alienation" restrictions included in the deed, there may be other hurdles that can complicate the disposal.

If another in-house user cannot be located, listing the space and/or property with a real estate broker may be part of the disposal strategy. The listing real estate broker should be chosen with the same care as the leasing or purchase real estate broker was chosen, as you, representing your organization or customer, now become a landlord or seller of the space or property, competing with other landlords and/or sellers in the local market. A subleasing model of before-tax income or loss or an acceptable sales price should be developed in accordance with corporate policies and procedures and what you, your customer, and the listing broker agree is realistic given market conditions (see Figure 9-5).

The timing and associated economic/real estate activity will indicate whether this is a "seller's" or a "buyer's" market. When you are subleasing, leasing, or selling space or property, market conditions and how anxious your customer is to divest the space or property will often affect the time it will take to dispose of the asset.

The expense items to be considered when subleasing space or leasing prop-

Figure 9-5. Sublease Analysis Spreadsheet.

XYZBLDG1.WK1 PAGE 1	SUBTENANT: C.O.D. CORPORATION—SUBLEASING P & L SUBLANDLORD: ABC COMPANY—FINANCIAL ANALYSIS #1	(NAME OF PREPARER) (DATE ANALYSIS MADE)

		ABC COMPANY Lease Information:	
Building & Address:	XYZ BUILDING, 1234 MAIN STREET	Lease Ends:	OCTOBER 31, 2008
City, St. & Zip:	CHICAGO, IL. 50515-1234	Total Leased Area:	25,250 Rentable Square Feet (R.S.F.)
Subl. Fl.(s):	7TH FLOOR (SUITE 703)	Rentable To	22,250 Usable Square Feet (U.S.F.)
Subleased Area:	17,022 Rentable Square Feet (R.S.F.) 15,000 Usable Square Feet (U.S.F.)	Usable Factor:	88.119%
		Current Lease Rate:	$19.00 /R.S.F.
Subl. Start Date:	NOVEMBER 1, 2002	Lease Rent Increase:	104.50% Per Lease Year
Subl. Term/End Date:	72 MONTHS—OCTOBER 31, 2008	Income Tax Rate:	0.34 % Of Before Tax Income Or (Loss)
Sublease Rate:	$20.00 /R.S.F.	Net Present Value:	0.08 %
Subl. Allowances:	$15.00 /R.S.F. For Upfit	Sublandlord Upfit:	$0.00 /RSF For Multi-Tenant Construction
Subl. Rent Increase:	103.50% PER SUBLEASE YEAR	Brokerage	6.00%
Subl. Rent	12 MOS.—RENT STARTS NOV. 1, 2003.	Commission	
Abatement:		Space Planning, Etc.	$0.75 /RSF
	2 MOS. IN 2002	Park. Sp. Cost Incr.	103.50% Per Lease Year
	10 MOS. IN 2003	# of Parking Spaces:	67 Cost/Sp./Mo. $30 Thru 10/03
# of Parking Spaces:	45 Cost/Sp./Mo $30 THRU 10/03		

(continues)

Figure 9-5. (Continued).

	Year 0	2002 (2 MO.)	2003 (12 MO.)	2004 (12 MO.)	2005 (12 MO.)	2006 (12 MO.)	2007 (12 MO.)	2008 (10 MO.)	TOTAL (6 YRS 0 MO)
Sublease Revenues:									
Rent Income		$56,742	$342,435	$354,421	$366,825	$379,664	$392,952	$336,956	$2,229,996
Parking Income		$2,700	$16,295	$16,865	$17,455	$18,066	$18,698	$16,034	$106,112
Less Rent Abatement		($56,742)	($283,708)	$0	$0	$0	$0	$0	($340,449)
NET REVENUES		$2,700	$75,022	$371,285	$384,280	$397,730	$411,651	$352,990	$1,995,659
EFFECTIVE RENT $19.54 /R.S.F.									
Tenant Part of Upfit Cost:	$0								
ABC COMPANY EXPENSES:									
Space Planning, Etc.	$12,767								$12,767
Brokerage Fee	$113,373								$113,373
Upfit/Depreciation	$255,337	$7,093	$42,556	$42,556	$42,556	$42,556	$42,556	$35,463	$255,337
Rent & Oper Expense	N/A	$53,904	$325,853	$340,516	$355,839	$371,852	$388,585	$335,874	$2,172,424
Parking Expense	N/A	$2,700	$16,295	$16,865	$17,455	$18,066	$18,698	$16,034	$106,112
TOTAL EXPENSES	$381,477	$63,697	$384,703	$399,937	$415,851	$432,474	$449,840	$387,371	$2,660,013
NET EFF. RENT $16.91 /R.S.F.									
CUM. BEFORE TAX INC.(LOSS):	($126,140)	($187,137)	($496,818)	($525,470)	($557,040)	($591,784)	($629,973)	($664,354)	
CUM. YEARLY INCOME (LOSS):	$0	($187,137)	($309,681)	($28,652)	($31,570)	($34,744)	($38,189)	($34,382)	
BEFORE TAX INCOME OR (LOSS):									($664,354)
INCOME TAXES:									$225,880
NET INCOME OR (LOSS):									($438,474)
Tenant Improvements:	($255,337)								
Add Back Depreciation:		$7,093	$42,556	$42,556	$42,556	$42,556	$42,556	$35,463	$255,337
NET CASH FLOW:	($255,337)	$7,093	$42,556	$42,556	$42,556	$42,556	$42,556	$35,463	($183,137)
NPV (THRU 10/31/08) =	($157,010)								

INITIAL MODEL FOR 7TH FLOOR

PROJECTED INCOME OR (LOSS) = ($664,354)

PROJECTED INCOME OR (LOSS) = ($670,354)

ADDITIONAL INCOME OR (LOSS) = $6,000

erty will include such items as the lease or mortgage payments for the remaining term of the obligation, insurance, a percentage commission for the listing real estate broker, space planning fees, permits, construction and depreciation costs, and income taxes, among other factors. Once you have found a tenant to sublease your surplus leased property, a sublease agreement should be prepared based upon your prime lease and your landlord's approval.

The expense items to be considered when selling a property will include such items as the mortgage payments, the cost of capital or interest, taxes and insurance, maintenance and operating costs, service contracts, a percentage commission to the listing real estate broker, and often a part of the closing costs.

A buyout of the lease is another option that may be viable if your landlord should need your space for an existing tenant or for a new tenant. If the landlord has too much vacant space, if there is an overabundance of similar space on the market, or if you are currently paying market or above-market rent, the landlord usually will not consider a lease buyout.

However, if the landlord needs cash, has a very qualified tenant ready to take over your space at a higher rate than you are paying, or can provide a more marketable space or contiguous floor area to sign a new tenant if your space is available, the landlord *may* consider a buyout of your lease. The buyout must provide the landlord with an economic benefit, and it is usually up to the tenant (you or your customer) to make the initial offer on the buyout amount. This cash buyout should take into account:

- The remaining value of the space at the current rate times the time remaining on the lease
- Plus or minus the remaining value of the space at today's market rate times the time remaining on the lease
- Plus a recapture of the value of the remaining undepreciated improvements made by the landlord
- Plus a recapture of the value of a pro rata amount of any other costs or cash inducements (moving costs, and so on)
- Plus a recapture of the pro rata value of the number of months of free rent (if any)
- Plus a recapture of a pro rata value of design and project management fees
- Plus a recapture of a pro rata value of the real estate commissions paid by the landlord
- Plus an estimated marketing cost to acquire a new tenant

All of these values are totaled, and the **net present value** (NPV) of this total will tell you or the landlord what the value today of the total is, taking into account the time value of money; it is the **breakeven point** for the proposed buyout. To obtain the net present value, you will need to determine the financial value of money today. This financial value of money is usually the rate of interest that your company or the landlord would have to pay in order to borrow money from a financial institution.

The breakeven point amount *can* provide a starting point for determining your initial buyout offer, which may be higher or lower than the breakeven amount. The landlord may or may not accept your initial offer, depending on the market, the landlord's need for cash *now*, and how much the landlord feels your company is willing to pay to get out of the lease. Again, your negotiation skills along with strategy and assistance from your real estate broker, can help in establishing your initial offer, subsequent offers, and your final offer.

A lease buyout can be very beneficial to your customer and your organization in that it removes a legal and financial obligation from today's balance sheet. It is important that you and your legal counsel review this document carefully to ensure that the buyout amount is the *final* payment and that your customer will have *no* further obligations to the landlord for this space. This document should remove all liability from your customer for *all* past or future additional rents, costs, expenses, liens, fees, taxes, or assessments. After the buyout is complete, it is not unusual to receive a bill(s) later for additional operating expenses, fees, or taxes on the space, and your buyout document should protect your customer from any further legal or financial requirements related to the space.

Example

ABC Company currently is a tenant in the XYZ Building, a downtown mid-rise building. The company is planning to relocate the operation in the XYZ Building to another city and believes that the relocation will provide considerable marketing and income opportunities. However, at the time the company will be relocating the operation, there will be thirty-six months remaining on the current five-year lease. The company does not want to sublease the space, but wishes to buy out the remaining lease commitment. The local real estate market surrounding the XYZ Building is soft, and the XYZ Building is 30 percent vacant. However, you understand that the landlord of the XYZ Building needs cash and might consider a buy-out of the lease, but will not make you an offer. What offer could (should) you make to the landlord?

Before you make an offer, you will need to take into account the issues that the landlord will consider, as described earlier. Based on the lease agreement, the following is one approach to looking at your and the landlord's remaining investment in the lease space:

- Total leased area: 25,550 rentable square feet (RSF)
- Current lease rate: $18.00/RSF
- Lease rent increase: 3% per year
- NPV rate: 8%

	2003	2004	2005	2006	Total
• ABC Company expenses	(9 mo.)	(12 mo.)	(12 mo.)	(3 mo.)	(3 yrs 0 mo.)
—Upfit/depreciation	$ 24,388	$ 32,518	$ 32,518	$ 8,130	$ 97,554
—Rent & operating expenses	$374,165	$513,852	$529,268	$133,288	$1,550,573
Total Expenses	$398,553	$546,371	$561,786	$141,417	**$1,648,127**

• Recapture expenses	(9 mo.)	(12 mo.)	(12 mo.)	(3 mo.)	(3 yrs 0 mo.)
—Recapture of undepreciated improvements	$ 8,130	$ 32,518	$ 32,518	$ 8,130	$ 81,295
—Recapture of 6 months free rent & 4 months marketing expenses	$337,357				$337,357

• Recapture expenses	(9 mo.)	(12 mo.)	(12 mo.)	(3 mo.)	(3 yrs 0 mo.)
—Recapture of fees & commissions	$ 6,676	$ 27,252	$ 27,997	$ 8,858	$ 70,783
—36 Months Recapture Costs					$ 489,435
Total Possible Buyout Obligation					**$2,137,562**

As you can see from this calculation, the remaining rent and depreciation on premises improvements due to the landlord over the 36-month period is $1,648,127. The recapture of prior expenses and projected expenses totals $489,435. So we know that the *total possible buyout obligation* may be approximately $2,137,562 in future dollars. If we take a net present value rate of 8 percent and apply this to the cash requirements for each year, we can determine the total dollar value that the future $2,137,562 represents today.

Once we have the possible buyout breakeven number, this number becomes the basis for the initial buyout offer to the landlord. It is not uncommon to offer the landlord one-half the breakeven number or less as an initial buyout offer and then, depending on the landlord's response, either continue with negotiations or call off the buyout process. Some landlords will negotiate and some will not, depending on what you are paying, their vacancy rate, their cash flow situation, their current debt service requirements, their relationship with their mortgage lender or financial partner, and the marketing prospects for the building and for leasing the space you propose to vacate at a higher rate than you are currently paying.

Sublease Analysis Spreadsheet

The *sublease analysis* as shown in Figure 9-5 was designed by one of the authors as a tool. It allows you to use a spreadsheet software program to help develop a model of the income or loss for a subleased property based on the local real estate market, competition, and the size/remaining time left on the current lease. The model can then be used to run numerous iterations to help you (the sublandlord) develop a subleasing strategy and run a pro forma for each particular proposed subtenant to help you make an informed management and real estate decision.

To use this spreadsheet format, you must have a basic knowledge of a spreadsheet software product such as Lotus or Excel, and of the modification and/or development of the spreadsheet formulas. Also, you should be familiar with the real estate terminology used and with lease and sublease analysis techniques.

The spreadsheet is set up for subleasing office space. You must be able to provide all the variables in the upper part of the spreadsheet shown in Figure 9-5.

- If some of the items do not apply to a particular analysis, a zero should be entered in the variable cell rather than leaving it blank.
- If an item or items do not appear on this spreadsheet, you should include them as a separate line item (e.g., electricity or real estate taxes); new items can be added. You must be aware of how these items will affect the existing formulas and the analysis results. Items in the spreadsheet below the line of asterisks should also be modified to suit the particular analysis.
- If the sublease term is less than six years, which most are, it will be necessary to modify the formula for the initial year to reflect the specific starting month and date of the sublease. The formula for the sixth year assumes a partial year and will need to be modified to meet the particular sublease termination date.
- Each year of the analysis may need to be modified manually to reflect the particular lease term.

Based on the variable items and the modifications to the cell formulas, the spreadsheet analysis should take place automatically as the input variables are entered. It is recommended that the initial results be checked manually to ensure that the modifications to the formulas reflect the correct sublease terms and expected income or loss.

The spreadsheet formulas use the variable information that is contained within the unprotected variable cells. The protected cells are the headings for variable or nonvariable items. Note that the variable information must be entered within the cell width and in the proper Lotus or Excel format for formula use to obtain a meaningful analysis.

The sublease analysis spreadsheet provides you with an organized methodology for establishing a subleasing program for each property to be subleased and will help you to understand the impact of each sublease on cash flow and on your company's or your customer's bottom line. The spreadsheet shown in Figure 9-5 is not fully automated, and you will need to spend some time reviewing how the spreadsheet works, the formulas used, and how best to tailor modifications to take advantage of the power and speed of this computer-aided real estate tool.

Other Expense Issues

When you assist your customer in moving to a new location, you should also review the lease to see if it requires any payments to the landlord after move-out to put the space back the way it was before your customer moved in, to pay for any cleanup of the vacated space, and/or to pay any special taxes or other expenses that the municipality may charge and for which the landlord can invoice your customer after move-out.

The lease may also cite the previous payment of a *lease deposit*, and that amount, which can be many thousands of dollars, should be due back to you or your client. The author has seen numerous cases where a customer has moved out of a space and did not request the deposit back. Few landlords go out of their way to ensure that deposits are sent back to vacating tenants unless the tenant requests the refund. It is always a good policy to keep a photocopy of the deposit check in the lease file, as some landlords have poor records that may not show that a deposit was paid by your customer three, five, or ten years before, when the space was first occupied.

Conclusion

This chapter has covered a number of financial issues that need to be managed and reviewed in a systematic manner. It is our opinion that millions of dollars are lost each year by organizations and made each year by landlords because the tenant does not review the lease and does not have an audit program to ensure that lease and related expenses are accurate and correct. Many accounts payable departments pay the bills they are requested to pay, and it is our opinion that the FM must be the person to review and audit all rent and related bills. The FM must also look at all leases to ensure that the landlord is meeting its physical and security requirements for the FM's customer. All future lease options, upfit allowances, purchase options, or option monies/space must be identified and budgeted for in a timely manner, and the FM must ensure that the customer is aware of related cost and business issues so that it can make the best strategic use of its lease obligations, both now and in the future.

10

Communications and Leadership

Pulse Points

- *The FM must be able to communicate with senior management and staff and to understand the business language that leaders use, especially in the analysis and decision-making processes.*
- *A top leadership priority for the FM should be communicating his leadership agenda to staff, management, and his customers.*
- *The FM should know how to communicate in business terms, written and spoken, to senior management and to related organization staff.*
- *The FM can use responsiveness as a communication tool to get timely financial and project information to the FM team, coworkers, customers, management, and suppliers.*
- *There are times when the FM must look at and understand what he or she can do to improve financial and operational performance in order to help the organization meet stated goals.*
- *The economic engine is what drives an organization's ability to continue in business and is part of what the FM must understand in the financial aspects of measuring success.*
- *The FM has many ways to share and communicate information, reports, events, and so on, whether in person on a one-to-one basis, via written material and/or a formal presentation, through staff, or through the Internet/Web site.*

Keywords

Communicating, leader, listening, sharing, preparing, alignment, stories, influencing, the language of business, delivering communication, automation, Internet, Web site, operational issues, strategic programs, proactive, voicemail, information, finance, great organization, economy, core values, purpose, service, learning, vision, mission, change, management, conflict, diversity, commitment, results, judgment, anticipating, technology, human resources, coalitions, systematic

Introduction

The ability to communicate effectively both orally and in writing is a basic business and *management* requirement for all FMs. This is especially important because the FM is a boundary spanner between the technical, business, and financial aspects of the FM services, communications, and products provided to the department's customers. The FM must be able to communicate with senior management and staff and to understand the business language that leaders use, especially in the analysis and decision-making processes.

To this end, this chapter will focus on the business communication and leadership skills that FMs must develop and use, both internally and externally, and will address some of the ways we believe the FM should be developing these skills.

Communications and Leadership

Today corporate leaders must cut through the clutter, focus their leadership agenda, and endlessly persuade. A top leadership priority for the FM should be *communicating* his or her leadership agenda to staff, management, and customers. Business leaders, including FMs, are under enormous pressure to sell their corporate strategies and financial requirements to their best customers, employees, and senior leadership. In an economic downturn, influence skills and communication only increase in importance.

The best leaders, whom FMs need to emulate, use a thoughtful and *systematic* approach to communicating their leadership agenda. They have mastered seven skills:

1. *Listen.* The leadership team has forged a new strategic direction. Now it's time to execute. But before executing the new direction, the FM must listen. Start with some inward reflection. Think through what you want to say and why. Once you have found your authentic voice, listen to others. Test arguments and explore new ideas. Far from being dogmatic or arrogant, the best FM communicators learn about the people they hope to influence—their needs, aspirations, and concerns.

2. *Prepare. Influencing* requires careful preparation and planning. Take time to research and develop ideas. Think through an influence strategy before starting to communicate. Don't go straight from inspiration to communication without preparation and testing.

3. *Align FM messages strategically.* Remember, everything the FM says and does sends a message: the FM's passion; the clarity of the FM's ideas, policies,

and business practices; the organization structure; who makes decisions; who gets promoted; and who gets fired. The best communicators ensure that all their messages—whether formal (corporate speak), organizational (policies and practices), or personal (what you say)—are aligned with the organization's core business strategies, their own personal values, and their behavior.

4. *Feel passionate.* The FM should pursue the ideas and values she or he feels passionate about and communicate that passion to others. If the FM does not do this, he will never connect emotionally with the audience and win them over to a shared *vision* and course of action. The best FM leaders draw upon their emotions to get buy-in from their customers. They understand that people's hearts and souls are often greater motivators than pure reason alone.

5. *Use vivid language and compelling **stories**.* In order to influence, the FM must position his arguments and present vivid supporting evidence. There is just as much strategy in how the FM presents his position as in the position itself. The FM should use graphics to enhance his or her message. And tell a story. Storytelling is a powerful tool in a leader's literary basket.

6. *Influence continually.* Seldom will the FM win over all the critical stakeholders to the leadership agenda on the first try. Rapid communication can never replace a systematic and thoughtful approach to winning people over to the FM's agenda. The best leaders view influencing as an ongoing process that is linked to a larger strategy for *change*. Persuasion often demands *listening* to the people the FM is trying to influence, testing the message, incorporating feedback, developing new messages, retesting, making compromises, and then trying again. Yes, this process can be time-consuming and difficult. But the credibility and influence the FM will gain will make it worthwhile.[1]

7. *Using the language of business.* The FM should look at all discussions, meetings, and presentations with or to management as opportunities to couch all strategic, budget, and operational arguments in financial terms as appropriate and use the *language of business* to sell them. It is important that the FM know the language of business and use it to provide training to the FM staff to help them in their FM development.

How to Talk to a CFO (Appendix A)

This is absolutely one of the finest articles ever written on communications for the FM. Thomas McCune, in presenting ten concepts, reinforces the themes of this book, stresses the importance of being able to communicate in business terms, and explains how to do this. Brutally frank and often funny, McCune's presentation is a classic that should be read and followed by all facility managers, particularly those who do not have a business degree. For more information, contact Thomas McCune at *www.AEPragmatics.com* or *www.ifma.org*.

Responsiveness: The Key to an Effective FM's Corporate Communication Effort

Today, an FM's ability to deliver a financial and business message and to communicate that message to customers and senior management depends not so much on the subtle intangibles of "positioning," but rather on the measurable immediacy of the FM's and the FM staff's responsiveness. Some organizations do not have a culture of financial or business responsiveness, and the FM and her or his staff must be aware of how much *information* can be shared with their customers.

In a high-pressure era of instant communications, round-the-clock deadlines, and global customers who are open when the FM's operations are closed, "right now" is often not soon enough. A "no comment" uttered by the FM organization on a financial or business issue can brand the FM and his operation as a failure or worse, even though the FM only meant to stall for a little time.

Yet it's hard to be responsive when customers are calling and want to know more financial details about an issue that they believe to be very important. The solution for the FM may lie in preparation, *automation*, the organization's *Web site*, and the ability to intelligently funnel callers to the right resource. Some FM organizations have developed an intranet Web site where their customers can view information and develop financial and project reports on demand. This permits the customer to review financial and/or project progress at any time. This customer *service* program has reduced the cost of FM department report development, reduced the number of reports sent out each month, and saved a large amount of paper, as the customer now decides what reports are important and prints what it needs.

The facility manager at times faces *operational* and technical *issues*, either internally to his customers or externally to his suppliers and the public, that can be equally daunting. What operational, financial, service, maintenance, safety, or emergency information should be provided, and with whom, when, and how should information be shared? The FM, in coordination with senior leadership, *human resources*, *finance*, public relations, marketing, and other departments, must ensure that the communications developed are in keeping with the organization's *strategic programs*. This requires that the FM be prepared to release information internally by:

1. *Being there first.* The FM and her staff must be aware of what is happening on all projects (both those that are being planned and those that are active), funding and related expense issues, and supplier and delivery plans, and must know what the physical situation is at all organization locations. This requires that programs for rapid communication among the FM, facility staff, security staff, and other internal departments and specific senior leadership when the issue warrants their notification be in place internally.

2. *Being prepared.* The FM and his staff should have a specific role in the corporate crisis communications plan that all organization managers are familiar

with. This regularly updated plan should detail both the internal contacts and the external steps that should be taken in the event of an emergency.

When Hurricane Andrew damaged the facilities of banking customers, many FMs and their suppliers immediately sent personnel to south Florida to help customers deal with the media and to answer questions like, "What happened to my money?"

3. *Making it easy.* What does it say about responsiveness if a company or an FM department doesn't post its phone number on its Web site? The more time internal customers and others must spend looking for information online or shuttling from one internal hand-off to another, the less responsive the FM and staff will appear, even though the information may be "right there."

4. *Being **proactive**.* The FM and his or her staff should, where possible, deliver answers before anyone has figured out what questions to ask, especially when funding, expense, or project factors may become an issue. Knowing about an issue in advance can help the FM frame the potential perception and even cauterize a problem before it grows, as you want the FM department to have the reputation of being a source of credible information. The FM should provide a list of frequently asked questions (FAQs) for customers to refer to as necessary.

Tell the truth. The FM should be honest and sincere with customers and management, especially when presenting the budget. Patiently reason your business case and demonstrate that you are not planning to jam your proposal or plan(s) down the throats of subordinates and/or peers. Know and be prepared with the answers to the typical what, who, where, when, why, and how questions that your customers and management may ask, and get to the point of your presentation as soon as possible.

5. *Being virtually available all the time.* The FM should automate the e-mail system so that it delivers an automatic response to messages, explaining why the FM is unavailable or suggesting alternative contacts. "Clone" an informed backup so that answers can be delivered when the front line is unavailable. When the FM is available, he should turn off the automated e-mail system and respond personally.

6. *Freeing callers from voicemail jail.* The FM must remember that *voicemail* automation can be a bane as well as a blessing. Undoubtedly, interactive voice response systems ("press 1 for . . .") save money, but at what cost in terms of frustration or delay? Don't let a prospect's first impression come from talking to a machine. The best solution, if the FM's organization can afford it, is to have all calls answered by a human attendant who is armed with a corporate organizational chart. The attendant can transfer the call to voicemail, relay the caller to the appropriate person, or take immediate action when required.

7. *Establishing online information bureaus.* Many FM departments have made immediate access to information part of their interactive financial strategies with their customers. An online intranet information bureau not only adds immediacy but can save money over the long term as well by providing organized information in the form of reports that the customer can obtain on a on-demand basis.

8. *Never saying "no comment."* A number of communication problems can be avoided by communicating factually in terms that the FM's customer can understand, especially when it comes to facility and project schedules, costs, staff, and related issues. FMs must put a premium on simple and direct language rather than legalese or engineeringese. It is important to be as forthcoming as possible. The more an FM-related event is shrouded in mystery, the longer it will linger. Avoid saying "no comment." Most people hear that and think, guilty as charged.

By establishing policies and procedures that facilitate responsiveness and intelligently using automation and the organization's intranet Web site to ensure access to information, the FM can use responsiveness as a communication tool to get timely financial and project information to the FM team, coworkers, customers, management, and suppliers.[2]

Conclusion

The FM has many ways to share and communicate information, reports, events, and so on, whether in person on a one-to-one basis, via written material and/or a formal presentation, through staff, or through the intranet/Web site. The financial, business, and leadership aspects of that communication must be delivered in language that the audience and users of the information will understand and will be interested in supporting or acting upon. Given the increasing competition for scarce resources both inside and outside of the organization, it is the FM's responsibility to effectively communicate all aspects of an issue to senior management and related department leaders in order to seek their support and to help them to make the best decision possible. How, when, where, what kind, and how much information is provided remains the FM's leadership responsibility, challenge, and opportunity.

Notes

1. Daniel Williams, "Communicate Your Leadership Agenda," *Executive Excellence, www.tolead.com.*
2. Nick Wreden, "Responsiveness: The Key to an Effective Corporate Communication Effort," Harvard Management Communication Letter, April 1999.

11

Trends in Facility Management

Pulse Points

- *The facility manager should understand which trends would be most appropriate for the organization and in what way, as these can affect the future, funds, and work of the FM and the staff.*
- *With third-party ownership programs, the FM's organization may no longer manage any space, may manage all the space, or may manage only some space.*
- *Many organizations are looking for legal and creative financing strategies to improve their market position.*
- *The FM may find himself negotiating energy acquisition from electricity or natural gas providers for his customer in order to stabilize pricing and reduce the potential for future price volatility.*
- *FM outsourcing companies focus on the non-core FM and corporate real estate parts of a potential customer organization.*
- *Over the past five years, as the Internet has taken root, e-commerce has changed the way we conduct business.*
- *The FM must know how e-commerce is affecting the organization and how to take advantage of e-business issues where and when appropriate.*
- *Specific FM trends may become an additional basis for business, and time will provide alert and curious FMs with information on how they can assist their organizations by using or assisting in the application of specific tools.*

Keywords

Trends, third-party ownership, REIT, e-commerce, energy deregulation, knowledge management, alternatives, financing, sale-leasebacks, synthetic leases, performance, electricity, natural gas, outsourcing, savings, ROI, operations, Internet, e-business, B2C, B2B, technology, digital, strategic planning, extranets, learning organization, culture, BVA, host data, portal

Introduction

An ongoing task for the organization's leadership is retaining and/or recapturing corporate equity wherever possible. Effective retention and/or recapture results in a number of financial processes through which the organization can obtain cash for its owned and in some cases its leased property. The FM should understand these processes and should understand which trend would be most appropriate for the organization and in what way, as these trends can affect the future, funds, and work of the FM and the staff.

This chapter will review financial and financial-related *trends,* such *as third-party ownership, energy deregulation, FM outsourcing,* and *e-commerce and facility management,* all of which can affect the available capital resources, services, expenses, and value of the facilities the FM and the FM department manage.

Third-Party Ownership

As discussed in Chapter 8, the CFO and the board of directors review proposed projects and decide on the best use of the organization's capital funds and resources. This includes both cash and fixed assets that the organization owns and/or leases. In their review of the status of funds and resources, the CFO and the board may choose to consider recapturing some or all of the capital monies that have been invested in property and buildings, the fixed assets.

A trend that started a number of years ago is the aggressive marketing by financial and real estate third-party service companies of programs under which the third-party company would purchase all or a part of an organization's portfolio of property and buildings and then lease all or part of that portfolio back to the organization for a long period of time—ten to thirty years. The third-party owner might also take on the organization's leased property obligations if the owner or landlord of the leased property agreed to the assumption of the lease.

With low interest rates and a healthy real estate market, the organization can gain a large infusion of cash (millions to billions of dollars) and eliminate the assets and associated liabilities from its balance sheet. It is no longer the owner of the formerly owned space and sometimes is no longer the prime tenant of the previously leased space, but instead is now a tenant or subtenant. In these third-party ownership programs, the FM's organization may no longer manage any space, may manage all the space, or may manage only some of the space. Often the third-party owner will manage the property with the organization as the tenant or will choose to find a landlord agency to manage the property for it.

After such a purchase, the FM may find that his position changes to one of managing a service contract with a landlord, he may control and provide services to some of the property, or he may be responsible for all of the organization's service as before, but no longer controls the property. With a third-party sale, the FM moves from being fully responsible for the property to being a representative of the tenant—the FM's customer. The agreement with the new third-party property owner may also give the organization the right to buy back some or all of the property back from the third-party owner after a specific period of time.

Should the organization choose to recapture capital in this way, the FM should be prepared to be part of the team negotiating the sale in order to ensure that the organization understands and supports the prices being offered for each facility or for a total block of space. The offer being made by the third party may be a good market price offer, but there are other issues that must be considered and addressed before accepting or rejecting an offer or negotiating further, and the FM's knowledge of the facility should enable the FM to see that these issues are dealt with.

Many organizations are looking for legal and creative refinancing strategies to improve their market position. There are a number of property development companies that can help their clients in *financing* and refinancing real estate assets through *sale-leasebacks*, leveraged leases, and *synthetic leases*.

These products may create significant *savings* and revenue opportunities. For example, through sale-leasebacks, organizations can reallocate capital that was tied up in real property to higher-earning parts of their core business. Furthermore, synthetic and leveraged leases can provide off-balance-sheet financing at extremely attractive rates.

In a sale-leaseback, the organizational owner of a property sells the property and simultaneously agrees to lease back the property or space in the building. Sale-leasebacks can further maximize economic benefits by utilizing a leveraged lease structure. In this instance, the investor, typically a finance subsidiary of a major industrial company, uses its own funds for only 5 to 10 percent of the total cost and borrows the remainder from third-party lenders (hence, leveraged). The leveraged lease provides superior economics because of the investor's earned tax deferral status, which allows for lower rents.

A synthetic lease, also called an off-balance-sheet loan, is a transaction that allows an organization to obtain off-balance-sheet financing for an asset while retaining the economic benefit (residual value) and the tax benefit (depreciation) associated with ownership. Unfortunately, accounting rules do not allow synthetic leases for sale-leasebacks, but they are increasingly popular for acquisitions and build-to-suits.[1]

Energy Deregulation

Energy is one of the largest operating costs the FM must budget for and manage. The onslaught of high prices and statewide power emergencies in California in 2001 had many analysts speculating about the source of the crisis, and the deregulation of the *electricity* industry took its share of the blame. Although the costs and benefits of deregulation have been debated since the passage of the National Energy Policy Act of 1992, there is still a great deal of uncertainty about how deregulation will affect consumers and organizations.

In the previous system of regulated monopolies managed by state government agencies, individual utility companies handled both the generation and the distribution of electricity and/or *natural gas*. Consumers usually had no choice—they had to use a designated local utility company. In addition, prices were controlled by state governments and were based on the local cost of service and a set limit on allowable revenue, so prices per kilowatt-hour of electricity or per cubic foot of natural gas varied across the nation. In some municipalities, water and sewer treatment was also controlled by city, county, or regional governments.

Energy deregulation allows multiple companies to supply the generation of electricity or natural gas in a competitive marketplace. Customers can choose a provider, in much the same way as they choose long-distance telephone service. In 1996, California and Rhode Island became the first states to pass legislation restructuring their electricity industries. Since then, almost all of the fifty states have enacted laws providing for similar plans or have begun to consider them. Some states have chosen to deregulate natural gas first and hold off on electricity deregulation until the lessons from other deregulated states have been publicized.

The history, growth, and operations of the electrical industry differ from state to state and often between power producers within a state, so the effect that deregulation will have on all consumers is very uncertain. Some people believe that market competition will drive prices down, and in certain locations that has been the initial result. However, diverse factors affecting free market pricing can cause price increases to be passed on to customers, resulting in increased energy costs. Also, although freedom of choice is often touted as a benefit, determining which is the "best" electricity or natural gas provider is a complex and difficult decision for most organizations.

In April 1998, California became the first state to put a working electricity deregulation plan into effect, and the 2001 electricity crisis created a storm of controversy about nationwide deregulation. California's problems, however, were mostly due to specific circumstances within the state. The main issue was that the existing supply didn't meet demand, resulting in higher prices. The situation had once been controlled by government-set price caps, but deregulation removed these limits and allowed generators to charge higher rates. Organizations and residents in certain areas of California saw their electric bills double and even triple after deregulation went into effect.

The FM who faces this challenge may find herself negotiating for her customer with electricity or natural gas providers in order to stabilize pricing and reduce the potential for future price volatility. From the demand side, FMs should be working to decrease demand by making buildings more energy efficient.

A U.S. government energy Web site that the FM might consider reviewing is *www.energy.gov*. The U.S. Department of Energy's Web site is *www.eia.doe.gov/ cneaf/electricity/chp_str/regmap.html*. This Web site consists of a U.S. map that the visitor clicks on in order to find out more about deregulation in that area. The information included for each state ranges from public benefits programs to pilot programs and retail access.

Another Web site that the FM may choose to visit is *www.epa.gov/energystar*, which is known as Energy Star. This is a voluntary partnership between the U.S. Department of Energy, the U.S. Environmental Protection Agency, product manufacturers, local utilities, and retailers. The partners help to promote the use of more efficient products by labeling them with the Energy Star logo and educating consumers about the unique benefits of energy-efficient products. The Web site includes links to products, manufacturers, retailers, and news.[2]

The trend toward energy deregulation can provide the FM with a great opportunity to reduce operational expenses, but the FM must also weigh the ramifi-
cations of stable supply at a market rate that may change in the short run and
hurt operational capability over a longer time frame.

FM Outsourcing

Each year FM outsourcing companies are invited formally via a request for proposal (RFP) or informally via a site visit to review selected FM *operations* for
many different types of organizations throughout the United States and Canada.
One consistent trend that comes up in all but a very few of the companies visited
is the lack of good, consistent, accurate, detailed, and reliable financial (budget
and expense) facility management data.

FM *outsourcing* has become a trend, as not only do outsourcing companies
have the expertise to advise organizations on new ways of making their facility
assets more productive, but most of these companies agree to be accountable for
implementing their recommendations and guarantee the outcomes. These companies argue that they can deliver measurably improved business outcomes for their
customers at a lower and predictable cost. Many of them manage millions of
square feet of facilities, and some even manage facilities around the world. These
FM outsourcing firms focus on the noncore FM and corporate real estate parts of
the organization and market their services via statements such as, "What we're
saying is, don't get caught up in all the details of managing your facility, leave
them to us."[3]

According to a May/June 2001 survey of facility managers on outsourcing,
eight FM functions are being outsourced by at least 45 percent of respondents.
And one FM function, custodial and housekeeping, was being outsourced by 72
percent of respondents.

"There has been a definite trend toward more outsourcing in recent years,"
concludes the survey report, published by Bethesda, Maryland–based FMLink
(*www.fmlink.com*), an online publication for facility and building managers. "The
importance of outsourcing in today's FM climate cannot be understated," FMLink
publisher Peter Kimmel said in discussing the survey results. The survey was
conducted online on the FMLink Web site, and 202 subscribers responded.

That growing trend means that FMs are spending significant amounts of time
in managing outsourcing contracts, the survey found. More than forty hours a
month of in-house staff time, in fact, was being spent in managing outsourced
contracts for three FM functions, respondents reported. Those three functions
were engineering, at forty-four hours a month; preventive maintenance, at forty-
three hours; and design and architecture, at forty-two hours.

The FM functions most frequently outsourced for all facilities were:

1. Custodial and housekeeping, 72 percent
2. Design and architecture, 65 percent
3. Landscape maintenance, 63 percent
4. Major moves, 54 percent

5. Security, 51 percent
6. Preventive maintenance, 50 percent
7. Engineering, 46 percent
8. Utilities maintenance, 45 percent

The survey states that 38 percent of FM operating budget is going to outsourcing, and it further suggests that FM outsourcing hasn't yet crested. According to the survey report, 36 percent of respondents said that within two years "they likely would be outsourcing at least one additional function that they are not outsourcing at present." The most likely candidate to join the outsourcing ranks over the next two years is preventive maintenance, picked by 40 percent of the group of respondents who anticipated increased outsourcing. Here's a more detailed look at the survey's findings:

• *Why outsource?* "The two most important reasons stated for outsourcing were 'cost savings' and 'the need for special skills, services or tools/equipment,'" the survey report noted. "In-house staff reduction," the third most frequent rationale for FM outsourcing, was "mentioned by significantly less respondents," according to the report.

• *What's outsourced?* The aforementioned "custodial and housekeeping" function is number one here, cited by 72 percent of respondents. Ranked next as most frequently outsourced FM functions are "design and architecture," cited by 65 percent of respondents, and "landscape management," cited by 63 percent.

• *What's most likely to remain outsourced?* The three "least likely services to be brought back in-house" are the three that are now most frequently outsourced: "custodial and housekeeping," "design and architecture," and "landscape management."

• *Where are outsourcing's greatest savings?* The greatest number of survey respondents reported cost savings in the three most frequently outsourced services. The order of the top three changes slightly, however, when they are viewed from the cost savings perspective. "Custodial and housekeeping" again ranks first, being cited by 52 percent of respondents. "Landscape management," however, ranks second for cost savings; it was cited by 34 percent of respondents. "Design and architecture" was the third-ranked area for reported cost savings, cited by 27 percent of respondents.

• *How are outsourcing contractors selected?* "Competitive procurement" ranked as "the most influential source for contractor selection," said the survey report. "Prior experience with the contractor" and "referrals" were respectively ranked the second and third most influential sources for contractor selection.

• *How are outsourcing contractors evaluated?* "The most important way to evaluate the contractor's performance was through direct oversight by the in-house FM staff," said the survey report. "Three other evaluation ways were listed as secondary: regular meetings with the contractor, staff surveys and/or customer complaint files, and performance-based measures."

• *What is the most difficult aspect of outsourcing?* "Selecting the right contractor" finished first, being cited by 39 percent of respondents. Ranked next, with 17 percent, was "managing the contractor," followed by "writing the proposal to select the contractor," with 13 percent.

• *Is outsourcing a different ballgame with "mission-critical facilities"?* Yes and no. "No single difference stood out between managing [mission-critical and non-mission-critical facilities]," said the survey report. "Forty-one percent said that there were no differences at all." On the other hand, the kinds of functions that were outsourced differed somewhat for mission-critical facilities, which were defined in the survey as "facilities that must be fully operational at all times." For example, "security," cited by 51 percent of respondents, moved from fifth to third place for mission-critical facilities. Similarly, "preventive maintenance" moved from sixth to fourth for mission-critical facilities. Conversely, the "major moves" function migrated in the opposite direction. Ranked fourth on the most frequent outsourcing list for all types of facilities, "major moves" drops all the way down to a distant eighth for outsourcing for mission-critical facilities.

• *What outsourced functions are most likely to be brought back in-house?* Nothing really seems to stand out in the survey. Granted, 24 percent of respondents said that they had "already brought back in-house a service that had been outsourced or would be doing so." "Cost" and "service quality" were "the two largest reasons by far" for bringing those functions back in, the survey report noted. The survey found no one area, however, that qualified as "most likely" to be returned in-house. Of the FM functions listed in the survey, none drew more than 7 percent of total respondents as a likely candidate to again become an in-house activity.

And that adds weight to another observation by FMLink's Kimmel on the 2001 survey results: "We also see continued major growth of the outsourcing industry, which until a few years ago, was populated by very few companies able to serve a nationwide clientele. Now many of the companies are global."[4]

The authors feel that outsourcing will continue to be an ongoing trend in FM and have been pleased to see that a number of FM professionals have taken the initiative in this area for their organizations. This is especially encouraging when we see FMs developing, implementing, and reviewing with their customers a set of meaningful FM performance measurements and metrics, including a formal and ongoing FM benchmarking scorecard program.

FM outsourcing is a fact of facility operations. The FM must review staffing and operational requirements to ensure that he proposes and implements outsourcing when and where it is appropriate and will serve the best interest of the organization. If the FM is not proactive in this area, senior management may make the decision without his input and/or support.

E-Commerce and Facility Management

Internet and business-to-business *e-commerce* have grown much more rapidly than anyone guessed even five years ago, spawning potentially new ways of communication, collaboration, and coordination among consumers, businesses, and trading partners. However, there are many different opinions about the importance of e-commerce in facility management.

Key Issues

1. *How is e-commerce being used today?* E-commerce is just beginning to emerge as a tool that can be used to help manage facilities. The most frequent application of e-commerce today is purchasing supplies and materials over the Web from a specific vendor. In addition to purchasing supplies and materials, the other top uses of e-commerce are accessing facilities manuals, publishing static project information on the Internet, purchasing supplies and materials through an Internet service that connects buyers and sellers, and taking interactive courses via the Internet.

2. *How will e-commerce be used in the next two years?* Some FMs have clear expectations that the use of e-commerce in facility management will grow substantially over the next two years and that it will significantly affect facility management practices.

3. *Who is using e-commerce?* There is substantial variability among industry groups regarding the use of e-commerce. Companies in the telecommunications (service providers) and information (data processing and services) industry groups tend to be relatively heavy users of e-commerce. Those in the vehicles and investment (all securities and investment services) groups reported relatively low use activity. Additional analysis suggests that companies that are ISO 9000 certified also may be more likely to adopt e-commerce.

4. *How effective is the use of business-to-business e-commerce?* Some FMs feel that e-commerce has not much improved their ability to manage cost or time issues effectively. However, they expect this to change in the next two years. The payoff for investing in e-commerce has not yet been clearly demonstrated. Some FMs agree or strongly agree that e-commerce has helped decrease the amount of time required to complete projects or that e-commerce has decreased the cost of purchasing supplies and materials. However, a majority disagrees or strongly disagrees with the idea that e-commerce has decreased the cost of facility maintenance and operations, decreased the total annual cost of facilities, decreased the cost of new construction projects, or decreased the cost of space management.

5. *What are the barriers to implementing e-commerce?* Some FMs feel that implementing e-commerce is a big problem, some feel that implementing e-commerce is somewhat of a problem, and some feel that implementing business-to-business e-commerce solutions is not a problem. The biggest specific problem in implementing e-commerce was reported to be the difficulty in integrating it with legacy systems. Other top problems included lack of a budget to invest in e-commerce, hard-to-customize software packages, cost of software upgrades, and cost of keeping building data current.[5]

The Impact of E-Commerce on Facilities Management

Over the past five years, as the Internet has taken root, e-commerce has changed the way we conduct business. E-commerce has two different aspects, business-to-consumer (*B2C*) and business-to-business (*B2B*).

Business-to-Consumer (B2C)

B2C selling online may not require a bricks and mortar store in a prime real estate location, but more and more e-tailers are finding that they still need all the back-end support that traditional retailers have. The old bricks and mortar companies that are going online have a better chance to be successful in the *digital* economy. They already have the infrastructure in place to handle shipping and returns, as well as the entire back-end support for the business.

Business-to-Business (B2B)

Business-to-business e-commerce is forecasted to reach or exceed $1.3 trillion by 2003. The B2B sector has really seen greater changes and savings from the "new economy." Internet- and intranet-based industry-specific exchanges—which are Web-based, real-time transaction systems characterized by industry-specific alliances, standard-setting bodies, and marketplaces—bring a whole new meaning to electronic data interchange (EDI).

This requires connectivity for all employees. It often goes hand-in-hand with paperless offices, which require less record storage, both on-site and off-site. Web-enabled replenishment systems allow a greater turnover of inventory. Some IT equipment companies have only four hours' worth of inventory on hand.

Demands on Facilities

Internet-driven facilities have to respond to the demands of connectivity, security, scalability, and the human factor. Connectivity in our buildings is getting increasingly important and will continue to do so. *E-business* can be conducted from anywhere in the world as long as FMs have connectivity through high-speed dedicated lines at a reasonable price.

Buildings with existing compatible and expandable local area networks (LANs) and wide area networks (WANs) can provide great cost savings. Mobile computing with wireless phones, personal digital assistants (PDAs) such as those developed by Palm, personal PCs, and laptops will increase with bandwidth. Rooftop space has become a valuable asset and is being leased out to wireless service providers.

Data and voice will more and more become bundled services, with Internet phones making real-time transmission of voice possible. The scalability of computer systems and office space is critical in the dynamic online economy. Today's computers with flat monitor screens have a smaller footprint and do not require rooms with raised floors and special air conditioning. While the equipment is more tolerant of environmental conditions, there is a high demand for computer security with e-commerce. Uptime is critical, and having a company's Web site down for fifteen minutes could drastically affect the company's stock price.

In addition to software and hardware protection, physical security and access control are critical. Another requirement is a cold or hot backup site. For security reasons, there has been an increase in intranet as opposed to Internet applications. Security issues also exist in the area of communication, both hard-wired and wireless. Cable modems, which may be seen as a solution enabling small firms to connect home offices, are another security risk to be faced. Security also includes the use of monitoring devices to control the access and movement of employees. The company also has to monitor e-mail and Web use to protect itself from potential lawsuits.

Businesses gather, analyze, and use competitive intelligence collected online to succeed in the global marketplace. Cyber-attacks can come from within the company (mostly by disgruntled employees), or from anywhere in the world.

Departments in Clickable Corporations

E-commerce has changed not just the sales and marketing departments, which now have to deal with online selling and a mobile sales force connected through wireless communications. Web-enabled databases have also changed the accounting functions, moving them away from legacy mainframe computers.

Even the job application process has gone virtual. Today, most companies have a résumé drop link on their Web site for electronic submission of résumés. Software packages can scan the résumés for buzzwords and match them with the company's employment needs. A lot of prescreening is now done electronically. The information about employees that is gathered when they are hired will be extended into a skills database that tracks the employees' education and skills as well as the results of their annual reviews and manages their careers.

Workspaces of the Digital Economy

Offices are changing in the e-commerce age. Telecommuting and mobile computing have led to new requirements for the office layout. Hoteling and sharing workspace can lead to not only less leased space but also smaller parking lots.

While the image of the corporate offices may be less important to the general public, it certainly plays an important role in recruiting and retaining hard-to-find employees. In a casual high-tech workplace, the importance of panelized individual offices has decreased. A fun space in a flexible office landscape may help knowledge workers to relax while working on deadlines and under pressure in an ever-changing high-velocity world. This may even include pet-friendly facilities, which some organizations have already provided for employees.

Industry-Specific Requirements

While the previous observations are broad, the following are more industry-specific effects of the digital economy for the FM:

- *Travel.* An increasing number of businesses, including airlines, rental car companies, and hotels, are encouraging online booking and ticket sales; this increases margins and reduces the necessity for travel agencies.
- *Financial institutions.* The popularity of online banking will increase, with the client's home office becoming a bank branch office. Traditional branches will decrease in number as a result of e-commerce, ATM machines, and supermarket branches. In the past, loan officers compared interest rates by calling; today, this has been replaced by scanning the Web sites of local and national institutions.

- *Retail.* Even the retail industry is experiencing the impact of e-commerce. We can shop for everything online, including prescription drugs and groceries that will be delivered to our doorstep. This may reduce the need for retail space, except for super centers and other consumer specialty stores.
- *Transportation.* An increase in shipping will be experienced as more people shop online rather than in stores. And companies will come to rely on shorter replenishment schedules. FedEx, UPS, and other such firms are responsible for shipping and distributions. Their facilities will experience an increase in size and efficiency. Warehouses will be optimized for order fulfillment, with truck loading software and terminals.
- *Real estate.* With the passing of the Digital Signature Act by Congress, real estate companies are now shifting their thinking from using the Internet as a marketing tool to using the World Wide Web as a tool in the facilitation of transactions. This will allow fewer agents to handle a larger number of transactions.
- *Manufacturing.* The manufacturing environment has changed greatly as a result of exchanges, which have made more and more products into commodities. Just-in-time inventory has led to smaller facilities and a greater reliance on transportation and information systems. Production and distribution have grown closer together.

The Future

The future will bring an increase in bandwidth, storage space, and mobile applications. Computers, communication, and consumer products are merging into smaller, more powerful polymorphic devices. Call centers and data warehouses are increasing in importance. Facilities are becoming more of a commodity, but location still remains the most important factor—even in a virtual world.[6]

The FM must know how e-commerce is affecting the organization and how to take advantage of e-business issues where and when appropriate. The e-business process for the FM department can provide many advantages, but it must be developed and implemented with support from senior management and related organizational departments (purchasing, finance, accounting, legal, IT, and so on).

Conclusion

This chapter discusses a number of trends in business and facility management that the FM should be aware of; the FM should also be proactive in determining how these trends can or should be applied. These trends have a basis in finance and business, as their application can affect the FM's organizational budgets, financial health, and competitive (for nongovernmental organizations) stance and reputation in the marketplace.

Specific FM trends may become an additional basis of business, and time will provide the alert and curious FM with information on how he can assist his organization by using or assisting in the application of specific tools. The FM is continually being expected to do more with less, and this can be achieved only by the smart application of knowledge gained through experience and the know-how to apply and address business and facility solutions from a strategic and an operational perspective.

We trust that the progressive FMs who have read this book will continue to work and lead their staff from the perspective of "I would rather be green and growing than ripe and rotting."

Notes

1. Trammell Crow Company marketing document, May 2002, Trammell Crow Web site, *www.trammellcrow.com.*

2. "Keeping Current: What Deregulation Means for the FM," paper, Trammell Crow Company Web site, May 2002.

3. Johnson Controls, Inc., facility management marketing Web site, *www.johnson controls.com.*

4. Jack Lyne, "Study: Facilities Management Outsourcing Rising, Hasn't Yet Crested," Sitenet Dispatch, *www.sitenet.com*, January 30, 2002.

5. Excerpts from the IFMA Research Report "The Impact of E-Commerce on Facility Management Practices, 2000."

6. Herman Greuwald, "The Impact of E-Commerce on Facilities Management," *Facility Management Journal*, January/February 2001.

Appendix A: How to Talk to a CFO

If you have worked in the world of facilities for any length of time, you have encountered at least one situation where a project you know is important has never been carried out because you couldn't get the money. Usually, it is the finance organization that is the "gatekeeper" to the corporate treasury where the money resides to perform your project. The most successful facilities people have learned to get the money they need by using some of the 10 concepts presented below:

1. To a financial officer, EVERYTHING is financial.
2. Learn the CFO's language.
3. Learn where you fit in the CFO's frame of reference.
4. Learn the time value of money.
5. If it's an expense eliminate it. If you can't eliminate it, minimize it.
6. If it's an investment, maximize the return on it.
7. Cash is king.
8. Hedge all risks.
9. Don't ignore politics.
10. Emphasize the corporation's welfare, not your division's.

Concept 1: To a Financial Officer, EVERYTHING Is Financial: Where you may see real estate, leases, and maintenance, the CFO sees assets, liabilities, expenses, and the effect they have on the corporation's share price. CFOs have this thought pattern beaten into them in business school and when they take the CPA examination. There is even a name for it: "The Shareholder Primacy Doctrine." This legal principle is often attributed to a 1919 court case named *Dodge v. Ford Motor Company, Inc.* However, the basic principle is much older. In *Dodge*, the court said that a corporation has only two real duties: to obey the law and to maximize shareholder value. In simplified terms, "maximizing shareholder value" means maximizng the share price and dividends, if the corporation pays dividends. More recent court cases have conceded that corporations may engage in charitable, environmental, and other "non profit" activities if these activities are "in good faith," "performed with ordinary care," and "reasonably believed to be in the best interests of the corporation." However, maximizing shareholder value remains the real mission of all corporations, even if their slogans talk about other things and they perform some eleemosynary activities on the side.

Even without the shareholder primacy doctrine, it is obvious that CFOs get hired and fired over money, not quality, customer satisfaction, employee satisfaction, or corporate image. They are simply not going to give you the money for your project or operation unless they can see how it improves the financial position of the company.

You must make your "pitch" to the CFO in financial terms. You need to master the financial frame of reference used by YOUR company. If your company is mostly "equity financed" (financed by the sale of stock) it may use "ROE" (return on equity) as its primary financial indicator. If so, make your pitch in terms of how it will affect ROE. If your company is mostly "debt financed" (financed by the sale of bonds or "commercial paper") it may use "ROA" (return on assets) or some variant thereof such as "RONABIT" (return on assets before interest and taxes). If so, make your pitch in terms of its effect on these indicators. This leads to our second concept.

Concept 2: Learn the CFO's Language: Using non-financial terms when communicating with the CFO will mark you as a non-financial manager, and therefore unworthy of serious notice. A glossary appears at the end of this appendix. It wouldn't hurt to memorize it. For example, don't use the word "cost." The income statement contains *expenses* so you should call them expenses. (However, "sunk cost" is OK to describe money that has already been spent and cannot be "unspent.") Other bad examples we have heard recently that hurt the CFO's ears include:

"Capital expense" There is no such thing. There are capital investments and there are operating expenses. Be clear which you mean. If it is a long-lived asset that must be depreciated over time, it is a capital investment. If it is a short-lived item that is consumed immediately, it is an expense.

"Profit" Believe it or not, even "profit" can be a questionable word, not because it is bad, but because there are so many different ways to calculate it.

A glossary of financial terms appears at the end of this appendix.

Concept 3: Learn Where You Fit in the CFO's Frame of Reference: Learn the basic structure of a financial statement. You don't need to know about journals, ledgers, debits, credits, and the detailed process that leads up to the creation of the financial statement, but you do need to know where your activities ultimately impact the financial statement. This is because while you are talking to the CFO, he or she is mentally tracing your activities to their "proper" place. An illustrated example of the financial statement appears later in this appendix.

Assets are real and financial things that the company owns or has a claim upon. Examples include cash, property, plant, equipment, accounts receivable, and loans the company has made to others. Almost all assets are good, but to the CFO short-term assets are the best. These include cash, accounts receivable, and othr highy liquid assets

---

Thomas McCune, *Proceedings of World Workplace 1999* (Houston: International Facility Management Association, 1999).

Figure A-1. Everything Is Financial.

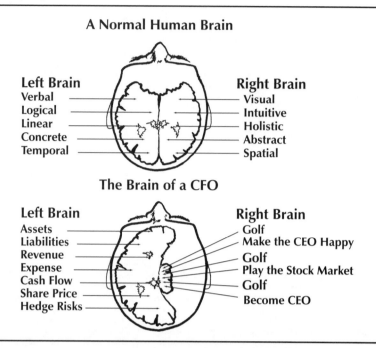

that can be quickly converted to cash. CFOs know that enough cash can get a corporation out of almost any problem. Several years ago, when Apple Computer was losing lots of money and was expected by some experts to fail, they put a photograph of a piggy bank on the cover of their annual report. The message was clear: "Ok, we've been losing money, but we're sitting on a big mountain of cash and we'll get through this thing."

Unfortunately, for facilities people, our assets are not short-term assets. Buildings and real estate are long-term assets. In fact, you frequently must use up short-term assets (cash) to acquire long-term assets (buildings). This is not necessarily bad. Just be aware that in the mind of the CFO, you are swapping the most desirable kind of asset for a less desirable kind. One good strategy is to talk to the CFO about how you effectively manage (from a financial point of view) a portfolio of assets for the corporation.

Liabilities are debts we owe to others. Like assets, liabilities can be divided into short-term and long-term. Short-term liabilities include accounts payable and short-term loans we must repay to others. Long-term liabilities include mortgages and bonds the company has sold that must be ultimately paid off. Some companies speak of being "highly leveraged." They imply that this is a good thing because they are using a lot of other people's money in relation to only a little of their own. This is fine, as long as the money is being used productively to generate income. However, if it is not efficiently generating income, the company is simply carrying a lot of unproductive debt.

Shareholder equity is the liability of the corporation to the shareholders in recognition of the fact that they are the owners of the corporation's wealth.

Together, assets and liabilities form the *balance sheet,* which represents the wealth of the corporation *at a point in time,* such as the end of a year or a quarter.

Revenue is money the corporation took in from the sale of products. Most CFOs never met a revenue they didn't like. Generally speaking, the more the better. Unfortunately for facilities people, most facilities do not generate revenue. This is certainly the case for "administrative" facilities such as the corporate headquarters. Even in the case of revenue generating facilities such as hotels, the facility is only part of the revenue generation process. Marketing, operations, and customer service all go into the mix that is required to generate revenue.

Expenses represent money we paid out to keep the business going. *Direct expenses* went for materials, labor, and other things that go directly into the products we sold. *Indirect expenses* went for labor and items that did not go directly into our products. Classic examples of indirect expenses include rent, depreciation, and facility maintenance. Other terms for "indirect expenses" include "overhead," "selling, general, and administrative expense," and "S,G,& A."

Together, revenue and expenses form the *income statement,* which describes the profitability of the corporation *over a period of time* such as a year, or a quarter. Revenue minus expense equals profit, also known as net income.

Concept 4: The Time Value of Money: Throughout most of recorded economic history, a dollar in hand today has been worth more than a dollar at some time in the future. (The only limited exceptions to this rule have occurred during major economic disruptions such as the great depression when "deflation" occurred, increasing the purchasing power of money over time.)

In purely economic terms, the reason for this is simple—if we had the dollar in hand today, we could use it to develop new products, market our goods, acquire other companies, otherwise fund the company's operations, or simply invest it. If we don't have the dollar in hand today, we need to borrow it from others, and they will demand interest on the loan of their money. Almost all companies use a *discount rate* to estimate the reduced value of future dollars. The simplest discount rate to use is the company's *cost of capital*. This is the weighted average "interest rate" on all sources of debt and equity financing used by the company. Many companies use a discount rate that is higher than their actual cost of capital to reflect various kinds of risk. These risks include the risk of non-repayment, risk of liability, and risk of business loss on the investment.

As a facilities person, you need to understand the discounting mechanisms used by your company. However, we believe that since facilities investments do not involve the types of business risks associated with new products, investments in facilities should be discounted at the company's weighted average cost of capital with no additional factors applied. We believe companies should analyze investments as follows:

$$\frac{\text{Non-revenue projects (facilities)}}{\text{discount rate}} = \text{weighted average cost of capital}$$

$$\frac{\text{Revenue-generating projects (\& products)}}{\text{discount rate}}$$

$$= \text{(weighted average cost of capital + risk factor estimated project-by-project)}$$

Concept 5: If It's an Expense, Eliminate It. If You Can't Eliminate It, Minimize It: Every dollar of expense is a dollar of lost profit. Therefore, a major component of the financial world view is that expenses should be completely eliminated insofar as possible. A classic example would be the corporate art program. In the mind of most CFOs this is a pure expense that contributes nothing to the generation of revenue. It is therefore a prime candidate for elimination.

Other expenses that cannot be completely eliminated should be minimized. The CFO knows that direct expenses such as raw materials which go into the company's products are not avoidable, but they can be minimized by competitive bidding, shopping around, and inventory control. The CFO also realizes that indirect expenses such as facility maintenance cannot be eliminated, but they are also prime candidates for minimization. As a practical matter, it is impossible to calculate a return on expenses for facility maintenance using any of the usual formulae.

At one extreme, you could assume that if you did not perform facility maintenance at all, the company's operations would eventually be shut down by regulators or litigation. Therefore, the "return" on facility maintenance would be the entire revenue stream of the corporation. In other words, the return on investment in facility maintenance would be almost infinite! No CFO is going to buy this argument.

A more reasonable argument is that the minimum threshold level of facility maintenance is an unavoidable expense to be minimized. But any maintenance effort above and beyond the minimum threshold level is an investment that should generate a return. For example, let's say that our union agreements require that the building be cleaned once per week. This is the minimum threshold level of cleaning. However, suppose our industrial safety experts demonstrate that cleaning three times per week will reduce the accident rate by a measurable amount. By factoring-in the cost of lost time, we can now calculate the return on the incremental investment in more frequent cleaning.

Techniques for justifying minimum threshold level expenses include:

- Benchmark the competition
- Examine regulatory constraints and alternative ways of complying with them
- Include all costs of non-compliance

Concept 6: If It's an Investment, Maximize the Return on It: Whereas the corporation minimizes expenses to the level necessary for operations, it invests money to create a return. The return can take many forms. Renovating a retail facility can improve sales revenue. Replacing inefficient HVAC equipment can reduce utility bills. In many cases, we are dealing with the incremental change in revenue or expenses due to our project as the return on the investment.

For example, if your utility bills are now $1,000,000 per year and you spend $700,000 on an HVAC upgrade project which reduces your utility bills to $850,000 per year, your investment is $700,000 and your return is $150,000 per year. You can use these numbers to perform an internal rate of return ("IRR") calculation or other analysis of return on investment.

Concept 7: Cash Is King: Your project may have wonderful "numbers" (low cost, high rate of return, whatever . . .). But if the company is short of cash, you may not get what you need to proceed with the project. In this situation, you may need to look at leasing, lease/purchase, swapping, non-recourse loans, or other mechanisms that do not require a large initial investment of cash. Your numbers may show that the lifetime value of these methods is actually more expensive than paying cash. However, if the cash is simply not available, they may make sense.

Always explore alternative financing mechanisms and at least have them in your "hip pocket" before making your pitch to the CFO.

Concept 8: Hedge All Risks: Again, your project may have wonderful "numbers." But the CFO has probably been through enough business cycles to know that things don't always go according to plan. That new office building that makes financial sense at 90 percent occupancy after an 18-month ramp-up doesn't look so good with 50 percent vacancy due to a hiring freeze.

The CFO has a whole department that hedges the financial risks of investments and foreign exchange. They even have their own strange language that includes words like puts, calls, straddles, and straps, not to mention the more commonplace options and futures contracts. Unfortunately our ability to use these strategies in corporate real estate is limited. About the only pure hedge we have is the "call" (an option to buy a specific property at a specific price within a given time frame).

About the best we can do to hedge risks in corporate real estate is to have an "exit strategy." If you have a sizeable portfolio, this can be accomplished by maintaining a mix of owned and leased properties with leases of varying durations. If the company needs to downsize, you can begin shedding the short-term leases as they expire and migrate into the longer duration properties. One element of this strategy is that you may have greater flexibility with owned properties than with long-term leases. Depending on market conditions, you may be able to sell a property you own faster, easier, and more economically than you can sublease (or buyout) a property with a long-term lease.

Concept 9: Don't Ignore Politics: Earlier, we said that to a CFO, everything is financial. We believe that down deep this is true. However, most people who have survived in the corporate world and risen to the position of CFO are at least competent at corporate power politics. In some cases, they are masters of corporate politics. Therefore, you too must play by the political rules.

The specific political rules are different for every corporation. Even within a single corporation, they change over time. Therefore, the first rule of corporate politics is to understand the politics of *your* company. Are there warring factions? (Probably.) Are there players who hold power disproportionate to their apparent status? (Possibly.)

How do you go about learning the corporate politics of your company? This is far more art than science. Spend as little time as possible at your desk. Go to every meeting and "extracurricular activity" you possibly can. Talk to everyone, but spend your time asking as many questions as possible and volunteering nothing. Align yourself with one or more factions if you must but never burn your bridges. Be a loyal subordinate. Don't get a reputation as a liar, squealer, or backstabber. Beware spies in your organization and purge them if found. Leave the more exotic power plays to the experts. There are numerous books on this subject in the business section of every bookstore. However, few improve on the classics such as *The Prince* and *The Art of War*.

A few general rules of politics that apply to almost any situation include:

Things change. One of the biggest mistakes you can make is to go to the big meeting with a bunch of project justifications based on old corporate objectives. They were possibly developed by the CFO's predecessor and are therefore automatically suspect. Last year, cash may have been tight and minimizing cash outflow by leasing may have been a winning strategy. But this year cash may not be an issue and stock price is the primary concern. This year the winning strategy may involve positively impacting earnings (and therefore stock price).

Make the CFO look good. After all, he or she is the CFO and you're not. You need to look like you understand finances, but not to the degree that you threaten the CFO. If he or she wants to lecture you a little bit now and then about finances, that's OK. Certainly don't try to bluff the CFO when it comes to financial matters. It's a pretty good bet that he or she genuinely knows a lot more about financial analysis than you do.

Get exposure. Several studies have indicated that the single biggest factor in getting promoted in any bureaucracy is simple exposure ("face time"). Use your projects and activities to gain as much exposure to the CFO and other senior executives as possible. If you behave yourself, the more exposure the better.

Make allies with other important divisions. In many corporations, organizations such as HR and Legal have significant power. Don't ignore them in your attempt to gain respect from the finance organization. After all, it is the decision to hire large numbers of people that drives the decision to add space. HR can be your best ally in the fight to add more and better facilities.

Concept 10: Emphasize the Corporation's Welfare, Not Your Division's: It is human nature to want to defend your "tribe" against competitors. Unfortunately, this instinct frequently goes awry in the corporate world and we begin viewing other divisions of the corporation as competitors. You may win short term battles against internal competitors. But in the long term you will greatly improve your position with the CFO by emphasizing the good of the entire corporation over the good of your division.

Useful Financial Rules

Measures of liquidity

Current ratio = current assets/current liabilities
Quick ratio = (cash + receivables + securities)/curr. liabilities

Measures of leverage

$$\text{Debt to equity ratio} = (\text{long term debt} + \text{value of leases})/\text{equity}$$

Measures of profitability

$$\text{Return on assets before interest and taxes (''RONABIT'')} = \text{EBIT}/\text{total assets}$$
$$\text{Return on equity (''ROE'')} = \text{net income}/\text{average equity}$$
$$\text{Return on investment (''ROI'')} = \text{net income}/\text{total assets}$$
$$\text{Return on investment (project)} = \text{uniform annual cash flow}/\text{initial investment}$$

Market measures

$$\text{P/E ratio} = \text{price per share}/\text{earnings per share}$$

Measures of operational efficiency

$$\text{Collection period} = \text{accounts receivable}/(\text{sales}/360)$$
$$\text{Inventory turnover} = \text{cost of goods sold}/\text{avg. inventory}$$
$$\text{Days inventory on hand} = 365/\text{inventory turnover}$$

Useful Financial Terms

Assets. Real, intangible, and financial items the corporation owns or has a claim upon. Assets traditionally appear on the left side of the BALANCE SHEET.

Balance Sheet. One part of the FINANCIAL STATEMENT which lists the wealth of the corporation at a specific point in time. Traditionally, ASSETS appear on the left and LIABILITIES on the right and the two must be in balance. EQUITY is a form of liability representing what the corporation owes to the stockholders.

Breakeven. The breakeven volume is the number of units the company must sell to recover its fixed and variable costs of production, at a given price. The breakeven price is the price the company must charge to recover its fixed and variable costs, at a given sales volume.

$$\text{QBKEVEN} = \text{FC} / (\text{P} - \text{AVC}) \text{ or } \text{PBKEVEN} = (\text{FC} / \text{Q}) - \text{AVC}$$

Cash Flow, Cash Flow Statement. Cash flow measures the profit of the company over a given time period in cash terms (as opposed to accrual terms). A CASH FLOW STATEMENT is generated by beginning with an accrual-based INCOME STATEMENT, and making the following adjustments:

- add back in non-cash expenses such as depreciation
- subtract increases / add decreases in operating assets
- add increases / subtract decreases in operating liabilities
- subtract cash going to / add cash coming from capital investments
- add cash coming from / subtract cash going to financing activities

Debt. An obligation or liability arising from borrowing money or taking goods on credit. Forms of debt include bank loans, bond sold to investors, and various types of "commercial paper." Debt holders are creditors of the company; stockholders are owners of the company.

Depreciation. A non-cash expense entered on the income statement to recognize the reduction in value of FIXED ASSETS due to wear and tear.

Discount Rate. The rate at which future cash flows are discounted because of the time value of money.

Income Statement. One part of the FINANCIAL STATEMENT which lists the REVENUE, EXPENSE, and PROFIT (or loss) of the company over a period of time. Traditionally, revenue appears on the right and expenses on the left.

EBIT = Earnings Before Interest and Taxes. (PROFIT before you subtract interest and tax expenses. It measures efficiency of operations independent of financial matters such as interest rates and tax rates.)

EBITDA = Earnings Before Interest, Taxes, Depreciation, and Amortization. (Profit before you subtract interest, tax, and non-cash expenses. It measures efficiency of operations independent of interest rates, tax rates, and capital investments in plant, equipment, and intellectual property.)

Equity. The "book value" of the company's stock. (Not the market value it is trading at on the stock exchange.) Equity holders are owners of the company.

Equivalent Annual Cost. The cost of obtaining and maintaining an asset annualized over its life (as if you were leasing it from someone else).

Expense. Payments made by the company to others for value received. DEPRECIATION is a "non-cash" expense used to estimate the decrease in value of a FIXED ASSET over time.

Financial Statement. A comprehensive description of the company's finances including the BALANCE SHEET, INCOME STATEMENT, and CASH FLOW STATEMENT.

Fixed Asset. An asset such as property, plant, equipment, or intellectual property that has a long life and cannot be expensed in a single year.

Fixed Costs. Costs which do not vary significantly in the short term with the volume of production. Property, plant, and equipment are examples.

Income Statement. One part of the FINANCIAL STATEMENT which lists REVENUE, EXPENSE, and PROFIT (or loss) of the firm over a period of time.

Internal Rate of Return ("IRR"). Mathematically, IRR is the discount rate at which the investment has zero NET PRESENT VALUE ("NPV"). If that is a little too abstract, you can think of it as "Return on Investment," although that is mathematically incorrect. IRR is used to compare and contrast different projects that the corporation could invest in. Higher is better. There is no formula for IRR, but spreadsheets can calculate it, iteratively.

Leverage. The ratio of total assets to total equity. A "highly leveraged" company will have high total assets in relation to low equity.

Liabilities. Any claims against the firm. Liabilities traditionally appear on the right side of the BALANCE SHEET.

Net Present Value. The initial cost of an investment (a negative number) plus the PRESENT VALUE of the future CASH FLOWS it will generate (a positive number).

Nominal Dollars. Dollars which are not adjusted for inflation or time value of money.

Opportunity Cost of Capital. The value of other opportunities you gave up to invest in the capital project in question.

Present Value. Future cash flows in terms of their value today, using a DISCOUNT RATE.

Real Dollars. Dollars at some other time adjusted to their value in current-day terms.

Revenue. Money (or other value) received for products sold to customers.

Time Value of Money. A dollar today is (usually) worth more than a dollar tomorrow, due to inflation, costs of borrowing, and risk. The DISCOUNT RATE measures the difference between current and future dollars.

Variable Costs. Costs which vary in the short term with the level of production. Raw materials are an example.

Your Place in the CFO's Frame of Reference

For a more complete version of this paper (free of charge) which contains mathematical formulae and worked-out examples, send a request to: Tom McCune, CEO/Senior Consultant, AE Pragmatics, Inc., San Mateo, CA, (aepragmat @aol.com).

Appendix B: Sample Facility Management Business Plan (Annex to the Company Strategic Business Plan and Annual Workplan)

Scenario

The Ingalls Company is an aggressively expanding retailer of home improvement products headquartered in the central United States. It currently serves about one-third of the country, and its ten-year business plan is to increase that geographic market to close to half of the United States and to expand into Manitoba and western Ontario in Canada.

Ingalls has struggled with both growth and strategic business planning. It has an industry-wide reputation for cost containment, particularly in the area of overhead. The company is in the fourth year of strategic business planning, but this is the first year that the facility manager has participated. The facility manager was included as a result of two factors: (1) cost overruns during the construction of the last distribution center and (2) upper management's realization that facility maintenance and repair has probably been underfunded and that this has resulted in some operational problems.

The facility manager has been in his position for about nine months and took the position after retiring from the Navy Civil Engineering Corps, where, in his last assignment, he was responsible for all facilities at Oceana Naval Air Station in Virginia. He is the first facility manager at Ingalls who has had facility management experience, and he reports directly to the CEO, who is the sole owner of this privately owned company. During the facility manager's final job interview with Ingalls prior to his hiring, it was emphasized that he was being hired for his ability to (1) reduce energy costs, (2) manage a substantial capital program, (3) upgrade the quality of Ingalls's facilities, and (4) reduce the backlog of maintenance. At the same time, he understands completely that this is a "lean and mean" organization that wants to minimize all administrative costs. Upon his arrival, he found almost no FM policies or procedures and no real FM staff. He is a member of the company's strategic planning group, and he seems to have established a good rapport with and gained the confidence of both his colleagues and the CEO.

Ingalls uses a very decentralized management model, so the facility manager is responsible only for corporate facilities (currently a dilapidated office building, a leased "back office" low-rise, and a smattering of leased office space) in rural Wisconsin and for the regional distribution centers, of which there are currently three. The distribution center at headquarters also includes a large maintenance facility. The facility manager has this model under study, since a major capital expansion will occur over the next ten years.

The corporate facility manager has the full range of facility responsibilities for corporate real estate, but he is not responsible for either security or office services such as reprographics and mail and messenger. He has thus far resisted any expansion of his duties beyond those associated with the buildings, but coordination problems, particularly with security and transportation services, have caused him to reconsider. Because he realized that a business planning cycle was upcoming and that he would be expected to contribute, the facility manager has concentrated on developing and obtaining approval for a capital improvement plan and a real estate and leasing plan. In addition, he has worked hard to convince his colleagues of the need for building condition assessments.

The facility manager has prepared his annual workplan for fiscal year 2003 and his strategic facility business plan for fiscal years 2004 to 2013. The latter projects an annual plan for fiscal years 2004 to 2008 and a "roll-up" projection for fiscal years 2009 to 2013.

The following facility management annual workplan and ten-year facility management business plan represent the facility manager's initial submission to the Ingalls business planning team. As such, the workplan provides a realistic projection of the facility department's needs and wants for fiscal year 2003 (within a reasonable range for the likely facility budget for that year), while the long-range facility business plan represents the best possible projection of FM needs by program for the next ten years.

Note: For illustrative purposes, we have included material in italics within the plans. This material would not appear in an actual annual workplan or strategic business plan. It is provided only as an explanation.

Annex F (Facility Management) to the Ingalls Company Ten-Year Business Plan

I. **Introduction.** This is a first attempt to produce a facility business plan to support Ingalls's strategic business plan. It is reflective of our philosophy that the proper management of our facilities contributes to corporate success and to the bottom line. Our goal in the facilities department is to:
    - Provide an efficient and cost-effective workplace
    - Provide outstanding customer service to our internal and external customers
    - Provide a safe and healthy environment for all Ingalls's employees
    - Considering the preceding factors, render all services in the most timely and cost-effective manner possible
II. **Environment**
    A. Company sales are expected to grow NLT 5 percent per year through the period of the study. (*From company business plan*)
    B. The company will expand into the Dakotas and Montana in FY 2003 and 2004; the Pacific Northwest in FY

2005 and 2006; Indiana and Ohio in FY 2007 and 2008; Iowa, Missouri, and Winnipeg in FY 2009 and 2010; and the rest of Manitoba, eastern Alberta, and western Ontario in FY 2011 and 2012. (*From company business plan*)

   C. For each two-year geographic expansion, a centrally located distribution center will be constructed. (*From company business plan*)

   D. The company wishes to be in owned space, with short-term leasing used only for unforeseen needs. The company wishes to be out of headquarters leased space by FY 2006. (*From company business plan*)

   E. Headquarters personnel spaces are limited to 1 percent less than business expansion projections throughout the period, i.e., if business expands annually at 5 percent, personnel increases are limited to 4 percent. (*From company business plan*)

   F. An austere, highly functional headquarters will be built in the Eau Claire–Chippewa Falls–Menomonie vicinity by FY 2006. (*From company business plan*)

   G. The company will conduct condition assessments of all company facilities starting in FY 2003. Assessments will be repeated every ten years. (*From FM staff*)

   H. Starting in FY 2003, the facility department will use a programmatic budget. (*From FM staff*)

   I. Starting in FY 2005, improving maintenance and repair based on the results of condition assessments will be emphasized. (*From FM staff*)

III. Assumptions

   A. Inflation will be 3 percent throughout the planning period. (*From company business plan*)

   B. FM cost inflation will be as follows:

      1. O&M: 3 percent

      2. Renovation and construction: 5 percent

      3. Leasing: 3 percent on existing leases; 5 percent on new leases

      4. Utilities

         • Gas: 4 percent

         • Electricity: 3 percent until 2006; 4 percent until 2010; 5 percent thereafter

         • Water: 2 percent until 2007; 3 percent thereafter

         • Planning and design: 3 percent (*From FM staff; approved by controller*)

IV. Constraints

   A. Administrative services will be outsourced to the extent possible. (*From company business plan*)

   B. All renovation and construction contracting will use local contractors chosen through a performance-based methodology. (*From FM staff*)

V. Discussion

   A. Scenarios

      1. Scenario 1

         • The department will be fully successful in meeting all of its goals. The business goals of the company and the department as spelled out in the Environment section of this plan will all be achieved and fully funded.

         • We will reduce energy costs at least 10 percent below those currently projected from current usage.

         • The backlog of maintenance will be reduced by 2008.

      2. Scenario 2. The department will be fully successful in meeting all of its goals. The business goals of the company and the department as spelled out in the Environment section of this plan will all be achieved *except that there will be no expansion into Canada.*

      3. Scenario 3

         • The department will be fully successful in meeting all of its goals except that the backlog of maintenance and repair will not be eliminated until 2010.

         • The business goals of the company and the department as spelled out in the Environment section of this plan will all be achieved *except that there will be no expansion into Canada and the headquarters completion will be delayed until 2012.*

   B. Impact on Programs of Each Scenario

      1. Scenario 1 enables the facility management department to meet all of its goals and best serve the company. In turn, it is the most expensive, although it also provides for energy savings (one of the FM department's goals). Starting in 2009, maintenance and repair costs should stabilize, since the backlog will have been reduced. This scenario alone ensures that the company will have facilities available where and when they are needed and that those facilities will be safe, secure, productive, and healthy.

      2. Scenario 2 also enables the facility management department to meet all of its goals and to serve the company well. Costs under this scenario will be less, since there will be no need for a Canadian distribution center, but that also represents a business loss for the company.

      3. Scenario 3 represents a plan to meet all FM goals, but on a slower schedule. Staff will have to use less well-maintained facilities for two more years. The greatest challenge will be maintaining a productive workplace for an additional four years in the existing headquarters and through short-term leasing. This will raise leasing costs. A hidden cost will be our inability to reduce energy costs because they are included in our full-service leases.

VI. Conclusion

   A. All scenarios can be supported by the FM department.

   B. Unless otherwise directed, FM department budgeting and planning will be premised on Scenario 1.

Appendixes:
1. Financial Displays (*only Scenario 1 displayed*)
2. Time-Phased List of Events
3. Personnel Projections
4. Space Inventory Projections

Annex F-1 (Financial Scenario 1) to the Facility Management Strategic Business Plan (2004–2013)

Accounts	2004	2005	2006	2007	2008	2009–2013
Overhead						
Personnel (Note 1)						
Costs	531.4	620.7	715.5	744.1	773.9	5727
FTEs (Note 2)	*8*	*9*	*10*	*10*	*10*	*50*
Office Equipment						
Purchase	37.4	75	40.5	0	44	344
Operations and Maintenance	25.8	23	28	29	35	250
Vehicular O&M (Note 3)	6	6.2	7	7.2	8	57
Studies, Design, and Engineering						
(Note 4)	20	41	20.8	42	22	79
Total:	620.6	765.9	811.8	813.3	882.9	6457
Operations and Maintenance						
(Note 5)						
Utilities						
Gas	78	85	101	105	127	671
Electricity	475	570	683	710	841	6429
Water/Sewage	31.5	39.1	47	48.4	56.9	373
Oil	0	0	0	0	0	0
Operations	201	235	282	290	339	1970
Maintenance	391	450	386	398	461	2970
Repair	307	320	390	402	474	3073
Custodial	331	402	475	489	564	3789
Moving	156	209	161	51	174	501
Total:	1970.5	2310.1	2525	2493.4	3036.9	19776
Noncapital Projects						
Construction	123	175	150	80	120	360
Renovation	103	105	109	50	52	550
Repair	130	133	136	111	114	550
Minor Construction	150	155	160	80	80	400
Equipment	85	103	106	20	103	272
Furniture	25	25	10	11	12	60
Design and Engineering						
(Note 6)	12	13				21
Total:	628	709	671	352	481	2213
Real Estate						
Leases	1872	36	0	0	0	150
Utilities (Note 7)	0	0	0	0	0	0
Alterations	57	30	0	0	0	120
Equipment	0	0	0	0	0	0
Furniture	0	0	0	0	0	0
Design and Engineering	0	0	0	0	0	12
Lease Income	− 23	− 18	0	0	0	0
Total:	1906	48	0	0	0	282
Grand Total:	5125.1	3833	4007.8	3658.7	4400.8	28728
Capital (Note 8)						
Construction	1750		1900		2300	4800
Alteration	125	130	135	140	145	800
Major Repair	125	132	141	50	53	295
Replacement	80	81	95	30	31	170
Equipment	93	96	101	50	52	290
Furniture	53	262	57	0	60	151
Design and Engineering	90	100	100	130	100	380
Total:	2316	801	2529	400	2741	6886

Notes:
1. Includes salary, benefits, training, and travel
2. FTE = Full-time equivalent personnel position
3. (For FM department only)
4. (Necessary preliminary work for major proposed projects; transferred to actual project budget if [a] the project is approved, [b] it is in the same budget year, or [c] it is a capital project.)
5. (FM department does not have responsibility for such functions as reprographics, mail, security, telecommunications, etc.)
6. (Not assignable to a specific project)
7. For non-full-service leases
8. (The capital program is normally planned and budgeted separately. For illustrative purposes only.)

Appendix F-2 to the Facility Management Strategic Plan (2004–2013), Time-Phased List of Major Events

2003

2004   Occupy distribution center for Dakotas/Montana.
Conduct condition assessment of one-third of buildings.

2005   Start construction of new headquarters.
Conduct condition assessment of one-third of buildings.
Order furniture and furnishings for new headquarters.

2006   Occupy distribution center for Pacific Northwest.
Occupy new headquarters.

2007

2008   Occupy distribution center for Indiana/Ohio.

2009

2010   Occupy distribution center for Iowa/Missouri.

2011

2012   Occupy Canadian distribution center.

2013

Appendix F-3 to the Facility Management Strategic Business Plan (2004–2013), Personnel Projections

2004   Hire facility manager.
Convert half-time maintenance mechanic to full-time maintenance supervisor.

2005   Hire building engineer/maintenance supervisor for headquarters.

2006   Hire construction/maintenance manager.

Appendix F-4 to the Facility Management Strategic Business Plan (2004–2013), Space Inventory Projections

Space Inventory (000 gsf)
(a/o last day of fiscal year)

	2004	2005	2006	2007	2008
Owned	280	350	420	420	490
Leased	53	9	0	0	0

	2009	2010	2011	2012	2013
Owned	490	560	560	630	630
Leased	0	0	0	9	9

Appendix C: Facility Management Workplan—FY 2003—The Ingalls Company (Note 1)

Accounts	$K	FTEs	Remarks
Overhead			
Personnel			
Costs	447.5		
FTEs		7	New FM; full-time maintenance person
Office Equipment			
Purchase	36		Priority 2
Operations and Maintenance	25		
Vehicular O&M	4.8		
Studies, Design, and Engineering			
Long-Range Real Estate Study			
and Plan	45		Priority 2
Energy Cost Reduction Study	37		
Location Study for Dakotas/Montana Distribu-			
tion Center	21		
Total:	**616.3**		
Operations and Maintenance			
Utilities			
Gas	72.5		
Electricity	412		
Water/Sewage	28.3		
Oil	0		
Operations			
Snow Removal	63		
Grounds Maintenance	31.3		
Safety Operations	36.3		Priority 2 to reduce
Environmental Operations	30		Priority 2 to reduce
Maintenance			
Preventive	57.2		
Scheduled	151		
"Catch-up"	125		Priority 2 to reduce
Repair	240		
Custodial	263		
Moving/Porter Services	151.8		
Total:	**1661.4**		
Noncapital Projects			
Construction	0		
Renovation			
Upgrade Headquarters			
Lobbies	31		
Renovate the Cafeteria	53		
Executive Area Upgrade	17		
Repair			
Recarpet Headquarters	63.8		Priority 2 to reduce
Resurface Parking Lot	37.6		Priority 1
"Catch-up"	23		Priority 1
Minor Construction			
Unassigned	35		Priority 1
New Security Stations	25.2		
Garage/Maintenance			
Facilities at Distribution			
Centers	89.1		Priority 2 to reduce
Equipment	83		Priority 2 to reduce
Furniture	21		Priority 1
Design and Engineering			
Headquarters Lobbies	3		
Cafeteria Renovation	4.3		
Executive Areas	1.7		

Accounts	$K	FTEs	Remarks
Security Stations	2.5		
Standard Garage/			
Maintenance Facility	7.5		
Building Assessment	11		
Total:	**508.7**		
Real Estate			
Leases	1800		
Utilities			
Alterations	55		Priority 1
Equipment	10		
Furniture	8		Priority 1
Design and Engineering			
Lease Income	− 22		
Total:	**1851**		
Grand Total:	**4637.4**		

Capital (*Would not ordinarily be shown in the annual workplan; for illustrative purposes only*)

Accounts	$K	FTEs	Remarks
Construction			
Alterations			
Major Repair			
Replacement	103		
Equipment			
Furniture			
Design and Engineering			
Design of Standard			
Distribution Center	120		
Site Adaptation of the			
Standard Plan for Dakotas/			
Montana	11		
Total:	**234.3**		

Notes:

1. Total budget 2002 ($K)
   a. Annual budget: 3,902.8 (*FY 2003 budget represents a 20% increase; not likely*)
   b. Capital budget: 103
   c. FTEs: 5 1/2
   d. Space
      (1) Owned: 280,000 gsf
      (2) Leased: 25,000 gsf
2. Priorities indicated in Remarks show how cuts would be taken if necessary. Priority 1 cuts would be taken first.

Appendix D: Facility Management Annual Budget—FY 2003—The Ingalls Company

Accounts	$K	FTEs	Expended This Month	Expended Year to Date	Variance	Actual Expenditure This Point Last Year	Actual Expenditure Last Month	Actual Expenditure Last Quarter	Remarks
Overhead									
Personnel									
Costs	447.5								
FTEs		7							
Office Equipment									
Purchase	29								
Operations and									
Maintenance	25								
Vehicular O&M	4.8								
Studies, Design and									
Engineering									
Long-Range Real Estate									
Study and Plan	38								
Energy Cost Reduction									
Study	37								
Location Study for									
Dakotas/Montana									
Distribution Center	25								
Total	**606.3**								
Operations and Maintenance									
Utilities									
Gas	72.5								
Electricity	415								
Water/Sewage	28.3								
Oil	0								
Operations									
Snow Removal	51								
Grounds Maintenance	31.3								
Safety Operations	40								
Environmental Opera-									
tions	33								
Maintenance									
Preventive	55								
Scheduled	151								
Catch-up	60								
Repair	240								
Custodial	252								
Moving/Porter Services	151.8								
Total:	**1580.9**								
Noncapital Projects									
Construction									
New Maintenance									
Shed	17								
Renovation									
Upgrade Headquarters									
Lobbies	32								
Renovate the Cafeteria	55								
Executive Area Upgrade	21								
Repair									
Recarpet Headquarters	60								
Resurface Parking Lot	41								
Catch-up	10								

Minor Construction
   New Security Stations   36
   Corporate Security
      Systems   17
   Garage/Maintenance
Facilities at Distribution
   Centers   92
Equipment   87
Furniture   37
Design and Engineering
   Headquarters Lobbies   4
   Cafeteria Renovation   4.3
   Executive Areas   2.1
   Security Stations and
      Executive Security   4.3
   Standard Garage/
      Maintenance Facility   7.5
   Building Assessment   18
      Total: **545.2**

Real Estate
   Leases   1800
   Utilities
   Alterations   32
   Equipment   10
   Furniture   0
   Design and Engineering   0
   Lease Income   −22
      Total: **1820**
        Grand Total: **4552.4**

Appendix E: Cost Justification

The ability to justify projects economically is an important skill. Companies set requirements for funds use far in excess of what is available in any one year. Two basic approaches have been developed to quantify the economic benefits of particular projects and to prioritize them. For instance, with the *accept-reject approach*, everything over a certain benchmark (benefit-cost ratio = 3.5, for example) is selected, and anything under it is rejected. Or the highest-ranking projects (rank-ordered by IRR, for example) up to the funds available are included in the budget; this is the *ranking approach*. Facility managers should be familiar with these analytical tools and should be aware of their strengths and limitations.

Cost justification is the term used for making decisions between competing proposed projects or go/no-go choices on specific proposed projects. Although the technique is most applicable to capital projects, it can be used whenever there is some degree of freedom to select among competing projects and the analytical time can be cost-justified.

Cost justification has these objectives:

1. Selecting the project with the highest potential for reward
2. Selecting the project that limits or minimizes financial risk
3. Prioritizing the projects competing for limited resources

The factors brought together to evaluate investment alternatives include the net amount of the investment required for a project, the returns or cash flows expected from an investment in the project, and the company's lowest acceptable rate of return on investment, or its cost of capital. The actual cost-evaluation tools we consider here are these:

- Average payback period
- Actual payback period
- Net present value
- Internal rate of return
- Benefit-cost ratio

The first two methods of evaluating investment alternatives are listed to provide a concept only—the idea that an investment must pay back over a period of time to be justified. Payback, however, is overly simplistic, and I do not recommend that anyone use it for making capital decisions.

Average Payback Period

Calculating an average payback period is a method for making an accept/reject decision or to select one project against a standard set by management:

$$\text{Average payback period (years)} = \frac{\text{Net investment}}{\text{Average annual cash inflow}}$$

Advantages	Disadvantages
• Simple to use	• Does not fully consider time value of money
• Considers cash flows	• Does not consider subsequent cash flow
• A measure of risk	• Cash inflows can be subjective

To use this device, select the project that meets or beats the predetermined maximum average payback period or best average payback period of alternative projects. See Figure E-1 for an example.

Figure E-1. Payback Period.

	Investment A	Investment B
Cost	$3,000	$7,000
Net annual cash flow	1,000	2,000
Payback period	3 years	3.5 years
Preferred investment:	Investment A	

David G. Cotts, *Facility Management Handbook*, 2d ed. (New York: AMACOM, 1999).

Actual Payback Period

This method uses the same data as the average payback period analysis but calculates an actual payback time. Actual payback is when the sum of prior cash inflow exactly equals the initial investment. The payback period is the time it takes to recover the cost of the investment through the net cash flow. The net cash flow consists of the after-tax value of savings generated by the project, and the tax write-off resulting from depreciation expense. To calculate the payback period, divide the annual net cash flow into the cost of the investment. A shorter payback period will be the investment alternative of choice with this method. A major drawback of the payback method is that ongoing long-term profitability is not included in evaluating the investment alternatives.

Advantages	Disadvantages
• Measures risk	• Does not fully consider time value of money
• Simple to use	• Does not consider subsequent cash flow
• Considers timing of cash flows	

To use the device, select the project that meets or beats the predetermined maximum payback period, or the shortest actual payback period among the alternatives.

Net Present Value

This analytic tool determines the dollar value, at time zero, of some future series of cash flows, discounted at the company's cost of capital. It measures expected future benefits (cash flows) against initial investment. The NPV method recognizes the time value of money. All the cash flows over the life of the investment are converted to present value. The present values of both cash inflows and the outflows are netted. If the NPV is positive, the investment alternative is good. If comparing two investment alternatives, choose the alternative with the higher NPV or lower negative NPV.

$$NPV = \text{Present value of future cash flows} - \text{net investment}$$

To calculate an NPV, you must know the initial net investment, the company's cost of capital, and future cash flows.

Advantages	Disadvantages
• Gives consideration to the time value of money	• Makes assumptions as to the cost of capital
• Considers all relevant cash flows	• More difficult to calculate; needs table of discount
• Commonly used and understood	factors

To use the device, select the project that has the highest positive NPV, or the smallest negative NPV from alternative projects. See Figure 5-2 for an example. The discounted cash flow can be complicated when you must take into consideration any salvage value of the investment and the annual depreciation amounts. Salvage value should be included as a cash inflow and converted to present value. Depreciation is not a cash expense; however, it does affect the tax expense by reducing the tax owed. So depreciation times the tax rate is a "cash inflow" to be converted to present value for each year depreciation is taken.

Internal Rate of Return

The IRR is the discount rate assuming an NPV of zero:

$$IRR = NPV = 0$$

To calculate the IRR of a project, you must know the initial net investment and future cash inflows. To make an accept/reject decision, you must know the company's cost of capital.

Advantages	Disadvantages
• Gives consideration to the time value of money	• Difficult to calculate without a good financial calculator
• Considers all relevant cash flows	lator
	• Less understood by nonfinancial managers
	• Assumes that all intermediate cash flows are reinvested at company's IRR

Once the IRR has been calculated for all competing projects, select the project that has an IRR greater than or equal to the company's cost of capital.

Figure E-2. Net Present Value.

Example:		Investment A	Investment B
Cost		$10,000	$11,000
Savings each year		$ 2,000	$ 4,000
Number of years with savings		4 years	4 years

(The discount rate is 10%.)

	Cost	Present Value Factor— P.V. of Inflow	Net Cash
Investment A	$10,000	$2,000 × 3.1699* = $ 6,340	($3,660)
Investment B	11,000	4,000 × 3.1699* = 12,680	1,680

Preferred Investment: Investment B

Present Value of $1 at Compound Interest

Periods Hence	4½%	5%	6%	7%	8%	9%	10%	12%	14%	16%
1	0.9569	0.9524	0.9434	0.9346	0.9259	0.9174	0.9091	0.8929	0.8772	0.8621
2	0.9157	0.9070	0.8900	0.8734	0.8573	0.8417	0.8265	0.7972	0.7695	0.7432
3	0.8763	0.8638	0.8396	0.8163	0.7938	0.7722	0.7513	0.7118	0.6750	0.6407
4	0.8386	0.8227	0.7921	0.7629	0.7350	0.7084	0.6830	0.6355	0.5921	0.5523
5	0.8025	0.7835	0.7473	0.7130	0.6806	0.6499	0.6209	0.5675	0.5194	0.4761
6	0.7679	0.7462	0.7050	0.6663	0.6302	0.5963	0.5645	0.5066	0.4556	0.4104
7	0.7348	0.7107	0.6651	0.6228	0.5835	0.5470	0.5132	0.4524	0.3996	0.3538
8	0.7032	0.6768	0.6274	0.5820	0.5403	0.5019	0.4665	0.4039	0.3506	0.3050
9	0.6729	0.6446	0.5919	0.5439	0.5003	0.4604	0.4241	0.3606	0.3075	0.2630
10	0.6439	0.6139	0.5584	0.5084	0.4632	0.4224	0.3855	0.3220	0.2697	0.2267
11	0.6162	0.5847	0.5268	0.4751	0.4289	0.3875	0.3505	0.2875	0.2366	0.1954
12	0.5897	0.5568	0.4970	0.4440	0.3971	0.3555	0.3186	0.2567	0.2076	0.1685
13	0.5643	0.5303	0.4688	0.4150	0.3677	0.3262	0.2897	0.2292	0.1821	0.1452
14	0.5100	0.5051	0.4423	0.3878	0.3405	0.2993	0.2633	0.2046	0.1597	0.1252
15	0.5167	0.4810	0.4173	0.3625	0.3152	0.2745	0.2394	0.1827	0.1401	0.1079
16	0.4945	0.4581	0.3937	0.3387	0.2919	0.2519	0.2176	0.1631	0.1229	0.0930
17	0.4732	0.4363	0.3714	0.3166	0.2703	0.2311	0.1978	0.1456	0.1078	0.0802
18	0.4528	0.4155	0.3503	0.2959	0.2503	0.2120	0.1799	0.1300	0.0946	0.0691
19	0.4333	0.3957	0.3305	0.2765	0.2317	0.1945	0.1635	0.1161	0.0830	0.0596
20	0.4146	0.3769	0.3118	0.2584	0.2146	0.1784	0.1486	0.1037	0.0728	0.0514

*The sum of the first four entries under 10 percent interest. Why?

Benefit-Cost Ratio

For very large projects, one way to reach an accept/reject decision is to calculate the BCR.

$$BCR = \frac{\text{Value of benefits of the project}}{\text{Costs of the project}}$$

Both benefits and costs are stated in constant-year dollars.

Implicit in such an analysis is that a wide variety of costs and benefits can be calculated. Ordinarily, calculating costs is much more straightforward than calculating benefits. As a minimum, a sophisticated economics staff is required to calculate benefits and costs. Which benefits and costs can be included is often stated in law or policy.

After the BCR for the project in question is calculated, the project is accepted based on whether the BCR exceeds a certain value fixed by policy. Seldom is a project with a BCR lower than 1.0 undertaken.

Preparing Financial Analyses

As noted in the descriptions of the cost-justification tools, there is considerable room for interpretation in obtaining or calculating costs, benefits, inflows, and incomes, compounded by the fact that the data are often incomplete. Because so much judgment is involved, you need to control the process carefully. If the calculations are done by an accountant or budget department analyst, then you must be prepared to live with the results. The issue is not one of honesty; it is one of balanced judgment. For example, carpet *can* last twelve to fifteen years, but my experience is that tolerance for it wears out after six years. No matter which analytical tool you use, the results will be dramatically different when six rather than twelve years is estimated for new carpet.

In their enthusiasm to purchase a new product, some facility managers rely on the vendor to furnish economic justification or perform the analysis in the company's format. This is frequently done to justify the higher initial cost of carpet tile over broadloom, for example. But there are a couple of risks to that action. First, it may not be possible to support those numbers to management when they are challenged. Second, the calculations might not be supportable at a specific location and situation.

Chargebacks

Charging business units for facility services is widely accepted in both the private and the public sectors. In a 1996 survey, 57 percent of all respondents reported some type of expense chargeback system in use for their services. There are three systems in place for administering the chargeback system.

1. Charge the actual cost of services plus perhaps an overhead charge.
2. Charge an allocation based on factors like space occupied or the number of employees.
3. A combination of the first two systems.

Appendix F: Life-Cycle Cost Analysis for the Beginner

One of the characteristics that distinguishes the professional facility manager is the ability to manage assets in a cost effective manner. The following are examples of cost related decisions that must be made:

- The choice between equipment purchase options
- Decisions about when to replace or repair
- Determination of the value of more efficient equipment
- Comparison of in-house versus out-sourced services
- Comparison with other company investment opportunities

Fortunately, when a basic knowledge of the concepts of present value, average annual cost, and internal rate of return is combined with a computer spreadsheet, the facility manager is able to reach a decision quickly and accurately. A computer spreadsheet is available from the author that will calculate the present value, the average annual cost, and the internal rate of return. It will also allow for tax depreciation and escalation of costs.[1]

The purpose of this presentation is to provide the facility manager with a working knowledge of three financial analysis tools combined with a spreadsheet that will convert annual cash flows into numbers suitable for comparison.

The objectives of this presentation are:

- An understanding of the terms: present value, average annual cost, and internal rate of return.
- The ability to determine when to use each of the above.
- An understanding of how to use the provided spreadsheet starting with the estimated annual costs, over the live of the items involved.

Simple Total Cost (Does Not Use the Discount Factor)

A common problem in facility management occurs when purchase decisions are made without consideration for the cost of operation. In the following example, two items are compared that have different initial costs and different annual operating costs.

The simple method has some serious deficiencies. It is not appropriate for comparison of options that have different lifetimes, it doesn't take into account the time value of money, and it doesn't allow for comparison with other projects. In the example shown in figures F-1 and F-2, the regular carpet has a lower first-cost and a lower cost over its shorter life. This can be misleading.

The Time Value of Money

Many states conduct lotteries where they advertise that the winning ticket is worth a million dollars. Instead of receiving a check for $1,000,000, the winner is awarded $50,000 a year for twenty years. However, if someone tried to sell the winning ticket, they would soon find out that it is only worth a little more than half a million. The reason for this is that cash in hand today can be put to work earning income and is therefore more valuable than the same amount of money to be received in the future. Consider the series of payments in the lottery example. The first check for $50,000 can be invested immediately and start earning money. As an example, let's say that it could earn 7 percent (or pay off a loan at 7 percent). Its **present value** is $50,000. The second payment won't arrive until next year. If you had $46,728.97 to invest at 7 percent for a year, it would be worth $50,000 when the next lottery payment arrives. The present value of the future payment of $50,000 is only $46,728.97. The present value of each of the

Figure F-1. Simple Life-Cycle Cost Method (Does Not Include the Discount Factor).

Description: High Quality Carpet

	Initial Costs	Annual Costs	Year 1	Year 2	Year 3	Year 4	Year 5	Year 6	Year 7	Year 8	Year 9	Year 10
Purchase	8000	Labor	800	800	800	800	800	800	800	800	800	800
Installation	2000	Materials	200	200	200	200	200	200	200	200	200	200
Other		Other										
	10000		1000	1000	1000	1000	1000	1000	1000	1000	1000	1000
Total Cost	20000											

1. By Professor John Preston, 122 Sill Hall, Ypsilanti, MI 48197. From *Proceedings of the Annual Conference, 1993* (Houston: International Facility Management Association, 1993).

Figure F-2. Simple Life-Cycle Cost Method (Does Not Include the Discount Factor).

Description: Regular Carpet

	Initial Costs	Annual Costs	Year 1	Year 2	Year 3	Year 4	Year 5	Year 6	Year 7	Year 8	Year 9	Year 10
Purchase	6000	Labor	1000	1000	1000	1000	1000	1000	1000			
Installation	2000	Materials	250	250	250	250	250	250	250			
Other		Other										
	8000		1250	1250	1250	1250	1250	1250	1250			
Total Cost	16750											

following payments becomes less and less until the value of the last payment the winner would receive in nineteen years is $13,825. The interest rate that we used to determine these lower values is called the **discount rate.** A more complete definition is contained in this excerpt from a finance text: "The **present value** of a cash flow is what it is worth in today's dollars. Present value incorporates the time value principle by **discounting** future dollars (computing their **present value**) using the appropriate discount rate (interest rate). In investment analysis, this discount rate is the cost of capital."[2]

The present value of the sum of the future payments could be calculated using the following formula (DR stands for discount rate).[3]

$$\text{Net Present Value} = \frac{\text{Payment 1}}{(1+\text{DR})} + \frac{\text{Payment 2}}{(1+\text{DR})^2} + \frac{\text{Payment 3}}{(1+\text{DR})^3} \cdots \text{Etc.}$$

This process is cumbersome and is far easier to do on a computer spreadsheet.

Consider the example of the carpet after the time value of money is taken into account (figures F-3 and F-4).

The regular carpet still appears to have the advantage. This is because we are comparing two products that have a different life. The present value method should only be used under the following circumstances:

- Two alternatives are being compared that will do the same job
- The expected lifetime of the alternatives is the same

If the expected lifetimes of the two alternatives are different, it would be misleading to compare them over the same length of time.

Figure F-3. Net Present Value.

Description: High Quality Carpet

Discount Factor 7.00%	Costs	Costs	Year 1	Year 2	Year 3	Year 4	Year 5	Year 6	Year 7	Year 8	Year 9	Year 10
Purchase	8000	Labor	800	800	800	800	800	800	800	800	800	800
Installation	2000	Materials	200	200	200	200	200	200	200	200	200	200
Other		Other										
	10000		1000	1000	1000	1000	1000	1000	1000	1000	1000	1000
Annual Present Values →	10000		935	873	816	763	713	666	623	582	544	508
Net Present Value	17024											

2. Lawrence D. Schall and Charles W. Haley, *Introduction to Financial Management* (New York: McGraw-Hill, 1983), p. 219.
3. Schall and Haley, p. 219.

Figure F-4. Net Present Value.

Description: Regular Carpet												
Discount Factor	7.00%		Year 1	Year 2	Year 3	Year 4	Year 5	Year 6	Year 7	Year 8	Year 9	Year 10
	Costs	Costs										
Purchase	6000	Labor	1000	1000	1000	1000	1000	1000	1000			
Installation	2000	Materials	250	250	250	250	250	250	250			
Other		Other										
	8000		1250	1250	1250	1250	1250	1250	1250			
Annual Present Values→	8000		1168	1092	1020	954	891	833	778			
Net Present Value	14737											

The Average Annual Cost

If you are comparing alternatives that will do the same job but have different lifetimes, then the average annual cost method is appropriate. This method also takes into account the time value of money and uses the discount rate. The difference is that it divides the net present value by the life of the item. This provides a value that can be used to compare options that have different life expectancies. The average annual cost method is preferred for the carpet example. As shown in figures F-5 and F-6, the average annual cost of the high quality carpet is lower due to its longer life and lower annual costs.

Internal Rate of Return (IRR)

If you have more than one use for your limited funds, you may have to choose between projects that do entirely different jobs. In this case you may view the problem as a choice between investments. Your initial cost is your investment (use a negative number) and your annual savings are your return (use positive numbers). Technically, the IRR is the discount rate that would yield a net present value of zero. It can be thought of as the rate your investment would earn if it were invested in this project. This number can be used to compare the earning potential

Figure F-5. Average Annual Cost.

Description: High Quality Carpet												
Discount Factor	7.00%											
Life	10		Year 1	Year 2	Year 3	Year 4	Year 5	Year 6	Year 7	Year 8	Year 9	Year 10
	Costs	Costs										
Purchase	8000	Labor	800	800	800	800	800	800	800	800	800	800
Installation	2000	Materials	200	200	200	200	200	200	200	200	200	200
Other	None	Other										
	10000		1000	1000	1000	1000	1000	1000	1000	1000	1000	1000
Equivalent Annual Cost	10000		935	873	816	763	713	666	623	582	544	509
Net Present Value	17024											
Average Annual Cost	1702											

Figure F-6. Average Annual Cost.

Description: Regular Carpet												
Discount Factor	7.00%											
Life	7		Year 1	Year 2	Year 3	Year 4	Year 5	Year 6	Year 7	Year 8	Year 9	Year 10
	Costs	Costs										
Purchase	6000	Labor	1000	1000	1000	1000	1000	1000	1000			
Installation	2000	Materials	250	250	250	250	250	250	250			
Other	None	Other										
	8000		1250	1250	1250	1250	1250	1250	1250			
Equivalent Annual Cost	8000		1168	1092	1020	954	891	833	778			
Net Present Value	14737											
Average Annual Cost	2105											

of different projects in your department or to help you in competing for funds within the company. Consider the proposed project to re-carpet an office space. The carpet must be replaced, so the real question is whether or not to spend the extra $2000 to get the high quality carpeting. Use the IRR method to determine the return on the **additional** $2000. Consider the additional expense to be an investment (−2000) and the lower annual cleaning costs (250) to be the return on the investment. Figure F-7 shows that the internal rate of return for this investment is only 4 percent.

Even though the higher quality carpet has a lower average annual cost, the extra money for the higher quality may be better utilized on another project. There are two more considerations before a final decision can be reached.

Figure F-7. Internal Rate of Return (IRR).

Description: Spend $2000 more on better carpet												
Discount Factor	7.00%											
Life	10											
	Initial Costs	Savings(+) and Costs(−)	Year 1	Year 2	Year 3	Year 4	Year 5	Year 6	Year 7	Year 8	Year 9	Year 10
Purchase	−2000	Labor	200	200	200	200	200	200	200	200	200	200
Installation		Materials	50	50	50	50	50	50	50	50	50	50
Other	None	Replace										
	−2000		250	250	250	250	250	250	250	250	250	250
Annual Present Values→	−2000		234	218	204	191	178	167	156	146	136	127
Net Present Value	−244											
Equivalent Annual Cost	−24											
Internal Rate of Return	4%											

Taxes

An important consideration for any organization that has taxable income is the effect of tax deductions. It is beyond the scope of this article to deal with this issue fully but there are some basic ideas that the facility manager must keep in mind.

- A capital asset loses its value over its lifetime.
- The lost value can be deducted from the company's profits.
- The tax that the company does not have to pay on those profits can be considered as a type of savings.
- The IRS has established lifetimes for different categories of capital assets.
- The amount of value deducted each year of the asset's life can be a simple percentage (straight line) or one of several other methods that deduct larger percentages in the early years (accelerated).

For example, the company buys an asset for $20,000 and the IRS allows a ten year depreciation life. If a straight line depreciation method is used, the company could deduct $2000 from its profits. If the company is paying a tax rate of 32 percent, this would mean an annual saving of $640.

It is likely that your company uses one of the accelerated methods to take advantage of the time value of money. If you are going to include tax savings as part of your analysis you should confer with your accounting department for advice.

Escalating Costs

Most financial texts assume that the cash flow resulting from an investment is fixed, that is, the dollar amounts are the same each year. This is not the case when your costs or savings depends on the cost of energy or labor. If an investment in a more efficient motor saves a thousand dollars worth of electricity in the first year, it will save more in the following years if the cost of electricity goes up. In order to take this effect into account when you are figuring your discount rate, you can substract the estimated escalation from the interest rate. For example, if the ordinary discount rate on money is 7 percent and you expect the cost of electricity to escalate at a rate of 4 percent each year over the life of the analysis, use a discount rate of 3 percent (7 percent − 4 percent). It is likely that there would be a different escalation rate for each item that constitues the annual expense of maintenance and operation. This method is proposed by BOMI (the educational institute of BOMA).[4] The final version of the spreadsheet allows the user to enter a separate discount rate for each type of annual cost or savings.

Figure F-8 illustrates the final version of the analysis that shows individual discount rates for labor, materials, and tax savings. The interest rate was assumed to be 7 percent. This was used as the discount rate for the tax savings because they are fixed amounts. An escalation factor of 4 percent was assumed for labor and 3 percent for cleaning materials. When substracted from 7 percent, the discount rates were 3 percent and 4 percent respectively.

Figure F-8. Life-Cycle Cost Analysis (Including Tax Benefits and Escalation).

Description: Spend $2000 more on high quality carpet

Life of the system	10				Year 1	Year 2	Year 3	Year 4	Year 5	Year 6	Year 7	Year 8	Year 9	Year 10
	Initial Costs	*Savings(+) and Costs(−)*												
Purchase	−2000	Item 1	Labor		200	200	200	200	200	200	200	200	200	200
Installation		Item 2	Materials		50	50	50	50	50	50	50	50	50	50
Other	None	Item 3												
		Item 4	Tax Savings		64	64	64	64	64	64	64	64	64	64
Annual Present Values			*Discount Factors*											
		Item 1		3%	194	189	183	178	173	167	163	158	153	149
		Item 2		4%	48	46	44	43	41	40	38	37	35	34
		Item 3												
		Item 4		7%	60	56	52	49	46	43	40	37	35	33
Totals	−2000				302	291	280	269	259	250	240	232	223	215

Net Present Value	561

Equivalent Annual Cost	56

Internal Rate of Return	5%

---

4. BOMI, *The Design, Operations and Maintenance of Building Systems*, RPA series, Vol. 2, Ch. 2, p. 39.

Conclusion

The final version of the spreadsheet includes present value, average annual cost, internal rate of return, tax savings, and individual discount rates adjusted for escalation. Use the following guidelines when deciding which method to use.

- Present value is useful when comparing items that have the same life and do the same job.
- Average annual cost should be used when two items that do the same job have different lifetimes.
- Internal rate of return can be used to compare different money saving opportunities. There must be a mix of negative numbers (investments) and positive numbers (savings).
- Tax savings should be considered if your company pays taxes.
- The discount factor should be adjusted if costs such as labor and energy are likely to increase.

Appendix G: Cost Containment Best Practices

Introduction

We are strong believers in the idea that we can learn from one another, but the profession seems to have taken some backward steps in this regard. We would hope that the International Facility Management Association would reinstate its annual Best Practices Forum. We learned much from our fellow practitioners at those forums. We note that the IFMA and the Federal Facilities Council have just formed a liaison relationship, and that is a step in the right direction. We hope that the U.S. federal government will do much more to publicize some of the truly great work that it has done on the management of large facilities, especially the publications, conferences, and work of the Federal Facilities Council.

Here are some of our favorites among the best practices that we have collected over our careers, with special emphasis on recent best practices and those that promise to help you contain costs. For each best practice, we have tried to give you a contact, and some of these are commercial firms. We do not endorse any product or service, but when the name of a commercial firm is given, it is because we feel that the commercial application is on the cutting edge of the field and is worth exploring.

As we reviewed the included best practices, we noted the high volume of references to U.S. federal facilities. This reinforces one of our major themes in this book: that there is a lot of innovative research and practice being done by U.S. federal facility managers. This information is largely available to others, *provided that you know where to look*. That is one of the purposes of this appendix: to guide you to these best practices in cost containment and better financial analysis.

We have tried to group the best practices by subject area. This list is by no means all-inclusive, but we are convinced that, if a facility manager were to implement one of these best practices each quarter for the next five years, he would be viewed as a cost-containment all-star within his company.

Activity-Based Costing and Budgeting

An Activity-Based Costing and Budgeting Process

Activity-based costing and budgeting is a less sophisticated form of programmatic budgeting. It gained prominence with the need to negotiate service level agreements with business unit managers. The greatest advantages to activity-based costing are that you must get your definitions right, you must make decisions on contentious issues such as overheads, it causes you to look at your work processes, and your costs will be transparent. For more information, contact Fred Klammt at *FredK@jps.net*.

Benchmarking

Jim Whiteside, "How Much Do I Cost?" FM Journal, March/April 1996, pp. 6–14.

This is one of the best articles on facility finances ever written. Jim Whiteside outlines how to calculate the true costs of doing business for each function of facility management. He then discusses such issues as multipliers, how to use cost data, nonproductive time, overheads, and how to tie cost to value. Getting good unit costs is dependent upon being able to pull costs out of the budget format easily and being able to divide them by a meaningful denominator. If this process is done correctly, those unit costs then become the basis for benchmarking. For more information, contact Jim Whiteside at *jwhitesi@amfam.com*.

Managing with Metrics

Costs are only one factor that should be measured. Customer satisfaction, effectiveness, and response also need to be measured. Whenever you develop metrics, you should use continuous process improvement techniques to refine them.

- Develop the metrics using your best judgment or as suggested by customers.
- Measure them in your environment.
- Present them within the department and to management for comment.
- Analyze and improve the metrics.

Once you are satisfied with any specific metric, you are ready for benchmarking.
For more information, contact Edward Pagliassotti at *epagliassotti@snet.net*.

Paul Tarricone, "Best Practices Make Perfect," Facilities Design and Management, March 1998, pp. 50–52.

This article is an excellent summary of the use of both best practices and benchmarking. Two special features are the "Thirteen Commandments" of best practices for planning and implementing FM technology and the benchmarking implementation process recommended by the IFMA. For more information, contact *www.fdm.com*.

Corporate Real Estate Performance Ratios, December 15, 2001, IDRC

This report contains benchmarking information that is too often ignored by facility managers, showing how facilities perform in support of the mission of the company. In addition, the information is international. Hopefully, the recent merger of IDRC and NACORE (now CoreNet Global) will not terminate the publication of this report. Not only is the report itself of value, but it also indicates corporate best practices by industry group. For more information, contact Conway Data, Inc., at *www.conwaydata.com.*

A Case Study of How to Make Financial Metrics Work for You

Once you have correctly identified and calculated significant benchmarks, they can be used in many ways. A major utility, by establishing key relationships between actions taken and results, achieved annual cost savings of more than 30 percent. For more information, contact G. Philip Booker at the Salt River Project at *gpbooker@srpnet.com.*

Capital Program Development

Barry Lynch, "Improving the Capital Budgeting Process," Proceedings of World Workplace 2001, Vol. 1, pp. 265–276

This presentation, by one of the real thinkers in the facility management profession, Barry Lynch, gives fifteen ways in which capital budgeting can be improved in the average company. It is also an excellent primer for anyone who is unfamiliar with construction project delivery methods, since Lynch lays out each method and indicates its strengths, its drawbacks, and its applicability. Lynch also incorporates sustainable construction, quality management, knowledge management, and serviceability tools and methods into the capital budgeting process rather than treating them as add-ons. For more information, contact Barry Lynch at *Lynchb@acninc.net.*

"Executive Guide—Leading Practices in Capital Decision-Making," GAO/AIMD-99-32, December 1998

This guide presents an integrative approach to capital program development based on the following principles:

- Integrate organizational goals into the capital decision-making process.
- Evaluate and select capital assets using an investment approach.
- Balance budgetary control and managerial flexibility when funding capital projects.
- Use project management techniques to optimize project success.
- Evaluate results and incorporate lessons learned into the decision-making process.

   This is an excellent guide to managing the capital investments of companies and government agencies. It could be the initial template for anyone who is charged with establishing a capital development program or reforming an existing one. It provides implementation practices for each of the principles listed here, with emphasis on using better up-front planning and decision making to save life-cycle costs. For more information, contact the U.S. Government Printing Office at *www.gpo.gov* or the Information Management Division, U.S. General Accounting Office at *www.gao.gov/AIMD.*

Report of the President's Commission to Study Capital Budgeting, *February 1999.*

While this report is focused on the U.S. government, its recommendations are generally applicable to capital budget development and implementation for all public- and private-sector organizations. Recommendations cover the following:

- Five-year strategic planning
- Benefit/cost assessments
- Capital acquisition funds
- Full funding for capital projects
- Adherence to scoring rules for leasing
- Trust fund reforms
- Incentives for asset management
- Clarification of the federal budget presentation
- Financial statement reporting
- Federal report card

   The report contains specific practices that should be employed in order to implement each of the recommendations and that, if employed, will result in cost containment. For more information, contact the U.S. Government Printing Office at *www.gpo.gov* or the White House Library at *www.library.whitehouse.gov.*

Capital Renewal

Recapitalization Rate

In planning or justifying major construction, renovation, or replacement projects or in analyzing a current inventory of facilities, the correct recapitalization rate is always an issue. Tradeline's archives currently contain several approaches to recapitalization: "Three Approaches to Setting Recapitalization Rates" and "What's the Number? The Problem of Planning for and Managing Waves of Expiring Assets" (you must be a subscriber to obtain these). The Tradeline Web site, *www.tradelineinc.com*, is one that we recommend that facility managers of medium and large facility departments bookmark and visit occasionally to check for publications and conferences. For more information, contact Tom Bogle at Koll Corporate Services (Atlanta) at *www.koll.com*.

Communications

"How to Talk to a CFO" (Appendix A)

This is absolutely one of the finest articles ever written on communications for the FM. Thomas McCune, in presenting ten concepts, reinforces the themes of this book, stresses the importance of being able to communicate in business terms, and explains how to do this. Brutally frank and often funny, McCune's presentation is a classic that should be read and followed by all facility managers, particularly those who do not have a business degree. For more information, contact Thomas McCune at *www.AEPragmatics.com* or *www.ifma.org*.

Contracting

Indefinite Demand, Indefinite Quantity (IDIQ) Contracting

Many facility managers in medium and large facility management departments face a high volume of work, demanding customers, and a situation in which the exact nature of all of the work is not always known. IDIQ contracting is ideal for such a situation. A contractor (or contractors) is selected for general excellence, an ability to be flexible, great partnering skills, and a bias toward strong customer service skills. Through either a blanket purchase or one of the unique forms of IDIQ contracts that are available, the contractor becomes the operational arm of the facility manager from at least the superintendent level on down. In certain cases, the contractor may be asked to provide project management. In order for IDIQ to be successful, both the facility manager and the contractor must be committed to partnering to serve the ultimate customer, must trust each other, and must be devoted to problem solving. For more information, contact the Center for Job Order Contracting Excellence at Arizona State University at *www.construction.asu.edu/ace*.

Job Order Contracting (JOC)

JOC is a specialized form of IDIQ contract that gives the facility manager slightly more control. During the contracting process, a standardized set of costs (the cost book) is decided upon. This can be a published set of costs (such as Means), or it can be unique to the customer. Bidding then becomes contingent upon a cost multiplier (coefficient) that is applied to the standard costs in the cost book. JOC has been used successfully in the public sector for over twenty years, but it has been slow to be adopted in the public sector. Cost savings of 8 to 12 percent have been documented, primarily as a result of the low administrative costs associated with JOC. In order for JOC to be successful, the facility manager and the contractor must be attuned to the same factors needed to make IDIQ successful, plus they need to have a process in place to handle work items that are not in the price book. For more information, contact the Center for Job Order Contracting Excellence at Arizona State University at *www.construction.asu.edu/ace*.

Performance-Based Contracting

As a result of studying JOC and why some contractors performed well and some did not, Dr. Dean Kashiwagi has developed a system, the Performance-Based Information Procurement System (PIPS), that allows the facility manager to select the best contractor for the job each time. PIPS is a system that is absolutely controlled by the facility manager but that uses an artificial intelligence system to select among contractors on the basis of very detailed contract-related information. The system has now been used on over three hundred contracts, and the results have been amazing. There have been beneficial consequences that were not even anticipated by Kashiwagi as he developed the system. Contractors have eliminated themselves during the process because they saw that they were unqualified to perform at the level expected. Former clients have provided legitimate references (both good and bad), not just pro forma responses. Design flaws have been addressed before the contract is signed, and risk has been almost totally shifted to (and accepted by) the contractor. Design and administrative costs have been reduced, and the facility manager's involvement has been focused on solving customer interface problems rather than on checking on the contractor. Projects are delivered on time and within budget and almost totally without change orders. For more information, contact the Performance-Based Studies Research Group at Arizona State University at *www.a-su.edu/pbsrg*.

Contracting and Acquisition Strategies for Federal Facilities

As this book is being written, the Federal Facilities Council is commissioning a report that will identify lessons learned by U.S. federal agencies using specific contracting methods, highlight issues related to performance-based contracting, and identify tools to support decision making for a particular project. For more information, contact Lynda Stanley at the Federal Facilities Council at *lstanley@nas.edu*.

Strategic Sourcing

Having a mandated requirement to consider the contracting out of service functions (referred to as A-76), the Navy has conducted over 126 cost comparisons and examined over 18,000 in-house positions for outsourcing. Despite impressive cost reductions and cost avoidance, the Navy concluded that competitive sourcing alone would not produce the type of savings desired. So the Navy launched an initiative called Strategic Sourcing, an overarching program for implementing infrastructure reform to achieve savings, streamline operations, and improve efficiencies at bases and shore facilities. The process begins with a review of all functions to achieve maximum operation efficiency and effectiveness and may include privatization, divestiture, sale of excess assets, business process reengineering, and forming partnerships with other services or the private sector. The Air Force has reached the same overall conclusion but is approaching strategic sourcing with the following four techniques:

- Employee stock ownership plans
- Transitional benefits corporations
- Bidding to goal
- Strategic partnering with the private sector

For more information on the Navy's approach, contact Capt. Phil Dalby at *Dalby@navfac.navy.mil*. For the Air Force's approach, contact Col. John Vrba at *John.Vrba@pentagon.af.mil*.

Delivering Major Infrastructure Projects

Both the public and the private sectors have concluded that we must get more infrastructure "bang for the buck." Low bid and design-bid-build will continue to have a future, but their applications will be greatly reduced. The time value of money, the cost of not doing business, and restraints on public spending require owners and their facility managers to seek new ways of delivering major projects. Professor John B. Miller of MIT offers a portfolio approach to providing infrastructure projects in his book *Principles of Public and Private Infrastructure Delivery* (New York: Kluwer Academic Publishers, 2000), which focuses on how to improve the project delivery process, with particular emphasis on how to control the cash flow. Through its Commonwealth Competition Council, the state of Virginia is putting some of these innovative delivery systems to work in everything from new roads to mental health facilities. For more information, contact Professor Miller at *http://kapis.www.wkap.nl* or Phil Bomersheim at the Commonwealth Competition Council at *pbomersheim@ccc.state.va.us*.

The Effect of Change Orders on Construction and Major Renovation Projects

Construction change orders are disruptive to the capital budget execution process and generally represent an inefficient and ineffective use of time and money. They can be as disruptive to the contractor as to the facility manager, although for too long contractors have "low-balled" project bids, planning to make their profit on change orders. This study, actually a master's degree thesis, looks at fifty-seven international projects to determine what can be done during planning and design to reduce change orders. For more information, contact Lt. Comdr. James Dempsey at *jdempsey@comdt.uscg.gov*.

Contract Documents

Improving the Quality Control of Construction Documents

Albert Antelman, AIA, has proposed an expert system to improve quality control for construction documents. By quality, Antelman means that the documents are accurate, have been coordinated, communicate well, are fair, are consistent, are standardized, are specific, are timely, and have been completed by a competent person. The CLIPS system takes construction documents from being merely the reference for construction to being an aid for commissioning and the basis of operations and maintenance throughout the life of the building. For more information, contact Albert Antelman at *antelmanab@nfesc.navy.mil*.

FM Contracts Online

Many FM services and products can be procured using standard contract forms that have been successfully used by others. The hard work has been done. All the user needs to do is fill in the blanks and make the documents site-specific. Contract forms are available at *www.aptek.net*. For more information, contact Fred Klammt at *FredK@jps.net*.

Cost Calculations

Mahlon Apgar IV, *"Uncovering Your Hidden Occupancy Costs,"* Harvard Business Review, *May–June 1993,* pp. 124–136

Despite the fact that we do not agree with all of the results that Mahlon Apgar hopes to achieve, this article is one of the classics in the field of cost containment. Apgar makes you look at your space in a quantitative fashion, as few of us have ever done, by concentrating on just what space is really effective for mission use. He stresses the 3 Ls—leasing, location, and layout—but he also addresses such issues as why we spend up to 30 percent of our space budget on lobbies and atriums. Apgar shows a prototype for a space budget that permits the examination of all space needs by function. For more information, contact the *Harvard Business Review* at *www.hbr.com*.

Recovering Costs

Some facility managers find themselves in a position where they can recover some of their costs by providing services to research projects or clients, who must reimburse the parent company or agency. This can be "found" and welcome money, but it must be properly calculated and will be subject to an audit, so record keeping by customer and by project becomes very important. For more information, contact Roy Davey at Facility Resources, Inc., at *rdavey@facilityres.com*.

Parametric Costing

During design, time can be saved and less expensive design alternatives can be adopted through the techniques called parametric costing and cost as (an) independent variable (CAIV). A knowledge base of similar projects or project components is used to analyze what will work best and what will cost the least for the new project under consideration before the project is specified. For more information, contact William J. Vitaliano at the Harris Corporation at *bvitaliano@aol.com*.

Customer Service

Stormy Friday and David G. Cotts, Quality Facility Management, *1995*

The authors of this book are the foremost advocates of the idea that total quality management in facility management starts with the customer. The book presents detailed instructions on how to plan, implement, and evaluate a customer service program within your organization. It has particularly insightful text on the role of marketing and marketing techniques in accommodating customers. For more information, contact Stormy Friday at *Stormy@The FridayGroup.com* or Dave Cotts at *dgcotts@aol.com*.

Design

Tax-Advantaged Design

Tax-advantaged design is an innovative practice that combines the creative talents of the designer and the analytical skills of the accountant to the advantage of the facility owner. Introduced early in the design process, tax-advantaged design can affect the current and future financial benefits of a new or substantially renovated facility. For more information, contact John W. Mason of KPMG Peat Marwick, LLP (Houston), at *www.kpmgconsulting.com*.

Document Management

Web-based Project Document Management

Organizations are taking a close look at the resources devoted to copying, faxing, and filing during major construction projects, particularly those managed through collaborative project management. With the Internet and intranets, all design and construction team members can use their own project and document management systems while sharing information with other team members through applications service providers using open architecture. Time and money can be saved by posting documents in the right location so that they are accessible to all team members who need them. For more information, contact e-Builders at *www.e-builders.net*.

E-Business

Robert E. Johnson, "Research on E-Business and Facility Management Practice," Proceedings of World Workplace 2001, *Vol. 2, pp. 77–83*

This presentation summarizes the practice of e-business as it relates to facility management to date.

- E-business is emerging as a major change agent in facility management.
- E-procurement is the most frequently used e-commerce application.
- The payoff for using e-commerce is near, particularly in purchasing, operations and maintenance, total facility costs, project management, space management, and construction management.
- Implementation, particularly with legacy systems and the lack of a specific budget, is a problem.

For more information, contact the IFMA Foundation at *www.ifma.org* or Robert E. Johnson at *http://archone.tamu .edu/~crscenter*.

E-Procurement

A number of firms have specialized in providing procurement and logistic support to facility managers, either for a specific situation, such as a new construction project, or for operations and maintenance. This can be particularly helpful in a new geographic area where the facility manager has not yet developed a vendor base. It also can reduce the dollar and space costs of maintaining inventory for operations and maintenance. For more information, contact Ariba at *www.ariba.com*, Datastream at *www.datastream.net*, FacilityPro at *www.facilitypro.com*, Graninger at *www .grainer.com*, or MRO Software at *www.MRO.com*.

Energy Management

Enterprise Energy Management

Systems are available to monitor energy use 24/7, capture energy use trends, capture historical data, and create needs profiles by process, time, or user. Using such a system can allow facility managers to both reduce and control energy costs, and these systems can be used both on a campus and for geographically dispersed facilities. For more information, contact *www.instepsw.com*.

Energy Deregulation—Actual Experience

Those facility managers who have actually sought cost savings in the deregulated marketplace have had mixed experiences. Because of stranded costs, deregulated utilities often are not offering the anticipated savings. They are, however, offering "value-added services" while "wanting to be your power partner." In order to realize savings, facility managers need to understand their energy usage and benchmarks prior to entering into negotiations. For more information, contact the IFMA Utilities Council at *www.ifma.org*.

Daniel Fisher, "Trading Places," Forbes, January 21, 2001, pp. 53–54

Even with all of the legal concerns about energy trading, facility managers are being asked to consider the energy purchasing options that have opened as a result of deregulation. This article presents a short primer on aspects of the business side of the energy industry. If they understand how the industry functions, facility managers will be able to make more knowledgeable decisions on energy purchasing. While not offering a "sure thing," this article indicates that stability is a major factor that FMs should seek out in their energy supplier. For more information, contact *Forbes* magazine at *www.forbes.com/forbes*.

John Preston and Timothy Walden, "Electric Rates: What You Don't Know Can Hurt You!" Proceedings of the IFMA International Conference, 1990, pp. 141–147

This article is another primer to help facility managers understand energy management under deregulation by understanding energy costs from the standpoint of the utility. The article contains an excellent description of terms and then applies those terms to an actual example. Included are several implementation steps that show how the user can control costs based on an understanding of what those cost are and how they are calculated. For more information, contact the International Facility Management Association at *www.ifma.org* or Eastern Michigan University at *www.emich.edu*.

Finding Value in Utility Deregulation and Dealing with ESCOs

Energy savings due to deregulation are available to facility managers, but FMs must know what they are doing. Some states have either slowed or stopped deregulation, however, as a result of the Enron debacle. Facility managers need to understand their usage in detail and then be able to negotiate a good service contract, with a cheaper rate being one of the elements to negotiate. In general, neither facility managers nor their procurement departments have the expertise to get the best possible energy contract package. For the first time at least, the use of a consultant to get the best possible energy contract can probably be justified. For more information, contact the Utilities Council at *www.ifma.org* or Craig Miller at *www.fdm.com*.

Energy-Efficient Lighting

Lighting consumes approximately 25 percent of the total electricity used in the business world. While many electrical utilities have severely curtailed or eliminated rebates for lighting efficiency improvements, new but mature technologies and lighting optimization still offer opportunities for savings. For more information, contact N. C. Bleeker at Philips Lighting at *www.philipslighting.com* or Brian Ostrowe at *bostrowe@aol.com*.

Energy-Conscious Construction

The bursting of the Internet bubble and the turbulence in the energy industry caused by both deregulation and scandal have left facility managers who are faced with major construction/renovation projects perplexed. How can we add value without adding cost? Some utility incentive programs still exist, but the key is often selecting a design team that is expert in energy-conscious design. For more information, contact James Berge at Fletcher Thompson Architects and Engineers at *jberge@ftae.com*.

Facility Management Technology

Analysis Required to Make Knowledgeable Purchasing Decisions

Personal experience, observation, and survey data indicate that the purchase and fielding of CAFM/CMMS continues to be done inefficiently and ineffectively. One consultant stated that because owners often bought more than they needed or were willing to maintain, more than two-thirds of all CAFM/CMMS software became "shelfware." A survey indicates that cost savings used to justify the purchase of CAFM/CMMS often were not realized, that those systems were not used to automatically generate unit costs (benchmarks), and that the really important savings that should have been used in justifying new systems were never even considered. For more information, contact Eric Teicholz at *teicholz@graphsys.com*, Philip Martin at *pmartin@synergisticfm.com*, or the IFMA Computer Applications Council at *www.ifma.org*.

Best Practices in FM Technology Management

In order to properly manage the introduction and implementation of FM technology, facility managers should do all of the obvious things like planning, developing specific measurable goals, and performing a cost-benefit analysis. Equally important, however, are having a healthy fear of data entry costs, having a bias for action, and constantly doing reality checks. For more information, contact Jeff Hamer at 1-818-991-9211.

Ten Ways to Save Money in CAFM Implementation

Most of your CAFM cost avoidance decisions must be made before the implementation of CAFM. If you have already built your CAFM database, most of your ability to avoid costs has been lost. CAFM and CMMS implementation remains highly unsatisfactory in too many situations because of both overhyping of system capabilities on the part of the vendor and unrealistic expectations on the part of the facility manager. For more information, contact James D. Filippi at Applied Data Systems at *jimf@adsi-fm.com*.

Intelligent Workplaces

Cost-Benefit Ratio Results

The premise behind the intelligent workplace is the concept that the intelligent building nurtures and grows a company's intellectual capital. The Center for Building Performance and Diagnostics at Carnegie-Mellon University has done cost-benefit analyses on a number of case studies of scenarios to increase workplace efficiency, from the use of systems furniture to providing raised floors. The results are of value individually and in total. For more information, contact Dr. Vivian Loftness at the School of Architecture, Carnegie-Mellon University at *www.arc .cmu.edu*.

Design, Operations, and Maintenance

With increased use of and dependence upon the Internet and the increase in the volume of e-business, buildings with adequate supporting infrastructure that is capable of high levels of reliability are essential. Having six-sigma building operations means that downtime must be virtually eliminated. This requires that we design, operate, maintain, and monitor building functions to a greater degree than we historically have done. Not doing so can be extremely costly. For more information, contact Andy Fuhrman at Gazelle LLC at *AndyF@gazellellc.com*.

Leasing

Enhanced-Use Leasing Authority

The U.S. Department of Veterans Affairs has implemented an enhanced-use leasing authority that permits a public-priority partnership to solve public-sector facility needs and excesses through leases of up to seventy-five years. If used properly, this practice can convert underperforming properties into productive assets and turn cost-generating facilities into revenue producers. For more information, contact the U.S. Department of Veterans Affairs at *www.va.gov/facmgmnt*.

Lease Management

Facility managers who control or have a large number of leases should track the significant provisions of those leases using an automated lease management system. Such an information system allows you to track options, expirations, occupancy data, payment history, and other such factors, and informs you of critical upcoming lease events at a time when you can react to them properly. Such systems are usually part of an overall total asset management system, but they can be used in a stand-alone mode as well. For more information, contact Ed Rondeau at *ed.rondeau@conway.com*.

Life-Cycle Management

Thomas P. Rozman, "Building Maintenance; Pay Me Now or Pay Me (Much More) Later," Proceedings of World Workplace 2001, Vol. 2, pp. 113–118

This presentation gives a concise explanation and examples of the use of life-cycle costing in the facility management area. In addition, it stresses the importance to the facility manager of being able to present arguments and justifications in ways that the upper management of his company, particularly the CEO, will understand. For more information, contact Thomas P. Rozman at *rozman@plymouth.soilmat.com*.

"The Army's Facility Construction and Maintenance Process; An Assessment," Logistics Management Institute, AR009TI, November 2000

While this report deals with some aspects of the design/build/operate/maintain cycle that are pertinent only to large government agencies, much of the material in it is pertinent to all medium and large facility organizations because it emphasizes using private-sector business concepts to better manage facilities. Of particular interest are recommendations on the development of requirements (something that is often done poorly in the private sector), better use of the Internet to link all interested parties during all phases of the life cycle of a facility, and establishing FM objectives and ways to ensure that they are carried out. For more information, contact the Logistics Management Institute at *www.lmi.org*.

Life-Cycle Maintenance Prediction Model

The U.S. Army Construction Engineering Research Laboratory (CERL) has developed a PC-based facility management resource prediction model for the owners of large facility inventories. The model will predict the actual activities required to maintain the facilities and the schedule for all of these activities for the next ten years. CERL should be a bookmarked site for every facility manager of medium and large facilities, as it has been a leader in developing automated condition assessment tools, many of which have been adopted directly by civilian firms. For more information, contact the U.S. Army Construction Engineering Research Laboratory at *www.cecer.army.mil*.

Comparison of Preventive and Reactive Strategies

Facility managers often hear consultants tell them that they should invest in preventive maintenance, but there is amazingly little data to support this recommendation. Using a boiler example, Glenn Robinson calculates a 29 percent reduction in life-cycle costs by performing preventive maintenance, without even considering the consequences of such things as an unexpected boiler failure during the dead of winter. For more information, contact *Glenn_Robinson@hsb.com*.

Justifying and Selling Your Needs to Management

Everything has a life-cycle cost. Methods for calculating that cost have been known for years, yet LCC is underused. It is not the methodology that is limited, but the ability of facility managers to sell their analyses. It is often necessary to sell more than just cost savings over time. For more information, contact Eric Truelove at IBC Engineering Services, Inc., at *ibc-m@execpc.com.*

Occupancy Costs

Measuring Performance Costs

Workplaces can serve many functions. They can be an aid in recruitment and retention. They should be safe and healthful and assist in productive work. Finally, they should be cost-effective. Several decades of research have gone into determining what works and what the associated costs are, based on experiences in both the United States and Canada. For more information, contact Judi Murtough at Public Works and Government Services Canada at *www.pwgsc.gc.ca* or Stan Kaczmarczyk at *www.gsa.gov.*

Designing to Reduce Occupancy Costs

Since facility departments are cost centers, every dollar saved for the company produces a dollar of profit. Design always represents trade-offs, but occupancy costs have not always been one of the cost avoidances in the design mix.

- Building and layout flexibility can be critical in reducing life-cycle costs.
- New, specifically designed space can often be a real cost saver.
- Modeling in the design phase can optimize operational efficiency.
- Meeting corporate financial goals should be an objective of design.
  For more information, contact Mark E. Glasser at ADD Inc. at *www.mglasser@addarch.com.*

Operating Budgets

Earnie Leake, "Management Strategies for Adding Value Through Facilities Operating Budgets and Leases," **Proceedings of the IFMA International Conference, 1990, pp. 83–98**

This presentation provides very basic tips and techniques for controlling lease and annual budget costs. These techniques are particularly helpful for the new facility manager entering the field who is dealing with a largely leased inventory. For more information, contact the International Facility Management Association at *www.ifma.org* or Earnie Leake at *earnie.leake@exodus.net.*

Outsourcing

Annual **Facilities Design and Management** *FM Outsourcing Survey, December 2001*

This annual survey and report gives insights into successful and unsuccessful FM outsourcing as seen through the eyes of facility managers. The results indicate what works (bundling services as opposed to the contracting of discrete services, for example), trends in outsourcing, and how outsourcing decisions are made. Noting what works and what does not work can be invaluable in containing costs as well as in outsourcing more effectively. For more information, contact *Facilities Design and Management* magazine at *www.fdm.com.*

Contracting Using a Business Case Analysis

With facility services increasingly being contracted out, facility managers need to use business tools to make contracting decisions. Three tools that should be considered to be a minimum to be used when hiring and controlling an FM outsourcing firm should be:

- Business case analysis
- Balanced scorecard
- A partnership agreement

This book spells out the elements of the business case analysis in detail. As indicated throughout the book, good business practices need to be applied to facility management as a result of the large amounts of resources involved. For more information, contact Johnson Controls Integrated Facility Management at *www.johnsoncontrols.com/ifm.*

Paul Tarricone, "The Single Life," Facilities Design and Management, February 1999, pp. 51–53

This article presents the pros and cons of the trend toward the use of full-service FM contractors, including data, examples, and interviews with some of the foremost FM consultants in the United States. For more information, contact *www.fdm.com* or Stormy Friday at *Stormy@TheFridayGroup.com* or Fred Klammt at *fredk@jps.net.*

What Works, What Reduces Costs, and Where Is Outsourcing Going?

There is little doubt that outsourcing is here to stay and, in fact, will continue for the foreseeable future, albeit with some adjustments. Outsourcing has been with us long enough now so that lessons can be learned from the experiences of facility managers to date. Contracts will be larger and more strategic, may cut across international borders, and will be for longer terms. Outsourcing firms will begin to be viewed as "in-house" providers. At the same time, where cost savings are not captured or service declines, certain functions may be brought back in-house. For more information, contact Ian Follett or Nancy Nauss of Facility Management Services, Ltd., at *fmsltd@fmsltd.com.*

Purchasing

Use of the Purchasing Card

For too many years, facility managers, often hampered by the purchasing regulations of their companies, have spent money on administrivia like excessive accounting and obtaining purchase orders for even exceptionally small and routine purchases. The use of credit and purchasing cards, even given their history of abuse, is a step in the right direction: toward spending FM dollars on bricks, mortar, and FM services rather than wasting them on administrivia. For more information, contact Robert Rusoff at Beckman Coulter, Inc., at *www.beckman.com.*

Quality Management

Stormy Friday and David G. Cotts, Quality Facility Management, 1995

This is the only book devoted to applying the concepts of total quality management to facility management. While many facility managers seem to think that total quality management is the "flavor of last month," they fail to understand that the quality and customer service bars have been raised substantially by the concentration on total quality management during the 1980s and 1990s. This book provides both theory and very practical applications and emphasizes both customer service and marketing as the basis for total quality management. For more information, contact Stormy Friday at *Stormy@TheFridayGroup.com* or Dave Cotts at *dgcotts@aol.com.*

Recycling

Maria Vickers, "The Intelligent Recycler," Today's Facility Manager, June 2000, pp. 21–29

Recycling programs of all types have had a mixed history. We personally have continued recycling at times when it actually cost our employers to recycle (cardboard boxes is one example) because (1) we felt that the market would come back (it did, but then it disappeared again) and (2) it was the right thing to do. Maria Vickers provides a step-by-step process for instituting a paper recycling program, easily understood definitions of paper grades, and an excellent list of other recycling resources. For more information, contact *mvickers@lucent.com* or *www.tfm.com.*

Space Planning

BestFit

It is far too simplistic to call BestFit a space planning tool. Developed by one of the true facility management research teams, Gerald Davis and Francoise Szigeti, BestFit, as the name implies, identifies what specific facility will best fit the needs of your organization. It can be used to evaluate an existing facility or to provide design criteria for the construction of a new facility. For more information, contact Serviceability Tools & Methods, Inc., at *info@st-m-serviceability.com.*

Strategic Facility Business Planning

Shore Facilities Capital Asset Management

The U.S. Coast Guard is developing a comprehensive method of assessing its facilities that utilizes condition assessment, strategic and tactical objectives, operational performance analyses, and a local commander's evaluation to guide decisions on both investment and reinvestment in shore-based facilities. This system pulls together the relevant portions of a large number of existing FM databases and evaluations and is being field-tested concurrent with the writing of this book. Ultimately, the idea is to convert all of the data into a mission dependency index that will permit an instantaneous decision on the wisdom of investing capital or renovation or maintenance money in a shore-based facility. If successful, this methodology has great potential for enabling the best use of limited facility funds. For more information, contact the SFCAM team at *www.comdt.uscg.mil.*

Sustainable Federal Facilities; A Guide to Integrating Value Engineering, Life-Cycle Costing, and Sustainable Development, *Federal Facilities Council, 2001*

This report details how life-cycle costing and value engineering should be used in the planning and design of public-sector facilities, but the techniques discussed are equally applicable to the private sector. The study goes into detail on the considerations for selecting the most economical options during the planning, design, and construction/renovation of facilities and contains a listing of actual projects from which lessons can be learned and how to access them.

If you are a U.S. federal facility manager, your organization should belong to the Federal Facilities Council. If you are not, you should visit its site frequently for its latest listing of publications and events, which are always substantive and helpful, particularly for the management of large facilities. For more information, contact the Federal Facilities Council, U.S. National Academy of Sciences at *www.nationalacademies.org/cets/ffc.nsf.*

Total Asset Management

Alan Edgar and Eric Teicholz, *"Accomplishing Total Asset Management,"* Proceedings of World Workplace 2001, *Vol. 1, pp. 255–266*

This presentation is an excellent primer for anyone who desires to bring comprehensive management to all company physical assets. It was made by two extremely savvy individuals who have experience both in managing facilities and in the supporting technology. It is a must read, and then *caveat emptor!* Starting with a definition of total asset management (TAM), the presenters provide the strategy and implementation steps that are necessary to make TAM work. Edgar and Teicholz also present a list of vendors and resources capable of assisting in TAM. This is a must read for anyone considering TAM. For more information, contact Alan Edgar or Eric Teicholz at Graphic Systems Inc., at *www.graphsys.com.*

An Overview of Facility Total Ownership Costs

This paper, submitted as part of the coursework for a master's degree, is one of the most detailed examinations of total ownership costs over long periods of time (a typical situation for the public sector). It discusses both management applications of the data and a simplified decision-making model. For more information, contact Lt. Comdr. James Dempsey at *Jdempsey@comdt.uscg.gov.*

Appendix H: Facility Accounting

ACCOUNTING

I. Accounting Basics

Accounting is a service activity involved in the reporting and interpreting of financial information for an organization. Accounting within an organization is termed "private accounting." In private accounting there are four basic types of accounting work.

- General Accounting—reporting on the organization as a whole
- Cost Accounting—reporting on product or service costs
- Budgeting—planning business activities in advance
- Internal auditing—verifying accounting accuracy and records

Facility accounting would fall under the umbrella of general accounting. Budgeting does include the facility area, but due to the length of subject matter to be covered, budgeting will not be discussed.

Business organizations can be broken down into three categories.

1. Sole Proprietorship—a business owned by a single individual
2. Partnership—a business owned by two or more individuals
3. Corporation—a business owned by shareholders and incorporated under the laws of a state or other jurisdiction. The business is a separate legal entity from its owners.

From this point on, I will assume all business organizations to be corporations.

II. Balance Sheet Equation

Accounting statements are the end result of general accounting work. They are used to show the profitability and financial health of a corporation. The Balance Sheet and Income Statement are the two most important financial statements. Each statement consists of an equation, the most important being the **Balance Sheet Equation:**

$$\text{Assets} = \text{Liabilities} + \text{Owners' Equity}$$

The **Balance Sheet** is a position statement on the business. It is a concise picture of financial position at a given point in time.

Assets—properties or economic resources owned by the business
Liabilities—debts of a business
Owners' equity—capital or claims of owners after liabilities have been paid.

By Heidi Lord Butler, from *Seminar Notes* (Houston: International Facility Management Association, 1989).

The **Income Statement Equation** is:

$$\text{Revenues} - \text{Expenses} = \text{Net Income (Loss)}$$

The **Income Statement** (or Profit and Loss Report) is a report on the profits or loss for a business over a stated period of time.

Expenses—goods and services consumed in operating a business or other economic unit.
Revenues—inflows of cash or properties received in exchange of goods and services.

Classification of Balance Sheet Items

A. *Assets*

1. **Current**—cash or an asset reasonably expected to be cash within a year or one operating cycle of the business, whichever is longer.

   Cash, accounts receivable, prepaid expenses, inventory, etc.

2. **Long-term investments**—assets that cannot be liquidated within a year.

   Stocks, bonds, long-term notes receivable, land held for future expansion, etc.

3. **Plant and equipment**—tangible assets having relatively long lives that are used in the production or sale of other assets or services.

   Land, buildings, equipment, plant assets, etc.

4. **Intangible assets**—assets having no physical existence but having value, because of the rights conferred as a result of their ownership and possession.

   Goodwill, patents, trademarks, copyrights, leasehold improvements, etc.

B. *Liabilities*

1. **Current**—a debt or obligation that must be paid or liquidated within one year or operating cycle, and the payment/liquidation will require the use of presently classified current assets.

   Accounts payable, notes payable, and other short-term debt.

2. **Long term**—liabilities that are not due and payable for a comparatively long period, usually more than one year.

   Mortgage payable and other long-term debt.

C. *Owners' Equity*

1. **Contributed capital**—amount of stockholders' investment. An example would be common stock.
2. **Retained earnings**—net income or loss retained by the business after the payout of dividends. Retained earnings are accumulated over the life of the business.

Double Entry Accounting

Businesses utilize a **double entry accounting system.** Double entry refers to the fact that you record each and every transaction as a **debit** and **credit,** with equal dollar amounts for both. For every transaction, debits are listed first and are recorded to the left. Credits are listed after debits and recorded to the right. To further understand double entry accounting, I have drawn a basic "I" account below.

Account

Debit | Credit

"I" accounts are simply a tool to help one better understand double entry accounting. A **journal entry** is the formal method used to record transactions.

Just like the game of monopoly, accounting has its rules as well. Memorize the following chart just as you would the rules of monopoly.

	Account balance	
Account	*Increases Are*	*Normal Balance*
Assets	Debits	Debits
Liabilities	Credits	Credits
Owners Equity	Credits	Credits
Revenue	Credits	Credits
Expenses	Debits	Debits

The normal balance of an account is whatever it takes (either a debit or credit) to record an increase.

Balance Sheet		*Income Statement*	
Assets	Liabilities	Expenses	Revenues
	Owners' Equity		

Journal Entries

Journal entries are used to record transactions in accounting. Journal entries must always have the same dollar amounts of debits and credits. Journal entries cannot be erased. Instead they must be corrected with a "reversing entry." Journal entries should never include cents (00) or dollar signs ($).

Some examples of journal entries and their "T" accounts follow.

ENTRIES

		Debit	*Credit*
Example 1: A business purchases $100.00 supplies on account.			
Entry—	Office Supplies	100	
	Accounts Payable		100
Example 2: A shareholder purchases $2000.00 of common stock.			
Entry—	Cash	2000	
	Common Stock		2000
Example 3: The business pays off the $100.00 balance on accounts payable.			
Entry—	Accounts Payable	100	
	Cash		100
Example 4: The business prepays the rent six months at a total cost of $2000.00.			
Entry—	Prepaid Rent	2000	
	Cash		2000
Example 5: The business makes a sale of $1000.00 paid by the customer on account.			
Entry—	Accounts Receivable	1000	
	Sales		1000
Example 6: The business borrows $10,000 long term to purchase a piece of equipment.			
Entry—	Equipment	10,000	
	Long-Term Debt		10,000
		15,200	15,200

Total Debits = $15,200
Total Credits = $15,200

Debits − Credits

"T" Accounts

	CASH Current Asset		SUPPLIES Current Asset		ACCOUNTS PAYABLE Current Liability		COMMON STOCK Owners' Equity		PREPAID RENT Current Asset	
	Dr	Cr	Dr	Cr	Dr	Cr	Dr	Cr	Dr	Cr
Example 1			100			100				
Example 2	2000							2000		
Example 3		100			100					
Example 4		3000							3000	
TOTALS	1100		100			0		2000	3000	

	ACCOUNTS RECEIVABLE Current Asset		SALES Revenue		EQUIPMENT Long-term Asset		LONG-TERM DEBT Long-term Liability	
	Dr	Cr	Dr	Cr	Dr	Cr	Dr	Cr
Example 5	1000			1000				
Example 6					10,000			10,000
TOTALS	1000			1000	10,000			10,000

Accounting Basics Exercise

1. Name five asset accounts.

2. Name three liability accounts.

3. Do assets have a debt or a credit balance
   Do liabilities have a debit or a credit balance?
   Does owners' equity have a debit or a credit balance?

4. Name two revenue accounts.

5. Name three expense accounts.

6. Write an entry for purchasing office supplies of $25 with cash.

7. Write an entry for purchasing a computer for $3000 on credit.

8. Write an entry for paying $600 on accounts payable.

9. What is the balance sheet equation?

10. Is the Income Statement for any given point in time or is it for a period of time?

Accounting Basics Answers

1. Cash, accounts receivable, supplies, inventory, building, land, equipment, patent, copyright, prepaid expenses, notes receivable, etc.

2. Accounts payable, mortgages, notes payable, salaries owed, taxes payable, unearned revenue, etc.

3. Debit
   Credit
   Credit

4. Sales, rents earned, interest earned, legal fees earned, revenue from repairs, commissions earned, etc.

5. Utilities, rent, supplies, salaries, taxes, phone, etc.

6. Office Supplies   25
       Cash   25

7. Computer   3000
       Accounts payable   3000

8. Accounts Payable   600
       Cash   600

9. Assets = Liabilities + Owners Equity

10. A period of time

III. Accounting for Plant and Equipment

Plant and equipment are tangible assets that are used in the production or sale of other assets and services that have a useful life longer than one accounting period.
    Characteristics of a plant asset:

- Has substance (physical)
- Must be in use or on stand by
- Has a service life more than 1 year

Cost of a plant asset includes all normal and reasonable expenditures necessary to get the asset in place and ready for use. Such as:

- Cost of a purchased asset includes invoice price less any discount, plus freight, unpacking, assembling, special base or foundations, and power connections.
- Cost of constructing a plant asset includes material, labor overhead, architectural fees, building permits, insurance during construction.
- Cost of land purchased for a building site includes real estate commissions, legal fees, title insurance, accrued property taxes, surveying, clearing, grading, draining, landscaping, or other costs that add a permanent value to the land. The cost to remove an old building is part of the cost, but land improvements (fences, parking lot surfaces, etc.) are not.

Capital vs. Expense

In properly accounting for plant and equipment, you need to know the difference between capitalization and expense. When you capitalize the cost of plant and equipment, the balance sheet is directly affected. The income statement is only affected through depreciation and write offs. By capitalizing an asset, the cost of the asset is allocated over several years, thereby having less impact on current income, and the tax deduction is spread out over several years. When you expense the cost, it is fully charged against the current year, thereby reducing current income and directly affecting the income statement.

Repairs and improvements to plant and equipment can be either expensed or capitalized depending upon the type of repair. For instance, if an extraordinary repair was made to a capitalized piece of equipment in order to extend its useful life, the repair would be capitalized. Or if a betterment was made to that piece of equipment, the cost would be capitalized as well. A betterment involves the cost to improve an existing plant asset's efficiency. Ordinary repairs such as cleaning or maintaining a plant asset are expensed.

Depreciation

Assets have a useful life that is quantifiable in terms of time or units of production. Depreciation is an estimated expense that recognizes that an asset's value diminishes as time passes on its productive life. Depreciation expense will be accumulated over the useful life of the asset and is the means by which the balance sheet value of the asset is reduced. The asset's original cost will remain intact on the balance sheet. However, a new account, **accumulated depreciation,** will appear on the balance sheet immediately following the asset. This account will show how much of the asset's useful life, in terms of cost, has been used. Keep in mind depreciation expense is simply an estimated figure to spread an asset's cost over its useful life. But for tax purposes, it is a very real expense to be fully deductible in the year depreciated. **Book Value** is calculated by subtracting accumulated depreciation from the assets original cost.

Make note: Land cannot ever be depreciated because the life of land is unlimited.

The journal entry to record depreciation expense is:

$$\text{Depreciation Expense} \quad \text{xxx}$$
$$\text{Accumulated Depreciation} \quad \text{xxx}$$

There are four types of depreciation methods.

1. **Straight-Line Method:** (Cost Salvage) ÷ estimated years of life

2. **Sum-of-the-Years-Digits Method:** Years of useful life remaining ÷ sum of the years digits = Depreciation Rate × Cost

3. **Declining-Balance Method Rate:** Rate × Book value
   (100% ÷ estimated years of service life)
   × 2 = Depreciation Rate × (Cost − Accumulated Depreciation)

4. **Units of Production Method:** (Cost − Salvage) ÷ estimated units of production = Depreciation per unit × units of production for the year.

Straight Line

(Cost − Salvage) ÷ estimated years of life.

Question: What is the annual depreciation expense for equipment A and B?

	Equipment A		Equipment B
Cost	$13,000		$4,200
Salvage	$3,000		$700
Life	5 years		7 years
Answer:	$2,000	a year	$500 a year

Sum of the Years' Digits

(Years of useful life ÷ Sum of the years' digits) × Cost − Salvage.

Question: What is the depreciation expense each year of useful life for equipment A and B?

	Equipment A	Equipment B
Cost	$11,000	$7,000
Salvage	$1,000	$1,000
Life	4 years	3 years

Answer:

Year 1	$4,000	$3,000
Year 2	$3,000	$2,000
Year 3	$2,000	$1,000
Year 4	$1,000	0

Declining Balance

$$2 \times (100\% \div \text{years of life}) \times \text{Book Value less accumulated depreciation.}$$

Question: What is the depreciation expense each year of useful life for equipment A and B?

	Equipment A	Equipment B
Cost	$20,000	$12,000
Salvage	$2,000	$1,000
Life	5 years	3 years

Answer:

Year 1	$8,000	$6,000
Year 2	$4,800	$3,000
Year 3	$2,880	$2,000
Year 4	$2,320	0

Units of Production

$$(\text{Cost} = \text{Salvage}) \div \text{estimated units of production} = \text{rate per unit.}$$

$$\text{Rate per unit} \times \text{production units for the year.}$$

Question: What is the annual depreciation expense for equipment A and B?

	Equipment A		Equipment B	
Cost	$11,000		$7,000	
Salvage	$1,000		$1,000	
Units of production	10,000	units	12,000	units
Units each year	2,500	units/year	4,000 units/year	
Answer:	$2,500	a year	$2,000	a year

Asset Disposal

Disposal of a plant asset can have significant impact on the company's reported income in the year of disposal. The impact can be favorable if the asset is sold for greater than its "book" value, or unfavorable if the asset is scrapped or sold for less than its "book" value. Some examples of journal entries to be made in these situations are below.

A Plant Asset is disposed of at "book" value.

Cash	xxx	
Accumulated Depreciation—Plant Asset	xxx	
Plant Asset		xxx

A Plant Asset is disposed of at more than "book" value.

Cash	xxx	
Accumulated Depreciation—Plant Asset	xxx	
Plant Asset		xxx
Gain		xxx

A Plant Asset is disposed of at less than "book" value.

Cash	xxx	
Accumulated Depreciation—Plant Asset	xxx	
Loss	xxx	
Plant Asset		xxx

Intangible Assets

Intangible Assets do not have a physical existence but have value due to the rights resulting from their ownership and possession. They are classified as non-current assets, recorded at cost and systematically amortized to expense over their estimated useful life. The entry to record amortization is:

Ammortization of Patents	xxx
Patent	xxx
(Straight-line method is normally used)	

Examples:

1. Patents—exclusive right to manufacture and sell
2. Copyright—exclusive right to publish and sell
3. Leaseholds—the right to possess and use properly. Payment of rent is capitalized and written off as rent expense
4. Leasehold Improvements—payments for alterations or improvements to leased property are capitalized and amortized in rent expense.
5. Goodwill—the difference between market value (true value) of the firm and the book value of assets minus liabilities.

Depreciation Exercise

A business has purchased a piece of equipment at a cost of $32,000. It has an estimated useful life of 5 years with a $2,000 salvage value. It has been estimated to produce 90,000 widgets over the next 5 years spread out as follows:

> 1st year—25,000 widgets
> 2nd year—25,000 widgets
> 3rd year—20,000 widgets
> 4th year—10,000 widgets
> 5th year—10,000 widgets

Fill in the chart below with depreciation expense each year, for each method.

Annual Depreciation Expense

	Straight Line	Sum of Years	Declining Balance	Units of Production
Year 1				
Year 2				
Year 3				
Year 4				
Year 5				

Questions:

1. Prepare first year journal entry using straight-line method.
2. What is the book value of the equipment at the end of year three using sum of the years' digits method?
3. Assume the equipment is sold for $5,000 at the end of four years and you were using the declining balance method of depreciation, prepare a journal entry reflecting the disposal of the equipment.

Depreciation Exercise Answer

Annual Depreciation Expense

	Straight Line	Sum of Years	Declining Balance	Units of Production
Year 1	6,000	10,000	12,800	8,333
Year 2	6,000	8,000	7,680	8,333
Year 3	6,000	6,000	4,608	6,667
Year 4	6,000	4,000	2,765	3,333
Year 5	6,000	2,000	2,147	3,334

1. Year 1 Journal entry using Straight-Line Depreciation Method

Depreciation Expense	6000	
Accumulated Depreciation		6000

2. $32,000 − $10,000 − $8,000 − $6,000 = $8,000

3. $32,000 - $12,800 - $7,680 - $4,608 - $2,765 = $4,147

Cash	5,000	
Accum. Depreciation	27,853	
Plant Asset		32,000
Gain		853

IV. Financial Analysis Techniques

Would you rather receive $1,000 today or $1,000 one year from now? You would probably answer "today," since you could invest that $1,000 to earn interest to make it worth more than $1,000 a year from now. This is the time value of money.

When analyzing investment related cash flows over time it is useful to discount them to their present value. The present value of a future cash flow depends upon:

1. the cost of the money (the interest rate of borrowing or the rate at which you could invest it elsewhere)
2. the time the future cash flow occurs.

To expand upon the above example:

Assume you can invest funds at 10 percent.
Assume you will invest $1,000 for two years.

The future value of $1,000 invested for two years is:

$$\$1,000 \times 1.10 \times 1.10 = \$1,210$$

To calculate the present value of $1,000 to be received in two years, simply do the reverse:

$$\$1,000 \div 1.10 \div 1.10 = \$826$$

This very basic principle is applied in the evaluation of investment related cash flow. The interest rate assumed varies depending upon the company's cost of capital (a combination of its cost of borrowing and how much it could earn by investing in other alternatives).

When allocating available funds to investment alternatives, financial analysis is often employed to determine what investments provide the most attractive returns. This allocation of funds is known as capital budgeting. There are several common tools used in capital budgeting to evaluate investment.

Payback Period

Payback period is the time it takes to recover the cost of the investment through the net cash flow. The net cash flow consists of the after tax value of savings generated by the project, and the tax write off resulting from depreciation expense. To calculate the payback period, simply divide the annual net cash flow into the cost of the investment. A shorter payback period will be the investment alternative of choice with this method. A major drawback of the payback method is that ongoing long-term profitability is not included in evaluating the investment alternatives.

Cost of Investment ÷ Net Annual Cash Flow = Payback Period

Example:

	Investment A	Investment B
Cost	$3,000	$4,000
Net Annual Cash Flow	$1,000	$2,000
Payback Period	3 years	2 years

Preferred Investment: Investment B

Rate of Return on Investment

The rate of return on investment (ROI) method takes into account earnings of an investment and the average value of the investment. Rate of return can be calculated by dividing the after tax net income by the average cost of the investment. The average cost of the investment is calculated by adding the initial cost of the investment and its salvage value and dividing by 2.

$$\text{After tax net income} \div \text{average cost of investment} = \text{ROI}$$

Example:

	Investment A	Investment B
Cost	$5,000	$7,000
Salvage	$1,000	0
After tax net income	$500	$1,200
ROI	14.3%	17.1%

Preferred Investment: Investment B

Discounted Cash Flow

The discounted cash flow method recognizes the time value of money. All the cash flows over the life of the investment are converted to present value. The present value of both cash inflows and outflows are netted. If the net present value (NPV) is positive, the investment alternative is good. If the NPV is negative, the investment alternative is not good. If comparing two investment alternatives, choose the alternative with the highest NPV or lowest negative NPV.

$$\text{Present Value of Cash Inflows} - \text{Present Value of Cash Outflows} = \text{Net Present Value}$$

Example:

	Investment A	Investment B
Cost	$10,000	$11,000
Savings each year	$2,000	$4,000
No. of years with savings	4 years	4 years

(The discount rate is 10%.)

	Cost	Present Value Factor = P.V. of Inflow	Net Cash
Investment A	10,000	2,000 × 3.1699 = 6,340	(3,660)
Investment B	11,000	4,000 × 3.1699 = 12,680	1,680

Preferred Investment: Investment B.

The discounted cash flow can be further complicated when having to take into consideration any salvage value of the investment and the annual depreciation amounts. Salvage value should be included as a cash inflow and converted to present value. Depreciation is not a cash expense, however it does affect the tax expense by reducing the tax owed. So depreciation times the tax rate is a "cash inflow" to be converted to present value for each year depreciation is taken.

Lease vs. Buy

Lease vs. buy decisions are nothing more than financing decisions. The asset will delinately become part of the business, but just how will that happen? Should the business use that asset for a fee each year, or should the business purchase the asset? There are benefits to both situations.

Advantages of owning

- You can take an annual depreciation write off.
- Property still has value at the end of a comparable lease period.
- You realize the full benefit of any appreciation in value.

Advantages of leasing

- Lease payments are fully deductible.
- There is no up front cash investment.

Present Value of $1 at Compound Interest

Periods Hence	4½%	5%	6%	7%	8%	9%	10%	12%	14%	16%
1	0.9569	0.9524	0.9434	0.9346	0.9259	0.9174	0.9091	0.8929	0.8772	0.8621
2	0.9157	0.9070	0.8900	0.8734	0.8573	0.8417	0.8265	0.7972	0.7695	0.7432
3	0.8763	0.8638	0.8396	0.8163	0.7938	0.7722	0.7513	0.7118	0.6750	0.6407
4	0.8386	0.8227	0.7921	0.7629	0.7350	0.7084	0.6830	0.6355	0.5921	0.5523
5	0.8025	0.7835	0.7473	0.7130	0.6806	0.6499	0.6209	0.5675	0.5194	0.4761
6	0.7679	0.7462	0.7050	0.6663	0.6302	0.5963	0.5645	0.5066	0.4556	0.4104
7	0.7348	0.7107	0.6651	0.6228	0.5835	0.5470	0.5132	0.4524	0.3996	0.3538
8	0.7032	0.6768	0.6274	0.5820	0.5403	0.5019	0.4665	0.4039	0.3506	0.3050
9	0.6729	0.6446	0.5919	0.5439	0.5003	0.4604	0.4241	0.3606	0.3075	0.2630
10	0.6439	0.6139	0.5584	0.5084	0.4632	0.4224	0.3855	0.3220	0.2697	0.2267
11	0.6162	0.5847	0.5268	0.4751	0.4289	0.3875	0.3505	0.2875	0.2366	0.1954
12	0.5897	0.5568	0.4970	0.4440	0.3971	0.3555	0.3186	0.2567	0.2076	0.1685
13	0.5643	0.5303	0.4688	0.4150	0.3677	0.3262	0.2897	0.2292	0.1821	0.1452
14	0.5100	0.5051	0.4423	0.3878	0.3405	0.2993	0.2633	0.2046	0.1597	0.1252
15	0.5167	0.4810	0.4173	0.3625	0.3152	0.2745	0.2394	0.1827	0.1401	0.1079
16	0.4945	0.4581	0.3937	0.3387	0.2919	0.2519	0.2176	0.1631	0.1229	0.0930
17	0.4732	0.4363	0.3714	0.3166	0.2703	0.2311	0.1978	0.1456	0.1078	0.0802
18	0.4528	0.4155	0.3503	0.2959	0.2503	0.2120	0.1799	0.1300	0.0946	0.0691
19	0.4333	0.3957	0.3305	0.2765	0.2317	0.1945	0.1635	0.1161	0.0830	0.0596
20	0.4146	0.3769	0.3118	0.2584	0.2146	0.1784	0.1486	0.1037	0.0728	0.0514

• Leases frequently come with maintenance contracts.
• You assume no risk of obsolescence.

To be able to make the correct decision, lease or buy, the net present values of cash flows for each situation should be compared. The one with the lowest net present value is the financially preferred option.

Leases can be broken down into two basic types—**capital lease** and an **operating lease.** A capital lease will meet one or more of the following criteria. An operating lease will not meet any of the criteria listed below.

1. Lessee will own the leased property at the end of the lease.
2. Leseee can purchase the leased property for less than the fair value during or at the end of the lease.
3. Lessee leases the property for more than 75 percent of the leased property's useful life.
4. The present value of the lease payments exceeds 90 percent of the fair value.

The following example illustrates a typical lease vs. buy situation.

Your company's lease is coming due next year and you need to decide whether you will remain at your current address and sign a new lease or move to a building which your company would then purchase. The cost of capital is 10 percent. The tax rate is 40 percent. The building would be depreciated using straight line with a $800,000 salvage value. Current IRS law regulates a building must be depreciated 31½ years, but for purposes of this example, the building will be depreciated only 5 years.

Alternative A: Sign a five year lease with annual lease payments of $700,000. Your company is currently in this building and will not need any major modifications to the building.
Alternative B: Purchase a building for $2,000,000 and spend another $600,000 in renovating for your company's needs.

Alternative A:

Years	0	1	2	3	4	5
Lease Payments*	(700)	(700)	(700)	(700)	(700)	
Tax Shield*	280	280	280	280	280	
Net Cash Flow	(420)	(420)	(420)	(420)	(420)	
Discounted Cash	(420)	(382)	(347)	(316)	(287)	
Cumulative	(420)	(802)	(1149)	(1465)	(1752)	(1752)

Alternative B:

Years	0	1	2	3	4	5
Buy Building*	(2000)					
Renovation						
Cost*	(600)					
Depreciation		(360)	(360)	(360)	(360)	(360)
Tax Shield*		144	144	144	144	144
Salvage Value*						800
Net Cash Flow	(2600)	144	144	144	144	944
Discounted Cash	(2600)	131	119	108	98	586
Cumulative	(2600)	(2469)	(2350)	(2242)	(2144)	(1558)

Preferred Alternative: Alternative B. Your company should move into the new building and make the purchase.

Ratio Analysis

Financial ratios can be calculated by combining various balance sheet and income statement items. These ratios can provide valuable insight into the financial health of a business, and can highlight problems and opportunities.

There is no "correct" value for each of the ratios explained below. Rules of thumb for what is appropriate vary by industry. Ratio analysis is most valuable when the ratios are compared to industry averages, key competitors, and/or the trends of the ratios over time.

1. Liquidity Ratios: measures liquidity

   A. $\text{Current ratio} = \dfrac{\text{current assets}}{\text{current liabilities}}$

   Measures short term solvency. Indicates the extent to which the claims of short term creditors are covered by assets that can be converted to cash within a year. A low ratio is not a healthy sign.

   B. $\text{Quick ratio} = \dfrac{\text{current assets} - \text{inventories}}{\text{current liabilities}}$

   An indication to creditors if the inventory would need to be liquidated in order to insure credit.

2. Asset Management Ratios: measures how effectively the firm is managing assets.

   A. $\text{Inventory Utilization} = \dfrac{\text{sales}}{\text{inventory}}$

   This measures if the size of inventory is appropriate in regard to sales. A low ratio would indicate the inventory carried is too large.

   B. $\text{Average Collection Period} = \dfrac{\text{sales}}{360} = \text{sales per day}$

   $\dfrac{\text{receivables}}{\text{sales per day}}$

   Measures the average length of time before account receivables are collected.

   C. $\text{Fixed Asset Utilization} = \dfrac{\text{sales}}{\text{net fixed assets}}$

   Measures utilization of plant and equipment. If the ratio is low, then the fixed assets may be under utilized.

   D. $\text{Total Asset Utilization} = \dfrac{\text{sales}}{\text{total assets}}$

   Measures utilization of all assets. If this ratio is low, not enough business is generated for the size of assets.

3. Debit Management Ratios: measures the percentage of total funds provided.

A. Total Debt to Total Assets $= \dfrac{\text{total debt}}{\text{total assets}}$

The lower the ratio, the greater the cushion against creditors losses in the event of liquidation. In other words, the business has more assets than debt.

B. Times Interest Earned $= \dfrac{\text{earnings before interest \& taxes}}{\text{interest changes}}$

Measures the extent earnings can decline without resulting financial embarrassment to the firm because of inability to meet annual interest costs. The higher the ratio, the better for the business.

4. Profitability Ratios: show the combined effects of liquidity, asset management, and debt management on operating results.

A. Profit Margin on Sales $= \dfrac{\text{net profit after taxes}}{\text{sales}}$

Gives profit per dollar on sales. If low, costs are too high or the sales prices are too low.

B. Return on Total Assets $= \dfrac{\text{net profit after taxes}}{\text{total assets}}$

Measures return on all assets.

C. Return on Common Equity $= \dfrac{\text{net profit after taxes}}{\text{common equity}}$

Measures rate return on stockholder's investments.

5. Market Value Ratios: gives management an indication of what investors think of the company's past performance and future prospects.

A. Price Earnings Ratio $= \dfrac{\text{price per share}}{\text{earning per share}}$

Shows how much investors are willing to pay per dollar of reported profits.

B. Market Book Ratio $= \dfrac{\text{stockholder's equity}}{\text{shares outstanding}} = $ book value per share

$\dfrac{\text{price per share}}{\text{book value per share}}$

If high, investors are willing to pay more than book value.

V. Summary—Questions

The Accounting Cycle

1. Journalizing—analyze and record daily transactions in the journals.
2. Posting—post the journal entries to the ledger accounts.
3. Preparation of the Trial Balance—summarize the ledger accounts and test the accuracy.
4. Preparation of a Worksheet—sort the accounts and their balances; adding adjusting entries and determine income or loss.
5. Preparation of the Balance Sheet and Income Statements—rearrange the worksheet information into the financial statements.
6. Adjust the Ledger Accounts—post adjusting entries to bring account balances up to date.
7. Close the Temporary Accounts—prepare and post closing entries to income statement accounts and transfer income or loss to retained earnings.
8. Preparation of a Post Closing Trial Balance—prove the accuracy of adjusting and closing entries.

Glossary

Accounting A service activity which provides quantitative information that can be useful in decision making. Recording, classifying, reporting, and interpreting the financial data of an organization.

Accrued Revenue   A revenue that has been earned but not yet received.

Accumulated Depreciation   An account on the balance sheet which shows how much of an asset's useful life has been used—in terms of cost.

Amortize   To write off as an expense a portion of the cost of an intangible asset.

Assets   Properties or economic resources owned by the business.

Balance Sheet   A position statement. A concise picture of financial position at a given point in time, showing assets, liabilities, and owner's equity.

Betterment   The cost to improve an existing plant asset's efficiency.

Bookkeeping   Recording transactions in accounting.

Book Value   The value of an asset according to the accounting records. Original cost − accumulated depreciation = Book Value.

Capitalization   Spreading the cost of an improvement to a plant asset over its useful life.

Capital Budgeting   The process of planning expenditures on assets whose returns are expected to extend beyond one year.

Capital Lease   A lease having the same economic consequences as a purchase.

Cash Flow   The amount of cash going in and out of a business.

Common Stock   A corporation's stock when there is only one kind.

Contra Account   An account which reduces the amount of an asset.

Contributed Capital   Amount of stockholder's investment.

Credit   To the right.

Debit   To the left.

Depreciation   The expiration of a plant asset's quantity of usefulness.

Dividends   A distribution of cash or other assets made by the corporation to its stockholders.

Expenses   Goods and services consumed in operating a business or other economic unit.

Extraordinary Repairs   Repairs made to a plant asset to extend its useful life at its current efficiency level.

Fixed Cost   A cost that remains the same regardless of production level.

Future Value   The value of present money in the future, if it were invested at "x" percent for "x" years.

Income Statement   A report on profits or (loss) for a specified time period.

Intangible Asset   An asset without physical substance but having value due to the rights of ownership and possession.

Journal Entry   An accounting record of a transaction with equal amounts of debits and credits.

Lease   A contract that gives one the right to use property.

Leasehold   Rights given to a lessee under terms of a lease contract.

Leasehold Improvement   Improvements made to leased property by lessee.

Ledger   A group of accounts used by the business to record transactions.

Lessee   The person or business using the property leased.

Lessor   The person or business owning the property leased.

Liabilities   Debts of a business or equity of creditors.

Liquidity   Amount of cash and assets that can be quickly turned into cash.

Market Value   The price of an asset in which it can be bought or sold.

Nominal Accounts   Income statement accounts.

Operating Lease   A lease that allows lessee only the use of the leased property for less than 75% of its useful life and less than 90% of the property's fair market value.

Ordinary Repairs   Repairs made to a plant asset to maintain its useful life at its current efficiency level.

Owner's Equity   Equity of owner of a business in the assets of the business.

Payback Period   The time it takes to recover the cost of the investment.

Posting   Transcribing debits and credits from the journals to the ledger.

Prepaid Expense   An asset that will be used in the operation of a business and will be an expense as it is used.

Present Value   The value of future money today, if it were invested at "x" percent for "x" years.

Real Accounts   Balance sheet accounts.

Retained Earnings   Net income or loss retained by the business after the payout of dividends.

Revenues   Inflow of cash or properties in exchange for goods or services.

Salvage Value   The dollar value of an asset after it has served its useful life.

Stockholder's Equity   The stockholder's ownership in a corporation represented by Common Stock plus retained earnings.

Trial Balance   An accounting work paper used to test the accuracy of account balances.

Unearned Revenue   Payment received in advance for goods and services to be sold.

Variable Cost   A cost that changes in proportion to production levels.

Worksheet   A working paper used in accounting to combine all information used to prepare financial statements.

Glossary

One of the continuing issues for facility managers in the area of financial management and budgeting is the FM's need to learn a new language, the language of business. We hope that this glossary, drawn from many sources, will assist the reader in using and understanding that language. In all cases, we have tried to use the least technical definition that retained the correct meaning of the term as it is used in the financial management of facilities.

We want to particularly thank Gerald Davis, Professor Michael Hoots, Heidi Lord Butler, Thomas Schleifer, ASTM, IFMA, the Institute of Management Accountants, and the Federal Facilities Council for help in defining these terms in ways that facility managers will understand.

For a broader glossary of facility management terms, see *The Facility Management Handbook*, 2d ed. For a primer on facility accounting, see Appendix H.

Above building standard Materials not included in the work letter that are subject to negotiation between the landlord and the tenant.
Accepted bid A bid that the owner accepts as the basis for entering into a contract with the party who submitted the bid.
Accounting cycle The complete sequence of procedures repeated, in the same order, during each accounting period; e.g., recording and posting transactions.
Accounts receivable The amount customers owe a business on current accounts.
Accrual A revenue or expense that has been earned but has not yet been received or paid.
Accrual basis of accounting The method of accounting based on incurred expenses and earned income for a defined period, regardless of whether the expenses or income have been paid or received.
Acquisition cost The costs directly related to the acquisition of a facility or related equipment and support. These typically include soft costs such as professional fees, option fees, incentive fees, security deposits, appraisal fees, and so on.
Activity-based accounting A technique in which the relationship between an activity and the resources needed to complete it is identified, and then the charges for that activity are based on the cost of those resources plus overhead and profit. Most chargeback systems are an attempt at activity-based accounting.
Actual cash value The actual value of property; current replacement cost minus depreciation.
Administrative approval An approval indicating that a work request has been processed correctly and that funding or level-of-effort floors or ceilings have been met.
Allocation Administratively assigning funds to a purpose.
Amortization of tenant allowances The return to the landlord over the term of the lease of those costs that are included in the landlord's building standard work letter and any other costs that the landlord has agreed to assume or amortize.
Amortization of tenant improvements An agreement by the landlord to pay for above building standard improvements and to amortize those improvements at a defined interest rate over a fixed term as additional rent.
Amortize To write off the cost of an intangible asset as an expense through periodic charges.
Annual budget See expense budget.
Annual expense A charge funded from the annual (expense) budget.
Annual value A uniform annual amount equivalent to the project costs or benefits throughout the study period, taking into account the time value of money.
Annual workplan A relatively constrained plan of facilities work, covering twelve to eighteen months, that includes both projects and operations and maintenance that the facility manager would like to accomplish during that period.
Annually recurring costs Those costs that are incurred in a regular pattern each year throughout the study period.
Approval level The upper limit that a designated manager is authorized to commit or expense.
Approvals Permissions to commit or expense funds by an appropriately designated manager.
Asset Something, such as a building or piece of equipment, that retains value for a period of time longer than one year after it is purchased.
Asset allocation
Asset management The process of maximizing the value of a property or portfolio of properties from acquisition to disposal within the objectives defined by the owner.
Assets Properties or economic resources owned by the business.

- **Current assets:** Cash and assets that can reasonably be expected to be turned into cash within a year or one operating cycle of the business, whichever is longer (e.g., accounts receivable).
- **Long-term investments:** Investments that will not be liquidated within a year (stocks, bonds, land held for future expansion, and so on).
- **Plant and equipment:** Tangible assets with relatively long lives that are used in the production or sale of other assets or services (land, buildings, equipment, and so on). A plant asset has substance, must be either in use or on standby, and has a service life of more than one year.
- **Intangible assets:** Assets that have no physical existence but have value because of rights conferred as a result of their ownership and possession.

Audit Formal examination and verification of accounts.

Balance sheet A position statement for the business. It is a concise picture of the business's financial position at a given point in time. Assets = Liabilities + Owners' Equity.
Base rental The initial rental rate, normally identified as the annual rent in a gross lease.
Base time (time zero) The date to which all future and past benefits and costs are converted when a present value method is used.
Benchmarking A comparison of activities, levels of performance, and other factors to a standard, whether external or internal.
Benefit/cost ratio (BCR) Benefits divided by cost, where both are discounted to a present value or equivalent uniform annual value. Normally a project with a BCR less than 1.0 will not be funded.
Bid A written response to an invitation for bid.
Bid bond A bond posted by a contractor competing for a project guaranteeing to the owner that, if the bid is accepted, the contractor will execute the contract.
Bid security A financial guarantee to the owner, submitted with the bid, that the contractor, if awarded the contract, will execute the contract in accordance with the contract documents.

Blanket purchase order (BPO)   An agreement, normally for a fixed time, for a purchase of low-dollar-value goods and services from a single vendor. BPOs are designed to fill anticipated repetitive needs for small quantities of goods and/or services.

Bond   A collateral agreement in which one party obligates itself to a second party to answer for the default of a third party.

Bonding capacity   The total value of bonds that can be underwritten for a particular contractor, based on the total volume of work that the contractor can support.

Book value   The value of an asset after the depreciation to date has been subtracted from the asset's original cost.

Breakeven analysis   An analysis to calculate the point at which the revenues from a new project just equal the project's fixed and variable costs.

Budget   The financial plan for allocating funds for specific activities during a specific period of time.

Budgeting   The process by which the funds required to carry out programmed objectives and workload are determined. The budget is arranged in a systematic manner by accounts that reflect the programs and also indicates the management and control systems to be used during execution.

Building economics   The application of economic analysis to the design, financing, engineering, construction, management, operation, or ownership of buildings.

Build to suit   An approach to real estate development that enables a corporation to assume ownership by having a developer hold ownership until the project is complete and ready for occupancy. It is a form of delayed ownership.

Building standard work letter   A document that delineates the type and quality of materials and the quantities to be furnished by the landlord as building standard.

Burn rate   The rate at which funds are expended during any given period. The start and end of fiscal years are typically times of high burn rates.

Business case   A type of analysis that shows, in both financial and qualitative terms, the advantages and disadvantages of a proposed action. Most companies and government agencies have a required format for the business case and specify the type of financial analysis required.

Business plan   A plan based on the mission and objectives of the business that shows what resources will be needed and in what time frame to implement the firm's business strategies.

CAFM   Computer-assisted facility management. Integrated facility management hardware and software that controls diverse facility management functions, most commonly space management, design, inventory management, work management, building operation, lease management, and financial management.

Capital account   An account giving the total amount of capital invested in fixed assets by the owners of a business; it includes real estate and equipment but excludes current assets.

Capital budget   The budgeting of assets whose returns are expected to extend beyond one year.

Capital cost   See capital expense.

Capital decision-making tools   There are two basic approaches to making capital budgeting decisions: the accept-reject approach and the ranking approach. The most commonly used tools for making these decisions are:

- **Average rate of return**
- **Average payback period**
- **Actual payback period**
- **Net present value**
- **Internal rate of return**

Capital expense   The cost to acquire, substantially improve, expand, change the functional use of, or replace a building or building system. Capitalization rules are driven by tax laws, so they vary among locations.

Capital lease   A lease having the same economic consequences as a purchase.

Capital planning   The planning of the major assets of the company and how they will be financed. Because of the financial impact of each capital project, these projects need to go through a capital development process that accepts or rejects them and prioritizes the accepted projects based on both financial analysis and qualitative factors. Most companies plan for at least five years.

Capital program   The totality of the capital planning process divided into execution years.

Capital project   A project that creates residual asset value for a company.

Capital review board   A management board that reviews all capital projects in the program and (1) assigns them to a year for execution and (2) decides among competing projects for execution, prioritizing them based on the financial and qualitative analysis presented for each.

Capitalization   Allocating the cost of an asset over several years, spreading both the effect on current income and the tax deduction. Capitalization affects the balance sheet.

Cash accounting   The method of accounting in which income is recorded only when it is received in cash and expenditures are recorded only when they are paid.

Cash flow   The amount of cash going into or out of a business or a project.

Change order   A written order from the contracting officer to the contractor modifying the quantity, quality, or method of work required in the contract.

Chargeback   An administrative mechanism for billing the costs of facility services back to the customers.

Claims   Amounts exceeding the contract price that parties seek to collect for delays, errors, unapproved changes, and other unanticipated losses.

Commitment   A funding obligation that has been entered into but has not been completely paid for or otherwise reconciled. A commitment is controllable only to the extent that the facility manager's firm can renege legally—for example, during a bankruptcy.

Competitive range   In procurement, the range within which bids that will be considered responsive, so that other factors of the bid will be taken into account.

Concessions   Inducements to sign a lease offered by a landlord to a tenant. Common concessions are free rent, extra tenant improvement allowances, payment of moving costs, and lease pickups.

Conditions of bid   Terms in the invitation to bid stipulating the manner in which bids are to be prepared, submitted, and processed.

Conditions of the contract   Articles in a contract defining or describing terms, responsibilities of the owner and the contractor, performance, payment schedules, and the like.

Constant dollars   Dollars of uniform purchasing power, indexed for general inflation or deflation.

Construction   The erection, installation, or assembly of a new facility; the addition, expansion, alteration, conversion, or replacement of an existing facility; or the relocation of a facility from one site to another. This includes equipment that is installed and made a part of such facilities, and related site preparation, excavation, filling, landscaping, or other land improvements.

Contingency funds   Funds allotted to cover unexpected costs that may be incurred throughout a period or a project.

Contract   A binding agreement between an owner and a contractor. There are a number of types of contracts:

- **Fixed price:** A contract that is not adjusted for the contractor's cost.
- **Fixed price level of effort term:** A contract obligating the contractor to a defined effort for a defined period for a defined, fixed amount. (Used primarily in research and development.)
- **Fixed price with performance incentives:** A contract that provides incentives for the contractor to surpass defined performance targets. If the targets are surpassed, the contractor's profit increases; if they are not, the contractor's profit decreases.
- **Fixed price with economic price adjustment:** A contract that provides for revision of the contract price in the event of defined contingencies.
- **Fixed price with firm target cost incentives:** A contract that provides at the outset a firm target cost, firm target profit, price ceiling, and formula relating final cost to target cost, establishing final price and profit.
- **Cost plus:** A contract that provides for the reimbursement of defined costs plus a fee, representing profit.
- **Cost plus aware fee:** A contract that provides for the reimbursement of defined costs plus a two-part fee: a fixed amount at the onset of the contract and an amount based on performance.
- **Cost plus fixed fee:** A contract that provides for reimbursement of defined costs plus a fixed fee.
- **Cost plus incentive fee:** A contract that provides for reimbursement of defined costs plus a variable fee that is dependent on cost or performance.
- **Cost plus cost sharing:** A contract that provides for reimbursement of a defined portion of costs, with no additional fee.
- **Time and materials (T&M):** A contract that provides payment to the contractor based on hours at fixed rates and cost of materials or other defined costs, including a profit factor.
- **Unit price:** A contract that provides the contractor a defined amount for every defined unit of work performed.
- **Indefinite demand, indefinite quantity (IDEA):** See indefinite demand, indefinite quantity (IDEA) contract.
- **Job order (JOC):** See job order contracting.
- **Performance based:** See performance-based contracting.

Contract bond   A guarantee that the contractor furnishes, indemnifying the owner against the contractor's failure to comply with the terms of the contract.

Contract cost breakdown   The contractor's itemized list, prepared after receipt of the contract, showing the cost of each element and phase of the project.

Contracting officer   A person who is officially authorized to bind a company to a contract.

Controllable cost   Costs that can be significantly affected by the actions of the responsible facility manager. The keys to identifying controllable costs are that (1) they are assigned to the facility manager and (2) they can be significantly influenced by the FM.

Cost   The price paid for the acquisition, maintenance, production, or use of materials or services.

Cost accounting   Reporting on product or service costs.

Cost avoidance   The prevention of costs greater than existing spending levels by adopting a proposed initiative.

Cost center   An organizational unit in which budgetary funding is used to sustain operations.

Cost containment   The control of costs relative to existing spending levels by adopting a proposed initiative.

Cost effective   The condition whereby the present value benefits of an investment exceed its present value costs, i.e., a big bang for the buck.

Cost model   The description of the project divided into discrete elements, with quantities and unit prices shown for each element.

Cost of capital   The rate of return that a business demands from an investment in order to accept the risk of making that investment.

Cost of ownership   The cost to the owner of owning the building, servicing existing debt, and receiving a return on equity. This also includes the costs of capital improvements, maintenance and repair, operations, and disposal.

Cost of providing the fixed asset   An amount that includes capital costs, mortgage costs, capital improvements, taxes, insurance, and depreciation charges. It does not include the lease costs, the security costs, or the relocation/rearrangement cost.

Cost reduction   The lowering of costs from existing spending levels by adopting a proposed initiative.

Cost saving   Money not spent by adopting a proposed initiative.

Current dollars   Dollars of purchasing power in which actual prices are stated in current terms, not adjusted for inflation or deflation.

Customer service agreements   Mini-contracts between the facility department and its customers for facility services.

Debt   A liability or obligation arising from borrowing money or taking goods on credit.

Debt financing   Raising money through borrowing and the issuance of a mortgage, bond, note, or debenture.

Debt management   The Finance Department's strategy for accumulating and paying down debt in order to ensure the financial viability of the company and to optimize its ability to borrow.

Debt service   The repayment of borrowed money and interest on the balance due.

Debt/worth ratio   Current debt divided by tangible net worth.

Decision analysis   A technique for making economic decisions in an uncertain environment that allows a decision maker to include alternative outcomes, risk attitudes, or subjective impressions about uncertain events in an evaluation of investments.

Deferred charges/income   Charges/income that are not chargeable to the fiscal period in which they were made.

Deferred maintenance   Maintenance that was not performed when it should have been or was scheduled to be but was instead put off or delayed until a future period.

Delegated contracting authority   The act of a contracting officer that gives limited contracting authority to an authorized line manager.

Depreciation   An estimated expense that recognizes that an asset's value diminishes as time passes in its productive life. There are four depreciation methods:

- **Straight-line method**
- **Sum-of-the-years'-digits method**
- **Declining-balance method**
- **Units of production method**

Design-build   A construction approach in which the owner buys both design and construction services from the same provider.

Differential price escalation rate   The expected percent difference between the rate of increase assumed for a given cost item (such as construction) and the general rate of inflation.

Direct expense   A cost that is directly attributable to an action. Often only variable costs are considered direct expenses.

Discount factor   A multiplicative number (calculated for a given discount rate and interest period) that is used to convert costs and benefits occurring at different times to a common time.

Discount rate   The rate at which future cash flows are discounted because of the time value of money.

Discounted cash flow   Cash flow with the time value of money taken into consideration.

Discounted payback period (DPB)   The time required for the cumulative benefits from an investment to pay back the investment cost and other accrued costs, considering the time value of money.

Discounting   A technique for converting cash flows that occur over time to equivalent amounts at a common time.

Discretionary cost   Costs that can be varied at the discretion of the facility manager without having a direct impact on operations. This is not to imply that changes in these costs will not someday affect operations. The direct correlation is just not apparent.

Disposition (disposal) expenses   Costs directly related to the disposition of the facility or the related equipment and support. They typically include professional fees for the facility and selling costs, transportation charges, accounting write-offs, and other such costs for equipment.

Due diligence   A type of research done before a major acquisition is initiated in order to assess building condition, environmental hazards, regulatory compliance, financial value, and other factors.

EBIT   Earnings before interest and taxes. One measure of the efficiency of operations.

EBITDA   Earnings before interest, taxes, depreciation, and amortization. One measure of the efficiency of operations.

Economic evaluation methods   A set of economic analysis techniques that consider all relevant costs associated with a project investment during the study period; comprising such techniques as life-cycle cost, benefit/cost ratio, saving to investment ratio, internal rate of return, net present value, and net savings.

Economic life   That period of time over which costs are incurred and benefits are delivered to an owner. It is often an assumed value established by tax regulations or legal requirements.

Efficient rent   The dollar amount per square foot per year that the tenant pays on average over the term of the lease, taking into consideration all stair-step leases and discounts.

Engineered cost   Costs that can be precisely determined and measured and are directly related to the outputs of the facility department. Changes in these costs have a direct impact on the ability to fund operational activities.

Engineering economics   The application of engineering, mathematical, and economic techniques to the economic evaluation of engineering alternatives.

Equity   An owner's right in a property after all claims against that property have been settled. Equity consists of contributed capital (normally stock) and retained earnings.

Equity financing   Raising money through the issuance of stock to or the receipt of monetary contributions by investors, who receive a share of ownership in the company raising the funds.

Estimating   The art of anticipating the cost of a project or line items in your budget.

Expected life   A term that is commonly, but not exactly correctly, used to mean economic life.

Expense allocation   The allocation of a pro rata share of all expenses or increased expenses to a tenant.

Expense budget   Also known as the operations and maintenance budget or the annual budget. The budget, arranged by programs, provided to the facility management department to operate, maintain, and repair (and normally do minor construction on) the owned and leased facilities of the company for the next fiscal period, normally twelve to twenty-four months.

Expense passthrough   Lease clauses that require a tenant to reimburse the landlord for expenses such as insurance and taxes beyond a fixed amount.

Expenses   Goods and services consumed in operating a business.

Expensing   Charging the entire cost of an asset against the current year, reducing current income and affecting the income statement.

Face rate   The identified rental rate in a lease that is subsequently discounted by concessions offered by the landlord.

Facility business planning   Preparing the facilities portion of the company business plan. For each company business plan, there should be a corresponding facility business plan or annex. This is not simply space planning, nor is it master planning, although both of those processes provide valuable inputs. All facility programs must be planned over the appropriate planning horizon.

Facility durability   The ability of a facility to maintain serviceability for at least a specified period of time.

Facility evaluation   A comparison, to a specified precision and reliability, of the qualitative and quantitative results of judgments, observations, measurements, analyses, or other tests against performance criteria established for a specified purpose.

Facility serviceability   The ability of a facility to perform the function for which it is designed, used, or required to be used.

Fair market value   The price at which a buyer and a seller who are under no compulsion to buy or to sell will trade.

Feasibility study   The study of a planned scheme or development, the practicality of its achievement, and its projected financial outcome.

FFE   Furniture, furnishings, and equipment.

Financial analysis   The examination and interpretation of financial statements or studies to evaluate the financial status of a business or a proposal.

Financial forecasting   Planning the finances of business operations for some future time period.

Financial ratios   Ratios between two ratios that show a significant relationship and are used as an aid to analysis and interpretation of the financial well-being of a company or function.

First cost   The cost incurred in placing a building or a building subsystem into service, including the cost of planning, design, engineering, site acquisition and preparation, construction, purchase, installation, property taxes and interest during the construction period, and construction-related fees.

Fiscal approval   The approval that verifies that funds are available to complete the project or to execute the budget.

Fiscal year   The accounting period of a company. Traditionally this has been twelve months (thus the term *fiscal year*), but some firms are now using six-, eighteen-, and even twenty-four-month fiscal periods. Many companies use the calendar year, but the U.S. government, for example, uses October through September as its fiscal year.

Fitup/fitout   Alterations and improvements to the base building and to the building systems, including demolition, where required, to prepare the accommodation for occupancy.

Fixed asset   An asset, such as property, plant, or equipment, that has a long life and cannot be expensed in a single year.

Fixed costs   Costs that are not directly related to the amount of goods or services produced.

Free rent   The period of time during which the tenant occupies the premises under the lease but does not pay rent.

Fungible   Interchangeable; to the facility manager, funds that can be moved from one account to another with no restrictions.
Future value   The value of present money y years in the future if it were invested at x percent.

General accounting   Reporting on the financial information of the organization as a whole.
Gross rental   A rental rate that includes normal building standard services provided by the landlord in the base year rental.
Guaranteed maximum cost   The amount defined in the contract between the owner and the contractor as the upper limit on the amount of money available for completing a project.

Hard costs   Costs associated directly with actual construction, leasing, maintenance, and upkeep.
Hierarchy of plans   The array of business plans in a company, often the strategic plan, the intermediate-term plan, the annual workplan, and the budget.
Hurdle rate   The minimum rate of return on investment that your company expects new investments to provide. Normally it consists of the cost of capital plus an administrative surcharge.

Improvement   A valuable or useful addition or alteration that increases the value or changes the use of a building or property; something more than mere maintenance, repair, or restoration to the original condition.
Improvement allowance   The estimated dollar value of the building standard work letter being offered by the landlord.
Income statement   A report on the profit or loss for a business over a stated period of time. Revenues − Expenses = Net Income (Loss).
Incremental cost/benefit   The additional cost/benefit resulting from an increase in the investment in a building project.
Indefinite demand, indefinite quantity (IDEA) contract   A contract form that meets user needs for a fixed term when neither the volume nor the types of services are known exactly.
Indirect expense   An expense that is not directly attributable to the action being analyzed.
Indirectly attributable costs   In leasing, costs that are allocated pro rata to all lessees.
Intangible assets   Valuables such as trademarks and copyrights accruing to a business.
Internal rate of return (IRR)   The discount rate that yields a present value of future cash inflows that is exactly equal to the initial net investment of a specific project (NPV = 0) This will be the return that your company expects your proposed investment to return and that it must return in order to exceed the company's hurdle rate.
Investment cost   The combination of first cost and later expenditures for upgrading, expanding, or changing the function or use of a building or building subsystem in ways that have substantial and enduring value (generally more than one year).
Invitation for bids (IFB)   A detailed prescriptive specification of bidding procedures and an invitation for contractors to submit bids.
Invited bidders   The only contractors from whom the owner will accept bids.

Job order contracting (JOC)   A competitively bid, fixed-price, indefinite quantity, long-term contract for multiple projects or services on an on-call basis through delivery orders. The contractor bids a coefficient that is applied to the customer-specified unit price book to calculate a lump-sum fixed price for each delivery order.

Labor and material payment bond   A bond that the contractor gives in which the owner is guaranteed that the contractor will pay for the labor and materials used in executing the contract.
Lease   A contract that gives one the right to use property.
Lease buyout   A cash inducement offered by a landlord to a tenant's previous landlord or by the tenant to the current landlord to cancel the remaining term of the tenant's lease.
Lease costs

- **Gross lease**—A lease that places all responsibility for operating costs on the lessor, who assumes the full risk of any increases in these costs.
- **Triple-net lease**—A lease under which operations costs are paid by the occupant.
- **Double-net lease**—A lease under which operations costs other than insurance are paid by the occupant.

Lease pickup   The landlord's commitment to assume the costs associated with paying a tenant's rent on premises to be vacated that are still under lease.
Lease-versus-buy analysis   An after-tax, incremental, present value comparison of cash flows resulting from purchasing an asset, on the one hand, or leasing the same asset, on the other hand.
Leasehold   Rights given to the lessee under the terms of a lease contract.
Leasehold improvement   Improvements made to a leased property by the lessee.
Lessee   The person or business using the property leased.
Lessor   The person or business owning the property leased.
Letter of agreement   A letter from one party to the other stating the terms of agreement between the two parties.
Letter of intent   A letter stating the intention of a party to enter into a formal agreement with another party. Such a letter is often used to get a project off the ground until a contract can be signed.
Liabilities   Debts of a business.

- **Current liabilities** are debts or obligations that must be paid or liquidated within one year or one operating cycle, whichever is longer, with the payment/liquidation requiring the use of assets that are presently classified as current assets (accounts payable, notes payable, short-term debt, and so on).
- **Long-term liabilities** are debts or obligations that are not due and payable for a comparatively long time, normally more than one year (mortgages, for example).

Lien   A court order restricting a party's use of property until the party has discharged a debt or duty.
Life-cycle costing   A technique of economic evaluation that sums the initial costs of an investment (less resale value) and the cost of replacements, operations (including energy use), and maintenance and repair of that investment (expressed in present or annual value terms) over a given study period.
Life-cycle costs (LCC)   Costs incident to the planning, design, construction, operations, maintenance, and disposal of a structure over time.
Liquidated damages   An amount of damages on a daily basis specified in the contract. This amount will be assessed against the contractor for each day beyond the contract completion date that the project remains uncompleted.
Liquidation value   The value of property sold to settle a debt.

Lowest first cost   A method of selecting goods or services by choosing those with the lowest cost at the time of purchase.
Lowest responsible bidder   The contractor who submits the lowest bid from among those whom the owner considers to be the least risky.

Maintainability   The capability of a system or facility to be maintained to a specified level of reliability, at a specified measure of cost or economy.
Maintenance   Work that is necessary to maintain the original, anticipated useful life of a fixed asset. It does not prolong the life of the property or equipment or add to its value.
Managing by metrics   A management technique which uses unit cost indicators to measure the efficiency an/or effectiveness of each organizational functions. Also called managing by the numbers.
Master plan   A technical plan for the use, restraints, phasing, and costs of a specific site. A master plan is not a business plan.
Mid-range plan   A facility business plan that projects programs three to five years into the future.
Minimum acceptable rate of return   The minimum percentage return required for an investment to be economically acceptable.
Mixed costs   Costs that are semivariable; they change in response to a change in the volume of the goods or services produced, but not proportionately.
Moving allowance   An offer by a landlord to pay all or part of a tenant's moving costs.
Multiyear agreements   Agreements made with vendors for goods or services for a period exceeding one year (often three years) in order to obtain favorable pricing.

Negotiated contract   An agreement developed without competitive bidding by negotiating specifications and terms. Such contracts are often used to obtain design services.
Net benefits/savings   The difference between the benefits and the costs when both are discounted to present or annual value dollars.
Net operating income (NOI)   Income remaining after all qualified operating expenses are subtracted from gross income.
Net present value   A calculation that determines the dollar value, at time zero, of some future sum of cash flows, discounted at the cost of capital (rate of interest).
Net rent   A rental rate that includes some services to be provided by the landlord; normally the tenant is responsible for the cost of janitorial and utilities services.
Net worth   The difference between the amounts of a company's assets and its liabilities.
Nominal discount rate   The rate of interest reflecting the time value of money stemming from both inflation and the real earning power of money over time.
Nonattributable costs   Costs that cannot be charged back to customers and must be borne by the facility department.
Nondiscretionary costs   Costs that cannot be varied at the discretion of the manager. Cuts in nondiscretionary costs will result in some impact on operations.
Nonrecurring costs   Costs incurred once, infrequently, or on an irregular basis during a facility's economic life.
Notice to proceed   A written notice from the contracting officer to the contractor that authorizes the contractor to incur obligations and proceed with work on the project.

Occupancy cost   The total cost incurred by a company or organization to provide space for operations. It includes all costs of operating the facility, plus the costs of providing the fixed asset.
Operations   Work that keeps the facility performing the function for which it is currently classified. This commonly includes the cost of utilities, work reception and coordination, moving, and work associated with building systems.
Operations and maintenance cost   The cost associated with the day-to-day operation of a facility. This includes all maintenance and repair (both fixed and variable); administrative costs; labor costs; janitorial, housekeeping, and other cleaning costs; management fees; and all costs associated with roadways and grounds.
Operations cost   See operations and maintenance cost.
Opportunity costs   The costs forgone by investing money one way rather than another.
Outsourcing   The provision of a bundle or a full range of services by a single contractor, so that the facilities staff is responsible only for managing the relationship with the contractor and monitoring the contractor's performance.
Outtasking   The provision of individual services by a service provider.
Overhead   Business expenses required for the operation of a business.
Owners' equity   The capital or claims of owners after all liabilities have been paid.

> • **Contributed capital** is the amount of the owners' investment, such as common stock.
> • **Retained earnings** is the net income or loss retained by the business after the payout of dividends.

Ownership costs   Costs resulting from owning the building, servicing existing debt, and receiving a return on equity. This also includes the cost of those capital improvements, repair, and upkeep that would not be considered standard operations and maintenance costs.

Pass-through costs   Costs that can be directly associated with a particular project, program, or cost center.
Payables   The amounts to be paid under a contract or agreement.
Payback   A technique of economic evaluation that determines the time required for the cumulative benefits from an investment to recover the cost of the investment and other accrued costs.
Payback period   The time it takes to recover the cost of an investment.
Performance-based contracting   A contracting method in which all aspects of an acquisition are structured around the purpose of the work to be performed (as opposed to the manner in which the work is to be performed or to broad, imprecise statements of work that preclude an objective assessment of contractor performance). It is designed to ensure that contractors are given the freedom to determine how to meet performance objectives, that appropriate performance quality levels are achieved, and that payment is made only for services that meet these levels.
Planned replacement   An advance plan to replace major components or elements of operating systems or buildings.
Planning   Developing a scheme to carry out the decisions of management. This includes a consideration of administration, human resources, facilities, communications, and logistics as well as operations.
Planning cycle   The time frame (1) during which any individual plan is developed and (2) considered by each type of business plan: workplan, mid-range plan, and strategic plan.
Portfolio   A group of securities, buildings, or other properties held by an individual or institutional investor.
Prebid (or preproposal) conference   A meeting held before bids or proposals are submitted to brief prospective contractors on the requirements for the bid or upcoming contract.
Prelease   Leasing of premises in a building that is under construction and is not yet ready for occupancy.

Preliminary pricing plan A plan showing enough detail to develop realistic estimates, determine the general construction and installation costs, and determine the level of build-out.

Preliminary project budget A budget developed on the basis of preliminary drawings; it is based either on similar project costs per square foot or on industry standards.

Present value The value today of money y years in the future if it were invested at x percent.

Price book In job order contracting, the book of standard rates for tasks provided by the owner and agreed upon when the contract is signed.

Pro forma statement A financial statement for an anticipated transaction.

Profit and loss statement (P&L statement) See income statement.

Profit center An organizational unit that generates income for a company.

Pro rata share The ratio of the rentable square footage of the building occupied by the tenant to the rentable area of the entire building.

Program One of the basic building blocks of facility management. A program is a logical grouping of work that has clearly delineated management responsibilities and resources committed to it. Do not confuse it with architectural, engineering, or interiors programming, which is the gathering of user requirements.

Programmatic planning and budgeting A system that does business planning by programs, which then become budget categories.

Programming Developing a scheme of actions designed to accomplish definitive and measurable objectives. It is specific as to time phasing and resources. Do not confuse this with architectural, engineering, or interiors programming.

Progress payment Money that the owner gives to a contractor, according to the contract, based on progress to date on the project.

Project Resources and activities used to achieve a specific set of objectives within a specified time schedule.

Project accounting Accounting for the costs of a project, organized according to the sections of the specifications standardized by the Construction Specifications Institute, the American Institute of Architects, or UNIFORMAT. Costs are normally downloaded to the corporate finance system monthly, quarterly, or at the end of the project.

Project work A request for work that costs more than a specific dollar figure or that changes the form or function of the facility.

Purchase order (PO) A written contract between the owner and a vendor using a standard form.

Purchasing officer A staff officer of the purchasing department whose primary duty is to purchases goods.

Rate adjustments In leasing, provisions for increases in the base rent, usually influenced by a prescribed index.

Rate of return on investment (ROI) A financial management technique that takes into account the earnings on the investment and the average value of the investment. ROI can be calculated by dividing the after-tax net income from the investment by the average cost of the investment.

Ratio analysis A form of financial analysis in which ratios are constructed and used to judge comparative performance.

Real dollars (Euros, yen, wan, etc.) Dollars (or other currency) at some other time that have been adjusted for inflation. (See current dollars.)

Recapitalization (For facility management only) Methodologies to determine how much should be invested annually in buildings and major equipment to maintain those capital items at a serviceability level equal to that when they were installed. One such formula says that owners should plan to invest 2 to 4 percent of the replacement value of a facility in maintenance and repair (less custodial and grounds maintenance, but plus a minor amount of construction/alteration).

Recapture Billing tenants for their pro rata share of increased operating expenses after those expenses have been incurred and paid for by the landlord.

Receivable That which is owed to a party.

Recurring cost A cost that occurs repeatedly during the life of an asset.

Repair Work that restores damaged or worn-out property to a normal operating condition. As a basic distinction, repairs are curative and maintenance is preventive. Repairs can be classified as minor or major. A major repair commonly exceeds one to two person-days of effort or exceeds the in-house capability to perform.

Replacement The exchange or substitution of one fixed asset, such as an item of equipment or a building component, for another that has the capacity to perform the same function. The replacement may be required as a result of obsolescence, wear and tear, or destruction of the item to be replaced. In general, replacement, as distinguished from repair, involves a complete, identifiable item.

Replacement cost All the costs associated with providing an equivalent building component replacement that are expected to be incurred during the study period and are included in the capital budget.

Request for information (RFI) An invitation to contractors to submit information about their firms. No proposal or bid is included.

Request for proposal (RFP) A document issued to prospective contractors that specifically defines the scope of the desired services and describes the evaluation criteria and method that will be used to select the contractor.

Requisition A written request within an organization for goods or services.

Resale value The monetary sum expected from the disposal of an asset at the end of its economic life, the end of its useful life, or the end of the study period.

Responsive bid A bid that meets all the terms and conditions of a solicitation.

Retainage Contract balances, specified in the contract, that are held back and not paid to the contractor until completion of the contract.

Return on assets (ROA) The net profit of a company after taxes divided by the total value of the assets employed to generate income.

Return on investment (ROI) The yield on an investment; the total profit of a company divided by the total amount originally invested to gain that profit.

Revenues Inflows of cash or properties received in exchange for goods and services.

Risk-adjusted discount rate A discount rate that has been adjusted to account for risk.

Risk analysis The body of theory and practice that has evolved to help decision makers assess their risk exposures and attitudes toward risk so that they can select the investment that is best for them.

Sale-leaseback A development method in which a company develops and completes a project and then sells it to a third party. The third party then executes a lease with the same company from which it purchased the building. That company then occupies the facility for the term of the lease.

Salvage value The dollar value of an asset after it has served its useful life.

Savings to investment ratio (SIR) A comparison of the projected cost savings from a proposal and the initial investment.

Sensitivity analysis A test of the outcome of an analysis by altering one or more parameters from their initially assumed value(s).

Service agreement   See customer service agreement.
Service life   The period of time over which a building, component, or subsystem provides adequate performance. It is not the same as economic life.
Shared tenant services   Services provided by a building to tenants, allowing the tenants to share the costs and benefits of sophisticated telecommunications and other technical services.
Shareholder value   The monetary value of a company's stock.
Short list   A list of vendors selected for further consideration following an initial review of all bids.
Simple payback period   The time required for the cumulative benefits from an investment to pay back the cost of the investment and other accrued costs, not considering the time value of money.
Soft costs   In facility management, and particularly project management, costs that are not directly attributable to construction, renovation, maintenance, and repair. The term is often used to mean overhead costs.
Sole-source procurement   A procurement that is awarded to a single vendor without competition.
Solicitation   A formal competitive procurement package consisting of applicable documents to obtain bids and proposals.
Space plan   The plan for the space assets of the company.
Stair-stepped rent   A rental rate that increases by fixed amounts during the lease term.
Statement of work   A document describing the services to be provided by the contractor in enough detail to permit the contractor to bid the work.
Strategic plan   For most businesses, the facility business plan that projects programs for the next five to ten years.
Subleasing   The leasing of space by a tenant to a subtenant, usually in accordance with the terms of the base lease. In most subleases, the tenant remains responsible for conformance with the lease.
Substantial completion   The point at which a designated expert indicates, in a certificate of substantial completion, that the work is sufficiently complete, as defined in the contract, for the facility to be utilized for its intended purposes.
Substitution and credits   The ability to substitute nonstandard materials for the landlord-supplied materials specified in the work letter, or to receive dollar amount credits for those materials if they are not utilized.
Sunk costs   Costs for fixed assets that have already been expended and therefore are not considered in financial decisions concerning future work.
Supplier   A firm that enters into an agreement with the department, the contractor, or a subcontractor to provide materials and/or equipment, either for use on a project or on a continuing basis.

Takeoff   The estimated amount of material needed for a particular project.
Technical approval   An approval indicating that a work request has received the appropriate technical review and design.
Tenant   An organization that has the rights and obligations of occupancy in a facility as specified in a lease or occupancy agreement.
Time value of money   A concept that says that an amount of money today is usually worth more than the same amount of money in the future as a result of the forfeiture of opportunity costs plus, in most recent history, the cost of inflation.
Triple net lease   A lease in which the tenant is responsible for all expenses associated with its proportionate share of occupancy of the building.
Turnkey   A project completed to the owner/tenant's specification and handed over complete, with little or no intermediate owner/tenant involvement.
Two-step bidding   A variation on formal bidding that is used when price is a dominant factor in the award but not the only factor. The first step is to establish the technical acceptability of each proposal. In the second step, bids are evaluated to determine the lowest-priced technically acceptable offer.

Unit cost   The cost of one unit of a good or service. Unit costs are commonly used in benchmarking.
Unprogrammed costs   Costs that were not anticipated or included in a budget but are incurred.
Useful life   The period of time over which an investment is considered to meet its original objective. The term is also commonly but not altogether correctly used instead of economic life.

Valuation   Methods of estimating the value, worth, or price of real property, a development, or a project.
Value engineering   The procedure for developing and evaluating alternatives to a proposed design that best fulfill the needs and requirements of the user/owner of the building.
Variable costs   Costs that vary directly and proportionately with the amount of goods or services produced.

Work letter   A document that indicates building standards plus any additional items to be paid for by the landlord or by the tenant; the letter specifies who is responsible for each item.
Worth   The value of an item as defined in monetary terms for a specific identified function.

Zero-based budget   A budget in which every line is prepared as if this budget year were the first year in which the budget was prepared.

Index